CHARLES WESLEY
THE FIRST METHODIST

1. Portrait of Charles Wesley as a young man painted by the most fashionable portrait painter of his time, Henry Hudson (1701–79). It now hangs in the Board Room of Epworth Press.

CHARLES WESLEY
THE FIRST METHODIST

FREDERICK C. GILL

ABINGDON PRESS
NEW YORK   NASHVILLE

CHARLES WESLEY : THE FIRST METHODIST

Copyright © 1964 by Frederick C. Gill

PRINTED IN GREAT BRITAIN

Contents

List of Plates

Acknowledgements

I gratefully acknowledge the help of the following: the Rev. Dr. Frank Cumbers and the Epworth Press for providing access to the Methodist Archives and Research Centre, permitting quotation from original manuscripts, and photographs; to his colleagues: the Rev. John C. Bowmer, M.A., B.D., who, in addition to help in the Archives, read the book in manuscript; Mr. F. G. Doubleday who was the first to suggest the subject, and Mr. L. E. S. Gutteridge for the loan of books from the Bretherton Library. The Rev. A. John Gedye, B.A., Warden of the New Room, Bristol, and Mr. John M. East and Mr. and Mrs. Garner, Caretakers of 4 Charles Street and the New Room, respectively; the Rev. Norman P. Goldhawk, M.A., of Richmond College; my old friend and former colleague, the Rev. W. Harold Beales, M.A.; Mrs. Alex Wilson of Garth House; the Rev. W. Harold Beales, M.A.; Mrs. Alec Wilson of Garth House; the Rev. Derek Wilson, for help in tracing the Gwynne family in Ludlow; Mrs. Grace J. Gwynne; Mr. J. D. Carleton, M.A., Headmaster of Westminster School; the Rev. W. Llewelyn Jones; the Rev. W. Lamplough Doughty, B.A., B.D.; the Rev. Harry Truelove for reading the proof; Mr. Michael Foxell for generous help, especially with the illustrations; Miss Joan Robinson, J.P. for typing the manuscript; and my wife for her unfailing patience and encouragement. If I have omitted to name any others to whom I am indebted I gladly acknowledge their kindness.

Plates

The publishers wish to acknowledge the sources of the following photographs, most of which were especially commissioned to illustrate this book, and to thank those who helped to obtain them: 1, 2*a*, 5, 6, 7, 11*a*, 12 and 14—Methodist Archives and Research Centre; 2*b*, 8, 9*b*, 10, 11*b*, 13—E. W. Tattersall; 3*a* and 3*b*—Beacon Press, Brecon; 9*a*—A. F. Kersting; and 15—Reece Winston.

Introduction

WHAT KIND of a man was Charles Wesley? His hymns have received generous and extensive treatment, but too little attention has been paid to other aspects of his life. Even his *Journal*, as readable, though less detailed and racy, as that of his brother, has long been unobtainable and I have been obliged to use a borrowed copy.

Unlike John Wesley, he has had few biographers, and their work is mostly out of date. The earliest was Dr. J. Whitehead in 1783. Thomas Jackson's three-volume biography (1847) is the most comprehensive, though hardly a critical assessment. More familiar is the shorter and useful *Life* by John Telford in 1886, revised and enlarged in 1900. The Drew Lectures of Dr. F. L. Wiseman, *Charles Wesley, Evangelist and Poet* (1933), makes no claim to be a biography, but discusses with critical insight selected aspects. More recently Dora Jones' study, *Charles Wesley* and Muriel Brailsford's *A Tale of Two Brothers* (1954) have appeared, both interesting and well-written, but covering familiar ground. Dr. Maldwyn Edwards' recent *Sons to Samuel* (1961) includes a welcome and perceptive tribute; and Dr. Frank Baker's Wesley Historical Society Lecture, *Charles Wesley as revealed by his Letters* (1948) offers a concise and reliable summary and is the best extant guide. I gladly acknowledge my indebtedness to the work of both these authors.

The brothers were so closely identified that it is difficult to write of one apart from the other, and in the process Charles' activities tend to become obscured. They have been obscured also by Charles himself as a result of his modesty, by the fact that we have no voluminous records as of John, and because those which have survived, including letters, are often undated and in some cases in shorthand difficult to decipher. And his published *Journal*, with intermittent gaps and an abrupt ending, covers only twenty years of his life. A further reason is the attitude (and negligence) of his family after his death, who deliberately withheld his papers from those who could have done justice to his memory. They were long kept in entire secrecy and many may have been lost or destroyed. He requested his wife to retain his journal—a thick octavo volume in his neat hand—in her own possession, but on her death her son Charles appears to have lost it. Later it was discovered lying, mutilated, among the straw on the floor of a furniture warehouse where some of the family goods were in store. The wonder is that it survived. It deserves to be republished.

Dr. Frank Baker, I understand, is engaged on the difficult but much-needed task of arranging and editing existing material. The result should greatly facilitate the work of future students. Original papers, unknown to the historian, may still be in private hands, and if so, information of such would be welcome.

My aim has been to meet the demand for a new and clearer image of the co-founder of Methodism, who deserves to be seen in his own dimension, distinct from that of John, and in the light of his own considerable achievement. His memory merits greater honour. He is presented here in his threefold character of Evangelist, churchman and poet. I have kept as far as possible to his own and contemporary records and allowed him to speak for himself. Only thus and by an objective approach can we correctly evaluate his character and work. In the result I hope that some prevailing misconceptions may be removed and a dim view be made clearer of one to whom, not only Methodism, but Christendom itself is so deeply indebted. In his hymns he has left behind him an imperishable legacy. And in this ecumenical age, we could do with a healthy injection of his apostolic vigour and catholic and evangelical spirit.

Chronology of Charles Wesley

1707	December 18	Born at Epworth
1716	April	Entered Westminster School
1726	June 13	Entered Christ Church, Oxford
	October 12	Birth of Sarah Gwynne
		Formation of the Holy Club
		Graduated B.A. (M.A. March 12, 1733)
1735	April 25	Death of his father
	September 21	Ordained deacon
	24	Appointed secretary to General Oglethorpe
	28	Ordained priest
	October 14	Sailed for Georgia (landed February 5, 1736)
1736	March 9	Began his ministry in Frederica
		First entry in his published *Journal*
	July 26	Returned to England (landed December 3)
1738	April 3	Resigned his secretaryship
	May 21	His "evangelical" conversion
1738–9		Assisted at St. Mary's, Islington
1739	May 29	First field preaching
	October 28	Opened his Bristol ministry
	November 8	Death of his brother Samuel
1742	July 30	Death of his mother
1744	June 25	First Methodist Conference
1747–8	September 9– March 20	First visit to Ireland
1748	August 13– October 8	Second visit to Ireland
1749		Publication of *Hymns and Sacred Poems*
	April 8	Marriage to Sarah Gwynne

13

1756	September–November	Last visit to the north of England
	November 5	His published *Journal* ends
1771		Removal to London
1784	September 1–2	John Wesley's first ordinations
1786		Attends his last Conference
1787	September	Last visit to Bristol
1788	March 29	Died in his eighty-second year
	April 5	Buried in Marylebone churchyard
1822	December 22	Death of his wife

Chapter One

EARLY YEARS 1707–1716

PREMATURE BIRTH—THE WESLEY PEDIGREE—EPWORTH—
UNCLE MATTHEW—FAMILY FINANCES—SUSANNA'S RULES—
THE RECTORY FIRE.

CHAPTER ONE

CHARLES WESLEY was his mother's eighteenth child. His premature arrival threw the Epworth household into no little confusion and anxiety, for he was born so small and frail that it hardly seemed he could live. For two months he neither cried nor opened his eyes, and it says much for his mother's care that he survived.

His earliest biographer, Dr. John Whitehead, says: "Mr. Charles Wesley was born December 18th, 1708, old style, several weeks before his time, at Epworth . . . He appeared dead rather than alive when he was born. He did not cry, nor open his eyes, and was kept wrapt up in soft wool until the time when he should have been born according to the usual course of nature, and then he opened his eyes and cried."

The date, however, is uncertain. Charles himself was never sure of his own birthday and there is a gap in the Epworth Church registers. Probably the date given in the records of Westminster School is reliable, which is December 18, 1707, and this is confirmed by Dr. Frank Baker's recent discovery of a transcript from the Epworth registers in the Diocesan Registry, Lincoln.

Among the stories of English rectories hardly one is more remarkable than that of Epworth. George Sampson in his Warton Lecture referred to the Wesleys as one of the most astonishing families this country has produced. Even Haworth Parsonage fails in comparison, for where Haworth produced a sporadic and dazzling brilliance, Epworth glowed with a clear and consistent flame which illumined the English-speaking world.

The Wesley pedigree on both sides was distinguished. Samuel Wesley, Rector of Epworth, came of the Westleys of Dorset, with a distant connection with the Wellesleys of Kildare. C. J. Stevenson in *Memorials of the Wesley Family* gives copious details, tracing Samuel's ancestors back to Guy of Welswe, near Wells, a tenth-century thane, a later descendant of whom married a Wesley of Westley Hall, near Bury St. Edmunds, from whom came the Wesleys of Bury and of Westley Hall, Shropshire.

17   CW—B

Later, according to Stevenson, from the same stock there was a Sir John de Wellesley, Sheriff of Kildare, a Sir William de Wellesley who fought in the Crusades, and a Sir Richard de Wellesley, head of the Wesleys of Dangan, Co. Meath, one of whom at a later period wished to adopt Charles Wesley as his heir. This Irish branch produced a Governor-General of India and also the Duke of Wellington.

Sir Herbert Wesley (or Westley) of the Dorset branch in the seventeenth century married a daughter of Robert Wesley of Dangan Castle. Their son Bartholomew, a physician and cleric, became Rector of Charmouth but lost his living under the Act of Uniformity in 1662, and was the grandfather of Charles Wesley. His wife was a daughter of Sir Henry Colley of Kildare, who was also probably a distant connection. Their son John (not to be confused with the founder of Methodism), although not episcopally ordained, held the living of Winterbourne Whitchurch in Dorset, from which he was removed, and was also four times imprisoned for refusing to conform. He married a daughter of Dr. John White, a well-known Nonconformist and a member of the Westminster Assembly of Divines. She was a niece of Dr. Thomas Fuller, author of *The Worthies of England*. And it was their son Samuel who forsook a Dissenting academy for Oxford, who for forty years was Rector of Epworth, and was the father of John and Charles Wesley.

Samuel's wife, Susanna, was one of the attractive daughters of Dr. Samuel Annesley, a cousin of the Earl of Anglesey and a former Vicar of St. Giles, Cripplegate and Lecturer of St. Paul's, who had also lost his living in 1662. He was of the order of Baxter, Goodwin and other Puritan divines, an outstanding character and noted preacher, as impervious to hardship as to public opinion, reading his twenty chapters of Scripture a day in a fireless study even in midwinter with the windows wide.

Thus on both sides of the Epworth ancestry there was the dual strain of good blood and hard living, and of distinguished Anglican and Puritan elements. And by a remarkable coincidence, both the grandfathers of John and Charles Wesley bore the same Christian name and surname—John White, Dr. Annesley's second wife (Susanna's mother) being a daughter of John White of Pembroke, Member of Parliament for Southwark and a strong Puritan who also, to carry the coincidence further, served as a member of the Westminster Assembly, acting as chairman of the Committee for Plundered Ministers.

Here, then, was the rock from which the Wesleys were hewn. And Charles was born into an unusual home, where grace accompanied spartan (though not drab) poverty, and where scholarship and gaiety combined with industry and piety. It was a happy household, despite its clash of strong personalities and the shadow of recurring misfortunes. Only ten of Susanna's nineteen children survived to maturity, though at one time there were at least thirteen alive together. They were days of large families and heavy infant mortality. Susanna herself was the twenty-second child in a family of twenty-four. The Minister who officiated at the baptism of yet another of Dr. Annesley's offspring was asked: "How many children has Dr. Annesley?" and replied: "I believe it is two dozen or a quarter of a hundred." At which John Dunton, a son-in-law of Dr. Annesley, remarked: "This reckoning of children by dozens is a singular circumstance," and added: "An honour to which few persons ever arrive."

Susanna's surviving children were gifted and attractive. It was their father's proud boast that his three sons received the best education in England; and they made good use of it. They must have been uncommonly clever, for good scholarships came their way, each excelled at school and university, and no father in such circumstances could have done more for his sons. The eldest, Samuel, became a King's Scholar and afterwards senior usher of Westminster School, then headmaster of Blundell's School, Tiverton. John was a Scholar of Charterhouse, Student of Christ Church and Fellow of Lincoln College. Charles was a King's Scholar and Captain of Westminster, and Student and, later, a tutor of Christ Church. But their education was for many years a heavy drain on their father's resources and partly explains his impoverishment.

The daughters were less fortunate, for on them, despite hardly less promising ability, fell the drudgery of the home—no small burden considering its numbers, its frequent childbirths, the size of the house, the extent of the glebe, and the additional care of the Rector's second parsonage in the adjoining parish of Wroot. They were a group of bright, high-spirited girls, some of them well-trained in the classics (Hetty could read the Greek Testament at the age of eight) and with a pretty turn for verse, and accustomed not only to household chores but to assist their father as amanuenses. It was a house of laughter, singing and unceasing industry. But unhappily no appropriate suitors came their way. Their isolated situation offered few social opportunities, and among other handicaps were their father's absorption in literary work to supplement his income, his prolonged absences in London representing the diocese as a proctor in Convocation, his imprisonment on one occasion for debt, and the fact that, faithful priest though he was, more often than not he was at odds with his parishioners.

Several of the girls left home, if only temporarily, like the Brontë sisters, to take posts in the neighbourhood, and one to start her own school. The youngest, Molly, married her father's curate, John Whitelamb, formerly a charity boy of the town whom the Rector had taken into his home and had assisted to an Oxford college. It was a happy union but ended before a year was out by her untimely death. Apart from her, and Kezzy who remained single, the sisters made ill-assorted marriages, in two cases desperately unhappy ones.

A letter from Susanna to her brother, Samuel Annesley tells its own story:

> My dear Emily, who in my present exigencies would exceedingly comfort me, is compelled to go to service in Lincoln, where she is a teacher in a boarding school. My second daughter Suky, a pretty woman and worthy a better fate, rashly threw herself away upon a man that is not only her plague, but a constant affliction to the family. The other children, though wanting neither industry nor capacity for business, we cannot put to any, by reason we have neither money nor friends to assist us in doing so. Nor is there a gentleman's seat in which we can place them, even as common servants, and that even you yourself would not think fit for if you saw them, so that they must stay at home while they have a home.

Of those hard days the eldest daughter, Emily, wrote:

> After the fire, when I was seventeen years old, I was left alone with my mother and lived easy for one year—but after we were gotten into our house, and all the family settled, in about a year's time, I began to find out that we were ruined. Then came on London journeys. Convocations of blessed memory, that for seven winters my father was at London and we at home in intolerable want and affliction; then I learned what it was to seek money for

20

bread . . . Thus we went on growing worse and worse; all of us children in scandalous want of necessaries for years together, vast income but no comfort or credit with it . . . My old belief yet remains that my father will never be worth a groat, as the saying is, and we of the female part of the family be left to get our own bread or starve as we see fit.

And this proved only too true.

As for the Rector, he never succeeded in securing the preferments his abilities deserved. He was received by the Queen and had distinguished literary and clerical friends. He loved the coffee house life of London, no doubt finding it a welcome relief from his parish. It was said by those who knew him that had he been more accommodating, less implacable in his opinions, he might have become a bishop. (His nomination for an Irish bishopric at the age of thirty-two was unsuccessful, probably on account of his youth.) But always he scorned the easy way, combining his parochial duties with those of a literary hack, fighting fire and flood in his water-logged parish, rowing by boat between his two livings or riding his cob by the swollen dykes, struggling with poor crops, sick cattle, low prices, and a sullen and unfriendly peasantry. But he was tough and courageous. Had he not once with disgust and contempt turned from his door his patron's mistress, saying that she was no fit company for his wife! And had he not in the hard days of his youth, moved by robust conviction, thrown aside his Nonconformist upbringing and walked from Dorset to Oxford with but forty-five shillings in his pocket to enter himself as a servitor at Exeter College! At one time he had served as a naval chapplain on a man-of-war. Such was the stuff of which the Wesleys were made.

He had, however, a poor head for business and few men in his position were ever more financially embarrassed. His two livings provided him with a reasonable income and by careful management and more capital he could have made his glebe pay, but always he was dogged by insolvency and with a Micawber-like air of philosophic cheerfulness and temperamental improvidence he pursued his erratic way.

His brother, Dr. Matthew Wesley, a prosperous London apothecary, on visiting the Rectory in 1731, when on his way to take the waters at Scarborough, was appalled by its poverty. His arrival had been a great occasion and Susanna wrote a lively account of it to John at Oxford: "My brother Wesley had designed to have surprised us, and had travelled under a feigned name." The news leaked out, however, through his manservant who had been sent on ahead, and Molly Wesley heard it in the market an hour before her uncle's arrival. "She, full of the news, hastened home, and told me her uncle Wesley was coming to see us; but we could hardly believe her. 'Twas odd to observe how all the town took the alarm, and were upon the gaze, as if some great prince had been about to make his entry."

For two days he regarded the struggling household with a jaundiced eye, then thawed in geniality and afterwards proved a generous friend. "His behaviour among us was perfectly civil and obliging. He spoke little to the children the first day, being employed, (as he afterwards told them), in observing their carriage, and seeing how he liked them; afterwards he was very free, and expressed great kindness to them all. He was strangely scandalized at the poverty of our furniture, and much more at the meanness of the children's habit."

He stayed again with them on his return journey, but finding two of his nieces had left for Lincoln lost no time in joining them, prolonging his stay there for four days and inviting them and their friends to share his meals at The Angel. But back in London he wrote a stinging rebuke to his brother, whose improvidence he considered irresponsible. "You have a numerous offspring; you have had a long time a plentiful estate, great and generous benefactions, and have made no provision for those of your own home, who can have nothing in view at your exit but distress. This I think a black account, let the case be folly, or vanity, or ungovernable appetites. I hope Providence has restored you again to give you time to restore this balance, which shocks me to think of." To which the ebullient though now ageing Rector replied characteristically, using the third person and calling himself John O'Styles: "If God has blessed him with a numerous offspring, he has no reason to be ashamed of them," and he sets before this *Severus Frater et Avunculus Puerorum* (as he calls him) details of his income and expenditure, beginning: "When he first walked to Oxford he had in cash £2. 5. 0. . . . He wrote a book which he dedicated to Queen Mary, who for that reason gave him a living in the country, valued at £200 per annum, where he remained for nearly forty

22

years, and wherein his numerous offspring amounted to eighteen or nineteen children. Half of his parsonage-house was first burnt, which he rebuilt; some time after the whole was burnt to the ground, which he rebuilt from the foundations, and it cost him above four hundred pounds, besides the furniture, none of which was saved."

The added living of Wroot brought little gain after paying a curate and with heavy losses through inundations of the glebe. "For the greater part of these last ten years he has been closely employed in composing a large book, whereby he hoped he might have done some benefit to the world, and in some measure amend his own fortunes. By sticking so close to this, he has broken a pretty strong constitution, and fallen into the palsy and gout. Besides this he has had sickness in his family for most of the years since he was married. His greater living seldom cleared above eighteen pounds per annum, out of which he allowed £20 per annum to a person [John White-lamb] who had married one of his daughters." And he concludes: "Let all this be balanced, and then a guess may be easily made of his sorry management. He can struggle with the world, but not with Providence. Nor can he resist sickness, fires, and inundations."

As far back as 1700 he had written to the Archbishop of York: "I must own I was ashamed, when at Bishop Thorpe, to confess that I was three hundred pounds in debt, when I have a living of which I have made two hundred pounds per annum, though I could hardly let it now for eight-score. I doubt not but one reason of my being sunk so far is my not understanding worldly affairs."

These letters give vivid glimpses of his circumstances. "Nothing to begin the world with, one child at least per annum, and my wife sick for half that time!" Fifty pounds expended on a journey to London and the cost of getting into his living, fifty pounds to stop the mouths of his more importunate creditors, a hundred pounds loan from a goldsmith, fifty pounds for furniture and to stock his glebe! "The next year my barn fell, which cost me forty pounds in rebuilding (thanks to your Grace for part of it)", and "ten pounds a year I allow my mother, to help to keep her from starving."

The Rector kept the Archbishop well informed of his circumstances and not all his misfortune could suppress his humour:

Last night my wife brought me a few children. There are but *two* yet, a boy and a girl, and I think they are all at present: we have had four in two years and a day, three of which are living. Never came anything more like a gift from heaven than what the Duchess of Northampton sent by your Lordship's charitable offices. Wednesday evening my wife and I clubbed and joined stocks, which came but to six shillings, to send for coals. Thursday morning I received the *ten pounds*, and at night my wife was delivered. Glory be to God for His unspeakable goodness! I am your Grace's most obliged and most humble servant, S. Wesley.

But two years later the position was no better. Susanna had borne him another child, who at three weeks old had been put out to nurse. It was during an election when the village was alarmed one night by a noisy disturbance, and the nurse, waking suddenly, had overlaid the child. "She waked and finding it dead, ran over with it to my house, almost distracted, and calling my servants, threw it into their arms. They, as wise as she, ran up with it to my wife, and before she was well awake, threw it cold and dead into hers. She composed herself as well as she could, and that day got it buried." And the Rector concludes: "All this, thank God, does not in the least sink my wife's spirits."

A month later he was in prison for debt and wrote from Lincoln Castle: "Now I am at rest, for I have come to the haven where I long expected to be. A jail is a paradise in comparison of the life I led before I came hither." He had been arrested in his own churchyard after conducting a baptism, and at the time he and his wife had only a pound between them.

His finer qualities, however, must not be overlooked. For years he ground out his two hundred couplets a day, working for his brother-in-law, John Dunton, a London bookseller, and along with him produced a periodical, *The Athenian Gazette*. He worked laboriously for twenty-five years at his voluminous Latin *Dissertations on the Book of Job*—a literary curiosity, on the publication of which Bishop Warburton remarked sarcastically: "Poor Job! It was his eternal fate to be persecuted by his friends." But Pope, an admirer of the Rector, commended it as a pious and good work and solicited subscriptions "for a good and honest man, past seventy and poor." The Rector also wrote the hymn: "Behold the Saviour of mankind" which survives in modern hymnals. And his affectionate letters of advice to his sons indicate that he contributed no less than Susanna to their training.

It was, however, with relief that, one by one, he saw his daughters married; and their suitors found an open door. As he wrote dryly to General Oglethorpe: "I thank God, I creep up-hill more than I did formerly, being eased of the weight of four daughters out of seven, as I hope I shall be of a fifth in a little longer." But we cannot forget his kindness to his aged mother and his gentle reminders to his sons to write often to their mother. "Reverence and love her as much as you can. . . . The more duty you pay her, and the more frequently and kindly you write to her, the more you will please your affectionate Father." His poem on a good wife reflects his own devotion to her:

> She graced my humble roof, and blest my life.
> Blessed me by a far greater name than wife.

It was a well-deserved tribute, and in more ways than one she was unique. She was of the quality of Monica, the mother of Augustine. And in toughness and courage she equalled her husband, though with less impulsiveness, more wisdom, and a greater serenity.

In looks she is said to have surpassed her sister Judith, who had been painted by Lely for his Gallery of Beautiful Women. She was well-grounded in Latin, was a woman of considerable ability, and words can hardly describe her diligence and devotion. Her journal and letters in their clear unaffected style still make good reading. And she was a born manager. Through all the years of the Rector's struggle and mismanagement it was her brave and unwavering spirit which steadied the life of the home and preserved its sweetness and strength. Full well the Rector knew the debt he owed her. And though the title of being the first Methodist must go to Charles, if by a Methodist we mean one who disposes a thing in an orderly manner, particularly in the practical expression of Christian piety, then the honour must be Susanna's, for method was the rule of her life.

The schoolroom can still be seen where each day from nine till twelve and from two till five, she taught her children; also the kitchen from which she ruled her household and where she

25

collected not only her family, but in her husband's prolonged absences, his neglected parishioners for Bible reading and prayer. So popular were these kitchen meetings that up to two hundred people would gather. Thus in family discipline, parochial fellowship, lay leadership, and the part a woman can play in the life of the Church, she anticipated in some measure the work of her two most famous sons.

Her wholesome rules on child training, so full of psychology and commonsense, are worth quoting at length, as they are too often quoted out of their context or misrepresented.

As soon as they were grown pretty strong, they were confined to three meals a day. At dinner their little tables and chairs were set by ours, where they could be overlooked; and they were suffered to eat and drink (small beer) as much as they would; but not to call for anything. If they wanted aught, they used to whisper to the maid which attended them, who came and spake to me. . . . They were never suffered to choose their meat, but always made to eat such things as were provided for the family. . . . Eating and drinking between meals was never allowed, unless in cases of sickness, which seldom happened. . . .

At six, as soon as prayers were over, they had their supper; at seven the maid washed them; and, beginning at the youngest, she undressed and got them all to be in bed by eight; at which time she left them in their several rooms awake; for there was no such thing allowed of in our house, as sitting by a child till it fell asleep . . .

In order to form the minds of children, the first thing to be done is to conquer their will, and bring them to an obedient temper. To inform the understanding is a work of time, and must with children proceed by slow degrees, as they are able to bear it; but the subjecting of the will is a thing which must be done at once; and the sooner the better. For by neglecting timely correction, they will contract a stubbornness and obstinacy which is hardly ever after conquered . . . They pass for kind and indulgent, whom I call cruel parents, who permit their children to get habits which they know must be afterwards broken . . . Whenever a child is corrected, it must be conquered; and this will be no hard matter to do, if it be not grown headstrong by too much indulgence. And when the will of a child is totally subdued, and it is brought to revere and stand in awe of the parents, then a great many childish follies and inadvertencies may be passed by. Some should be overlooked, and taken no notice of, and others mildly reproved.

26

I insist upon conquering the will of children betimes, because this is the only strong and rational foundation of a religious education; without which both precept and example will be ineffectual. But when this is thoroughly done, then a child is capable of being governed by the reason and piety of its parents, till its own understanding comes to maturity, and the principles of religion have taken root in the mind.

I cannot yet dismiss this subject. As self-will is the root of all sin and misery, so whatever cherishes this in children insures their after-wretchedness and irreligion. Whatever checks and mortifies it, promotes their future happiness and piety.

As soon as they could speak they were taught the Lord's Prayer. They were very early made to distinguish the Sabbath from other days. They were quickly made to understand that they might have nothing they cried for and instructed to speak handsomely for what they wanted.

There was no such thing as loud talking allowed of. Every one was kept close to their business, for the six hours of school; and it is almost incredible what a child may be taught in a year; by a vigorous application, if it have but a tolerable capacity and good health . . .

Lying was prevented by each being told that confession and promise to amend would avoid a beating. Every act of obedience, on their own inclination, would be commended and frequently rewarded. Nothing, not so much as a farthing or a pin, must be taken without the owner's consent. And promises must be strictly observed. "Never," says Susanna, "were children better disposed to piety."

There was no repressive sense of fear or of authority, no unnecessary suppression. And although she was preoccupied with conduct and discipline to the exclusion of broader social and aesthetic interests, which reflects her main limitation, who can doubt her sound instinct? Judged by results, her rules were effective. In a cynical age and in a rough community she preserved the virtue of her children; and they, far from feeling inhibited, developed in natural goodness, full of high spirits, each strongly individualized in personality and self-expression, and abounding in family loyalty and affection. Their father, despite his erratic temperament, was a strong formative influence in their lives, but their mother by these sensible and sustained

27

methods nourished qualities of character which they never lost, and principles of conduct from which they never diverged, and which later marked the strong family life and ethical vigour of Methodism.

In 1709 Epworth Rectory went up in flames. "I suppose you have already heard", Susanna wrote to her son Samuel, "of the firing of our house, by what accident we cannot imagine; but the fire broke out about eleven or twelve o'clock at night, we being all in bed, nor did we perceive it till the roof of the corn chamber was burnt through, and the fire fell upon your sister Hetty's bed. She awaked and immediately ran to call your father, who lay in the red chamber; for I, being ill, he was forced to lie from me . . . We had not time to take our clothes, but ran all naked."

The story of John Wesley's providential rescue is familiar, but Charles, who was seventeen months old at the time, was no less mercifully preserved and owed his escape to a maid who carried him out of the burning building in her arms. Susanna herself, who was again pregnant, nearly perished. In the confusion she was cut off from the rest, and with the fire up to her knees, had been unable to open an outside door. For a short while she was missing, during which the Rector searched frantically for her among the crowd which had gathered. "When I came to her," he wrote afterwards to the Duke of Buckingham, "her lips were black. I did not know her." He adds that little remained to be salvaged, "not a rag or a leaf," apart from a little lumber. "Everything was consumed to ashes, for the fire was stronger than a furnace, the violent wind beating it down upon the house." But the letter ends, as usual, on a buoyant note: "All is lost. God be praised." His spirit was irrepressible.

Such then was the background of Charles Wesley's earliest years. So far we know little of him, but can picture him as a bright and lively child in a happy if circumscribed home in an isolated and a flood-ridden area, with poor facilities for travelling (the Wesleys kept no carriage), with no outside cultural opportunities and few, if any, congenial families with which to associate. It was a household preponderantly female. The eldest son was already in London, but John and Charles were soon to join him, and both there and in Oxford the boys of the family moved in a different world.

Chapter Two

WESTMINSTER AND OXFORD
1716–1735

BROTHER SAMUEL—WESTMINSTER SCHOOL—DR. BUSBY—A
SCHOOLBOY'S INSCRIPTION—A FORTUNE DECLINED—STUDENT
OF CHRIST CHURCH—EIGHTEENTH-CENTURY OXFORD—
AFFAIR WITH AN ACTRESS—COTSWOLD INTERLUDES—THE
HOLY CLUB.

CHAPTER TWO

FOLLOWING THESE troubled years, Samuel, the eldest son, knowing his father's straitened circumstances, generously made himself responsible for Charles' maintenance and education. The Rector deeply appreciated his kindness, writing to him in 1732: "You have been a father to your brothers and sisters, especially the former, who have cost you great sums in their education, both before and since they went to the University. Neither have you stopped there, but have shewn your pity to your mother and me in a very liberal manner, wherein your wife joined with you, when you did not overmuch abound yourself."

Samuel, who was Charles' senior by seventeen years, was by now ordained and senior usher of Westminster School, and lived in Dean's Yard. He was a fine classicist, with distinguished friends. Like his brothers he was deeply religious, though with no liking for their unconventional evangelism, and was equally interested in social reform. While at Westminster he formed the first free dispensary in England, which developed into St. George's Hospital. A flagstone in Westminster Abbey is inscribed with the names of four of his children.

Westminster, an ancient foundation of unknown date, which had grown out of a school attached to the former Benedictine Monastery, had been served by famous headmasters, and, greatest of all, the redoubtable Dr. Busby who died at the age of eighty-eight in the fifty-seventh year of his headmastership, having made the school the most famous in England. That was in 1695, twenty-one years before Charles' entry.

Busby was a hard flogger who, according to Dr. Burney, "could correct in a very liberal manner". But under him the school flourished and expanded, despite the violent political changes of the period which threatened its independence. When asked how he had managed for over half a century to weather the stormy disruptions of the Civil War and the Restoration, with three different dynasties and forms of worship, he replied: "The *fathers* govern the nation; the *mothers* govern the fathers; but the *boys* govern the mothers; and *I* govern the boys."

He was succeeded by Thomas Knipe, who was followed by Robert Freind—a pale shadow compared with Busby, but a welcome relief. As one put it:

> Forget at length your fears, your panic end,
> The monarch of this place is now a Freind.

He was headmaster during Charles' time at the School. Westminster was also remarkable for the unusual number of distinguished men among its former scholars, such as Ben Jonson, George Herbert, Gibbon, Wren, Locke, Dryden, and many others.

This was the school to which Charles Wesley came at the age of nine. For his first five years he lodged with his brother, but from 1721, as a King's Scholar, his board and education were free and he shared the old dormitory for the King's Scholars which then stood in Dean's Yard and which had been the granary of the monastery. He obtained seventh place among the nine Scholars admitted that year. It was a coveted honour, keenly competed for, and carried the strong likelihood, given normal application, of a university scholarship.

The school has in its possession a Book of Common Prayer which belonged to Charles, presented to it by Mr. F. B. Gordon during its wartime evacuation to Lancing. On the top right-hand corner of each page is a letter, forming a sequence which when pieced together makes the following inscription: "*E libris Caroli Wesley Hujusie Ecclesiae sancti Petri Collegiati Anno Domini* One thousand seven hundred and twenty one. Charles Wesley his book who is of Saint Peter's College, Westmonster [*sic*] Amen." Its mixed Latin and English, its ingenious concealment and the pun in its deliberate misspelling make it a typical schoolboy's effort.

Charles applied himself with diligence and in 1725 became Captain of the School. He was active and high-spirited, a bonnie fighter and had a generous spirit. Like his father he was impulsive and hot-tempered, and more than once he engaged in a fight on the Green within the cloisters. Once it was in defence of a new boy whose strong Scottish accent and the fact that he was a Jacobite had made him an object of ridicule. Charles befriended him, and in after years was more than repaid, for the boy, James Murray, became Lord Mansfield,

2a. Susanna Wesley, the mother of John and Charles. The date of this portrait is unknown, presumably early 18th century.

2b. The famous John Adams-Acton memorial in Westminster Abbey to John (right) and Charles Wesley. It was unveiled in 1876.

3*a* & *b*. Garth House, the home of the Gwynne family, as it is today. The partly castellated outer wall can be seen in the foreground. *Left*, the hall and staircase. Here Wesley came to woo and eventually marry Sally.

Lord Chief Justice; in legal problems Charles was able to turn to him for help, and in their old age they resumed their earlier intimacy.

Charles also took part in the annual Latin play. He had the reputation of being "arch and unlucky", which we may take to mean full of fun and of pranks which often landed him in hot water. He had his father's gift of humour and a strong social disposition. The school life was spartan, beginning with the rising bell at 5.15, followed by ablutions in the cloisters, Latin prayers and Greek grammar until breakfast at eight—the boys were kept strictly to the speaking of Latin, and Charles, like his two brothers, became a proficient classical scholar. The school day ended at eight in the evening when the boys went to bed.

A curious family incident occurred around this period. A letter reached the Rector of Epworth from Garret Wesley, a wealthy childless Irishman and distant family connection, inquiring if he had a son called Charles and offering financial aid towards his education along with a suggestion of adopting him and making him his heir. No undue excitement seems to have followed what could hardly have been unwelcome to a penniless and heavily encumbered parson, but the Rector apparently was less eager to be relieved of a son than he had been of his daughters. It says much for his unselfish nature that there was no greedy grasping at this sudden promise of affluence for Charles, whom he left to decide for himself. Charles appears to have been equally uninterested. He was now well established at Westminster, with prospects of Oxford opening before him, and although Garret Wesley came over to see him, he declined the offer. We are given no details of how far the proposal went or what conditions, if any, were imposed. At all events Charles seems to have had no regrets, and Garret Wesley in his search for an heir adopted Richard Colley, an even more distant relative than Charles, on condition that he changed his name to Wesley. To complete the story, this Richard Colley not only inherited his estates but was later created Baron Mornington, and was the grandfather of the Duke of Wellington, who was first entered in the Army List as Arthur Wesley, which he later changed to Wellesley—probably the original form of the family name. Charles Wesley, in his old age, and the second Lord Mornington were neighbours in Marylebone and close friends.

In 1726 Charles gained a studentship at Christ Church,

CW—C

Oxford, securing first place among the Westminster candidates. It was worth about £100 a year. Thus all three of Samuel's sons were Christ Church men. And among Oxford Colleges, Christ Church predominated, not only because of its architectural magnificence and its lavish hospitality to distinguished guests, but equally for its high reputation for scholarship.

Oxford in some respects has little changed; the Colleges, the courts and quadrangles which the Wesleys knew, still preserve their ancient form, and the outline of the old town remains; otherwise all is transformed, and Charles Wesley would hardly recognize it. In his day it was small and compact, unlike the sprawling city of today. It was noisy with the rattle of iron wheels upon the cobbles, and offensive at times from the stench of household garbage emptied into the runnels of the streets.

Academically it was far less demanding. Its leisure and lethargy encouraged the lazy, while its disregard of discipline and its farcical examinations discouraged serious learning and piety. This partly explains the formation of the Holy Club by Charles Wesley and like-minded students for the better use of their time in methodical study and prayer. Even the authorities showed a similar concern by issuing the following appeal against prevailing corruption and infidelity, the Dean of Christ Church alone among the Heads of Colleges refusing to allow it to be exhibited in the hall of his College: "Mr. Vice-Chancellor, with the consent of the Heads of Houses and Proctors, has thought fit to recommend it, as a matter of the utmost consequence, to the Tutors of each college and Hall in the University, that they discharge their duty by a double diligence, in informing their respective pupils in their Christian duty, as also in explaining to them the articles of the religion which they profess, and are often called upon to subscribe, and in recommending to them the frequent and careful reading of the Scriptures, and such other books as may serve more effectually to promote Christianity, sound principles, and orthodox faith. . . ."

Specific instances of declining standards are given in Dr. V. H. H. Green's book *The Young Mr. Wesley*, such as the reputation of the President of St. John's as a heavy gambler, a chaplain of Merton accused of sexual vice, and even worse scandal at Wadham whose Warden, after arrest, escaped abroad. Dr. Green finds that the real weakness of the University at this period lay in its lack of any real incentive to research, its perfunctory teaching, the failure of the examination system, and its too rigid insistence on the study of Aristotle and formal logic, leaving little stimulus for wider studies or original work.

This then was the Oxford in which Charles found himself and he loved it, welcoming every outlet and opportunity it offered to his keen and eager spirit. For the first time he tasted the pleasures of freedom, no longer under the tutelage of a much older brother. He found Oxford society congenial. He liked good company, enjoyed gay discourse, was never at a loss for friends, and was soon the centre of a lively group. Never again would he relax with such eager spontaneity or carefree happiness as during this first year at Oxford, when work and piety for the moment receded into the background and he indulged in a gay and innocent round of excitement. It was a natural reaction after his strenuous years at Westminster and the spartan background of Epworth. When John, who was of a cooler and less impetuous nature, frowned on these diversions, as he called them, Charles retorted with spirit: "What, would you have me be a saint all at once?"

There were excursions to London, as in January 1730 when, in the company of his brother and William Morgan, he left Oxford at five a.m., passed through Beaconsfield and arrived at Samuel's house in Westminster in the late afternoon. They paid a round of calls on old friends, enjoying tea and cards with one, supper and music with another, and a family visit to Uncle Matthew. They saw the Latin play at Westminster School, visited the House of Commons and went to the theatre. Charles seems to have been mildly involved with a young actress, Molly Buchanan, then appearing in *The Virgin Queen* at the Theatre Royal in Lincoln's Inn. Apparently she had a scheming mother—a Shakespearian actress, who encouraged Charles' attentions, but he withdrew in time. "My eyes were partly opened by my last saving journey to London." Was Mrs. Buchanan over-pressing? "To do the Old Lady justice, she did give us opportunities enough could I but have had the Grace to have laid hold on them and but for my strange College dullness Molly might have made something of me . . . Hints were lost upon so strange a Fellow as I was, and as such no doubt I have been since sufficiently laughed at." We should

35

like to know more of this incident, but the pretty actress flits across the stage all too quickly, and we are left only with Charles' disillusion.

Meanwhile bracing letters came from his father, urging him to cultivate piety as well as learning and to take plenty of exercise. "You must find time every day for walking . . . a little more exercise now and then will do you no harm. You are now launched fairly, Charles. Hold up your head, and swim like a man; and when you cuff the wave beneath you, say to it much as another did, *'Carolum vehis, et Caroli fortunas'* [Thou carriest Charles and Charles' fortune]. But always keep your eye fixed above the pole star; and so God send you a good voyage through the troublesome seas of life, which is the hearty prayer of your loving father." And: "Bear no more sail than is necessary, but steer steady."

John had just been elected Fellow of Lincoln and, as Greek Lecturer and Moderator of the Classes, was now well established and with a rising reputation in the University. But about this time he had left Oxford for a year to act as curate to their ageing father. The old man, palsied and declining, but game as ever, had written to his sons: "My hide is tough; and I think no carrion can kill me. I walked sixteen miles yesterday; and this morning, I thank God, I am not a penny worse." A further letter gives news of his fall from a horse: "My old nag fell with me, trailed me by my foot in the stirrup about six yards, trod on my other foot, but never hurt me."

Charles, in the meantime, who could never long be idle, after the novelty and freedom of his first year had settled down with new diligence to his work, and it was during this fresh application to his studies and in his brother's absence that he adopted a new way of life. "Diligence led me into serious thinking. I went to the weekly sacrament, and persuaded two or three young students to accompany me, and to observe the method of study prescribed by the statutes of the University. This gained me the harmless name of Methodist." Oxford, as we have noted, was hardly a hive of strenuous activity (there were, of course, notable exceptions), and here was a modest and conscientious move towards the University's true function. But even more significant is that in this revealing comment of Charles Wesley we find the germ of Methodism. In our search for Methodist origins we may overlook or underestimate this simple statement, but bearing in mind also the methodical routine of his mother, here is their primary source. It is true the name was not new and had been applied at earlier periods to odd groups and sects, but it never survived, as in this case, and fixed itself in history for generations to come.

Now for Charles all was changed, and like a seedling the little group began to grow. We hear of no sudden enlightenment, no swift and overpowering illumination, but of single-minded and undramatic application to their immediate duty. Basically this was the foundation, and later, linked to active evangelism, the very substance of Methodism. The name itself conveys the meaning. No new theology was involved, no break with the Church, no revolt against tradition. Methodism meant discipline, self-discipline, a resolute sense of duty and responsibility, a life of regular devotion and active witness. Before the outbreak of a nation-wide enthusiasm, the long itineraries and rousing multitudes, we find a student quietly applying himself with dedicated diligence to his appointed task, and out of such austere and patient pursuit of discipline and duty Methodism first arose, attracted its earliest followers and gained its now familiar name.

This, of course, is by no means the whole explanation, nor does it cover the many tributaries that swelled the flood tide of revival, but we misunderstand its nature if we fail to hold clearly in our minds this small and dedicated group which, led by Charles Wesley and at first hardly numbering half a dozen, formed in an indifferent and even hostile atmosphere a cell of serious study, methodical piety and Christian activity. Methodism was to take many shapes and forms (surprisingly diverse), but here was its initial quality and spirit.

Charles lost no time in informing John of this new development and from this point came into much closer relation with him. Hitherto his brother Samuel had been his mentor and guide, but from now on, through natural circumstances, John's influence is predominant, and at times to the point of domineering. The following extract from a letter to John at Epworth shows how gladly Charles turned to him: "God has thought fit, it may be to increase my wariness, to deny me at present your company and assistance. It is through Him strengthening me I trust to maintain my ground till we meet. And I hope that, neither before nor after that time, I shall relapse into my former

37

state of insensibility. It is through your means, I firmly believe, that God will establish what He has begun in me; and there is no person I shall so willingly have to be the instrument of good to me as you. It is owing, in great measure, to somebody's prayers (my mother's most likely) that I am come to think as I do; for I cannot tell myself how or when I awoke out of my lethargy—only that it was not long after you went away."

John had urged him to keep a diary and this he found irksome. John was a great diarist—his journals comparable with those of the best diarists of the day. Almost to his dying day he noted down with scrupulous care every date and detail of his activities. With Charles it was otherwise, and his *Journal* covers only half his career. How shall he set about it? he asks. What exactly must he record? And, because John used shorthand, what cipher should he use? "If you would direct me to the same, or like method to your own, I would gladly follow it, for I am fully convinced of the usefulness of such an undertaking. I shall be at a stand until I hear from you."

Meanwhile he continued to influence more of his friends, and John, on his return, assumed the leadership, greatly to Charles' relief and to the advantage of the group which benefited from his status in the University. It became known as the Holy Club, though other names were scornfully applied. "Here is a new set of Methodists sprung up," said one of Charles' fellow-students. The first two members after Charles were William Morgan, a Commoner of Christ Church, who came of an Irish family, and Robert Kirkham, whose father was Rector of Stanton in Gloucestershire. Morgan, whose health was frail and who died shortly afterwards, was zealous in works of charity and was the first to interest the Wesleys in prison visitation. Another early member was John Gambold, a servitor of Christ Church. On hearing of "the whimsical Mr. Wesley and his pious extravagances", he had consulted him, and Charles, with characteristic modesty, had referred him to John, saying, "He is somewhat older than I and can resolve your doubts better." Gambold has left this clear description of Charles: "He was a man made for friendship; who, by his cheerfulness and vivacity, would refresh his friend's heart; with attentive consideration, would enter into and settle all his concerns; so far as he was able, would do anything for him, great or small; and, by a habit of openness and freedom, leave no room for misunderstanding."

Among them also was a young servitor of Pembroke, George Whitefield, whose career was as remarkable as that of the Wesleys. He had served as a pot-boy in his mother's inn in Gloucester, and with little education and a background very different from Charles Wesley's had managed to reach Oxford. "Never a poor creature," he says, "set up with so small a stock." He was so poor he was obliged to wait on the wealthier students for what money he could earn; so lost in an atmosphere of extravagance and impiety that in winter he sat alone, cold and miserable, in his fireless study; so withdrawn from the life around him that he was regarded as "a singular odd fellow". Like Gambold, he admired the despised Methodists and longed to join them, but was held back by poverty and inferiority.

His *Journal* gives a factual contemporary account:

> The young men (the despised Methodists) were then much talked of in Oxford. I had heard of, and loved them before I came to the University; and so strenuously defended them when I heard them reviled by the students, that they began to think that I also in time should be one of them. For above a twelve months my soul longed to be acquainted with some of them, and I was strongly pressed to follow their good example, when I saw them go through a ridiculing crowd to receive the Holy Eucharist at St. Mary's. At length God was pleased to open a door. It happened that a poor woman in one of the workhouses had attempted to cut her throat, but was happily prevented. Upon hearing of this, and knowing that both the Mr. Wesleys were ready to every good work, I sent a poor apple-woman of our college to inform Mr. Charles Wesley of it, charging her not to discover who sent her. She went, but, contrary to my orders, told my name.

On hearing this, Charles, who had noticed the lonely student on his walks and at the parish Communion, invited him to breakfast the following day. And Whitefield continues: "I thankfully embraced the opportunity; and, blessed be God! it was one of the most profitable visits I ever made in my life."

Charles was the instrument of his conversion. He befriended him and lent him books, of one of which Whitefield records: "I never knew what true religion was till God sent me that excellent treatise by the hands of my never-to-be-forgotten friend. . . . From time to time Mr. Wesley permitted me to come unto him, and instructed me as I was able to bear it. By

39

degrees he introduced me to the rest of his Christian brethren. They built me up daily in the knowledge and fear of God. . . . I now began, like them, to live by rule, and to pick up the very fragments of my time, that not a moment of it might be lost. . . . Their hearts glowed with the love of God."

Many came amongst them for a while and fell away. The displeasure of a tutor, the contempt of a friend, academic success, dirt thrown at them in the street, proved too much for them. As for the rest, Whitefield adds: "The world, and not themselves, gave them the title of Methodists, I suppose from their custom of regulating their time, and planning the business of the day each morning. Mr. John and Charles Wesley were two of the first that thus openly dared to confess Christ; and they, under God, were the spiritual fathers of most of them."

But to associate with them required courage. "I had no sooner received the sacrament publicly on a weekday at St. Mary's, but I was set up as a mark for all the polite students to shoot at. By this they knew that I was commenced Methodist, for though there is a sacrament at the beginning of every term, at which, especially the seniors, are by statute, obliged to be present, yet so dreadfully has that once faithful city played the harlot, that very few Masters, and no undergraduates but the Methodists attend it. Mr. Charles Wesley, whom I must always mention with the greatest deference and respect, walked with me, in order to confirm me, from the church even to the college. I confess to my shame, I would gladly have excused this; and the next day, going to his room, one of our Fellows passing by, I was ashamed to be seen to knock on his door."

This was hardly surprising, for he underwent a period of irritating persecution, including the disfavour of the Master of his College and the withholding of tips for his menial tasks as servitor. But he never forgot Charles Wesley's kindness, and though serious doctrinal differences divided them in later years, his gratitude and affection remained unimpaired. And he more than repaid his indebtedness when he persuaded the reluctant Wesleys to follow him into the fields with the Gospel and provided them with their first open-air multitudes.

Nor must we forget that just as Charles was the founder of the Holy Club, so also was he the main influence in the conversion of Whitefield who became the outstanding Christian orator of the century ("unrivalled in eloquence," said the Earl of

Chesterfield); he crossed the Atlantic thirteen times, pioneered in America, founded schools and orphanages, raised immense sums for charity; and won multitudes for Christ.

The Methodists followed a strenuous and consistent routine, including early rising, Bible reading and academic study, regular Communion, the observance of fasts and Church festivals, and sick and prison visitation. They read together devotional classics and shared Christian fellowship. They met in each other's rooms, but their main centre was John Wesley's study, still to be seen, in the inner quadrangle of Lincoln College.

But they must not be regarded only in terms of austerity. They were neither sour puritans nor pious sentimentalists. Their enthusiasm found a healthy outlet in social and philanthropic as well as evangelistic activities. There was no aloofness from the world except in the times allocated to study and prayer. They sought out the needy and illiterate, giving generously out of their own meagre income. (Once the Wesleys walked from Oxford to Epworth and back to save horse hire, in order to swell the fund they had established for the relief of the poor.) And they sought authority for what they did, consulting the Bishop of Oxford and securing his blessing. It would be quite wrong to think of them as religious busybodies or frenzied fanatics. Their main singularity was that they were out of tune with contemporary cynicism and indifference, and sought a recovery of personal discipline and social responsibility. This was the point of conflict. A Methodist, as defined by John Wesley, is one that lives according to the *method* laid down in the Bible.

Perhaps they were over-zealous, at times tactless—common faults of youthful enthusiasm—and maybe they over-emphasized their mission, but how otherwise could they have succeeded? Old Samuel Wesley at Epworth, nearing the end of his stormy life, followed the group with interest and blessed it from afar. The other Samuel in Tiverton regarded it coldly, but the Rector wrote to John: "I hear my son has the honour of being styled the Father of the Holy Club, and if it be so, I must be the Grandfather of it," and: "I have the highest reason to bless God that He has given me two sons together at Oxford to whom He has given grace and courage to turn the war against the world and the devil."

There were other occasions—pleasant interludes, when they carried their gaiety and their mission further afield, to the Kirkhams at Stanton, to the Griffiths at Broadway Vicarage, and to the Granville family who were then living in Buckland, one of whom, Mary (Pendarves), a young widow, became afterwards the famous Mrs. Delany. Here was good company and open hospitality, with picnics and dancing, with mild flirtations and serious discussion, and against a welcome background of charm and elegance after the harsher realities of Epworth. Romance was in the air in those halcyon Cotswold days, and those villages in their lovely setting are for ever associated with their bright company. They gave each other classical names, Charles being known as Araspes, though he figured less prominently (though no less actively) in this agreeable group.

About this time the old Rector died. He had been taken ill in 1735 and after eight weary months had died in the following year. Game to the end, striving to complete his work on Job and with difficulty taking his pulpit, weakness finally overcame him, and Mrs. Wesley sent for her sons, "Everybody observes his decay but himself." John and Charles were with him to the last, and Charles sent a full account to his brother at Tiverton. "You have reason to envy us, who could attend him in the last stage of his illness . . . The fear of death he had entirely conquered . . . He often laid his hands upon my head and said, 'Be steady. The Christian faith will surely revive in this kingdom; you shall see it, though I shall not.' " Words strangely prophetic! And to John he said more than once, "The inward witness, son, the inward witness; this is the proof, the strongest proof of Christianity,"—a familiar theme of later Methodism.

The Press paid generous tributes to the passing of "the Rev. and learned Samuel Wesley, a man of considerable learning and great ingenuity" and "a person of singular parts, piety and learning". The break-up of the home followed. His debts amounted to above £100, a creditor seized his livestock on the day of his funeral, and his letters and papers were sealed until the eldest brother's arrival, to whom Charles ends his letter: "If you take London in your way, my mother desires you would remember she is a clergyman's widow. Let the Society give her what they please, she must be still in some degree burdensome to you, as she calls it. How do I envy you that glorious burden and wish I could share in it! You must put me in some way of getting a little money, that I may do something in this shipwreck of the family for somebody, though it be no more than furnishing a plank."

For a time, Mrs. Wesley went to live with her daughter Emily in Gainsborough. Fortunately she had a life interest in £1,000 left to her by her brother's widow. Meanwhile the two brothers returned to Oxford, but within six months had embarked for America.

Chapter Three

AMERICAN JOURNEY 1735–1736

A RELUCTANT ORDINAND—THE HOLY CLUB MOVES OUT-
WARDS—COLONY IN THE MAKING—GOSSIP AND INTRIGUE
—OGLETHORPE'S ANTAGONISM—NO KETTLE FOR CHARLES
—ILLNESS—BOSTON HOSPITALITY—STORMY VOYAGE—A
PLAUSIBLE ROGUE.

CHAPTER THREE

THE AMERICAN journey was ill-starred from the outset. What prompted it and why did they leave Oxford where they were well established and with good prospects? John was in an unsettled mood. Having resisted his father's wish to succeed him at Epworth, he had been attracted to the headship of Skipton Grammar School and then had toyed with the idea of taking a College living. The number of his pupils had declined, relations with colleagues were not easy on account of his religious enthusiasm, and the future of the Holy Club was uncertain. The proposal, therefore, of missionary work in America came at an opportune moment and offered an escape from present problems as well as a promising field of evangelism.

General Oglethorpe, Member of Parliament, an ardent and impulsive reformer, of commanding presence and romantic ideals, had established three years earlier a colony in Georgia for the settlement of debtors released from prison and other displaced persons. Land had been granted, a Charter had been obtained, subscriptions had been raised, public interest had been stirred, and some forty families had already been settled along with a number of Continental refugees who had been victims of religious persecution. Every male emigrant was supplied with basic needs—a watch, musket, bayonet, hatchet and other tools, an iron pot, a frying pan, and a daily supply of rations, soap and lamp oil for a year.

Oglethorpe, as Governor, found himself with a rag-tag community in an undeveloped area, and, fired with enthusiasm, had returned home to report progress and to find suitable and hand-picked helpers. His first choice fell on John Wesley. He had heard of the Holy Club, had been a friend of his father and a subscriber to his book on Job, and Samuel Wesley at Tiverton was among his admirers, having composed a wildly romantic poem in praise of the new Colony.

The proposal he put to John was that he should go out as an S.P.G. missionary, John's main interest being to evangelize, not the settlers, but the Indians. He hesitated on account of his widowed mother, but her Spartan reaction, when consulted, left no room for doubt: "Had I twenty sons, I should rejoice that they were so employed, though I should never see them more." This decided him and he embarked with a high sense of mission.

Meanwhile, what of Charles? Oglethorpe was now a national figure and his project had excited the interest of other members of the Holy Club who found in it a new outlet for their enthusiasm. Two of them, Benjamin Ingham, newly ordained, and Charles Delamotte, the son of a London merchant, arranged to accompany John, and Oglethorpe invited Charles Wesley to go out as his personal secretary, though no man was ever less fitted for the post. It is doubtful whether he was really eager—even Ingham thought there were heathen enough at home and Charles was certainly not anxious at the time to be ordained, but John rushed him into it, urging his ordination before leaving England. Charles' reluctance is seen in a letter he wrote to Dr. Chandler: "I took my degrees, and only thought of spending all my days in Oxford. But my brother, who always had the ascendant over me, persuaded me to accompany him and Mr. Oglethorpe to Georgia. I exceedingly dreaded entering into Holy Orders, but he over-ruled me here also, and I was ordained deacon by the Bishop of Oxford, and the next Sunday priest by the Bishop of London." The ordinations took place in Christ Church, Oxford.

Of the real nature of the enterprise the Wesleys had not the faintest idea. It was the dawn of Romanticism with its image of the "noble savage", and John Wesley, caught up in the fervour of this unrealistic dream, anticipated a virgin land where natives led simple and uncorrupted lives, a field ripe for evangelism. There would be plain fare, living on water and the fruits of the earth. And no women!—except of a different species. He would thus be able "to attain such a purity of thought as suits a candidate for that state wherein they neither marry nor are given in marriage, but are as the angels of God in heaven". Thus he wrote to Dr. Burton, before he sailed. And never was a man to be more disillusioned.

Charles showed nothing of this unrealistic attitude, which suggests that he had more commonsense; he was certainly less naïve. In the same letter, however, John gives his chief motive, namely that of saving his own soul. "I hope to learn the true sense of the gospel of Christ by preaching it to the heathen." And Charles became his reluctant accomplice.

The Holy Club hardly survived their departure. There were good reasons, as most of its members were leaving Oxford; Clayton to Manchester, Gambold to Stanton Harcourt, and others to follow their various careers, mostly in church livings. Only Whitefield remained—the last of the Oxford Methodists, and he, helped by James Hervey and Charles Kinchin, maintained Wesley's relief fund for the poor of £40 per annum, and his two or three charity schools. His *Journal* in 1736 records: "My dear and honoured friends, the Reverend Messrs. John and Charles Wesley, being now for some time embarked for Georgia, and one or two more having taken Orders, the interest of Methodism, as it was then and is now termed, had visibly declined, and very few of this reputed mad way were left at the University." But it was hardly a disintegration, as its spirit was now more widely dispersed and slowly (and in some cases remarkably) became effective elsewhere.

But not in Georgia. The failure of the Wesleys' journey was inevitable, partly owing to their strong personalities, partly to their hitherto cloistered and academic lives, and partly to the shapeless and primitive nature of the community in which they found themselves. Had they been lesser men they might have succeeded, and a pair of mild young curates might have suited Oglethorpe better.

The party of four sailed from Gravesend on October 22, 1735, but were delayed at Cowes until December 10, where Charles preached several times in the parish church to crowded congregations. The firm hand of John Wesley can be seen in the following declaration solemnly signed by the four friends while walking in the Isle of Wight:

In the name of God, Amen. We, whose names are underwritten, being fully conscious that it is impossible, either to promote the work of God among the heathen, without an entire union among ourselves, or that such a union should subsist, unless each one will give up his single judgment to that of the majority, do agree, by the help of God:—first, that none of us will undertake anything of importance without first proposing it to the other three;—secondly, that whenever our judgments differ, any one shall give up his single judgment or inclination to the others;—thirdly, that

CW–D

in case of an equality, after begging God's direction, the matter shall be decided by lot.

John Wesley
Charles Wesley
Benjamin Ingham
Charles Delamotte.

The passengers consisted of a group of Moravian missionaries and emigrants whose strong piety and gracious character made a lifelong impression on the Wesleys, and an ill-assorted company of wastrels and misfits, with whom they had little in common and who gave a cool response to their pastoral ministrations. Two contentious women, one being Mrs. Hawkins, the wife of a surgeon, were particularly unpleasant, even vicious, at first imposing on the Wesleys and then, when blandishments failed, showing animosity.

For two months the boat ploughed across the Atlantic bearing its odd assortment of missionaries and fugitives, though it was a five months' voyage from the time of sailing. Five months of inactivity in congested quarters with so many disagreeable passengers, with an ill-mannered crew and the added nightmare of a storm which nearly sent them to the bottom, followed by a hurricane which tore the mainsail to shreds, with mountainous seas ablaze with lightning, produced, not unnaturally, frayed nerves and strained relations. The four friends, however, pursued their Oxford routine of study and devotion, gave what pastoral care they could, and John managed to learn German.

Charles, a creature of moods, began a long and melancholy letter to his friends, Sally and Anne Kirkham, his heart still in the Cotswolds, as in the lurching vessel he poured out his nostalgia. "Besides you two, I have no relations, no friends in England, whom I either write to, or find any ease in thinking of. And for you I pray continually." And, as the boat approached land: "God has brought an unhappy, unthankful wretch hither, through a thousand dangers . . . In vain have I fled from myself to America; I still groan under the intolerable weight of inherent misery. If I have never yet repented of my undertaking, it is because I could hope for nothing better in England—or Paradise. Go where I will, I carry my Hell about me. Nor have I the least ease in anything, unless in thinking of S[elima] and you."

It was hardly a cheerful mood in which to begin his mission, and not one in which he could hope to succeed. What was the "Hell" he carried within him? Had the storm unnerved him? From his brother's *Journal* we learn how nearly fatal it was—of towering seas and terrified passengers, all save the calm Moravians. Had the vicious words and violent passions unleashed in shipboard gossip and scandal affected him? Was it, more likely, realization of the plain fact that in coming to Georgia he had made a mistake and that his life had taken a serious misdirection?—quite obviously he had not wanted to come.

All were contributory factors, intensified by seasickness, making each step now a mockery and delusion. Lacking his brother's harder nature and possessed of a deeper sensibility, he faced the future with foreboding. Yet hope was never far removed and irresistibly breaks through this revealing patchwork of emotion. The sight of land restored his good spirits; now he had reached a crisis which only God could resolve, and the issue would soon be determined. "For I am come to a crisis. The work I see immediately before me is the care of fifty poor families (alas for them that they should be so cared for!) . . . Among these I shall be either converted or LOST . . . The whole bent of my soul is to be altered. My office calls for an ardent love of souls, a desire to spend and to be spent for them, an eagerness to lay down my life for the brethren."

Despite its mixed sentiments, this protracted letter reveals Charles' determined spirit and the deep sincerity with which he both embarked upon his work and sought a more satisfying faith.

His *Journal* opens on the day he landed in Frederica, after spending a month with John in Savannah, Oglethorpe and Ingham having gone on ahead. "Tuesday, March 9th, 1736, about three in the afternoon, I first set foot on St. Simon's Island, and immediately my spirit revived. No sooner did I enter upon my ministry, than God gave me, like Saul, another heart . . . The people, with Mr. Oglethorpe, were all arrived the day before. The first who saluted me on my landing was honest Mr. Ingham, and that with his usual heartiness. Never did I more rejoice at the sight of him. . . . The people seemed overjoyed to see me. Mr. Oglethorpe in particular received me very kindly."

Charles plunged at once into his work, holding a conference with his parishioners, reading prayers the same evening in the open, and at daybreak the following morning outside Oglethorpe's tent in a heavy downpour. John had remained in charge of the parish in Savannah, and Charles was in the coastal garrison town on St. Simon's Island, where Oglethorpe had his headquarters, a hundred miles to the south, which meant a ten days' journey.

Within two days of his arrival he was astonished to find Oglethorpe at loggerheads with him. "In the evening I had the first hard word from Mr. Oglethorpe, when I asked him for something for a poor woman. The next day I was surprised by a rougher answer, in a matter that deserved still greater encouragement. I know not how to account for his increasing coldness." And when he approached him later "the hurricane of his passion drove me away".

Why this sudden unpleasantness on the part of the General? Though of a generous nature, he was irascible and impulsive, a little vain, somewhat boastful and easily imposed upon. His nerves at the time were on edge, for he was harassed and hard-pressed, the Colony being on a war footing. British gunboats patrolled the river and he was constantly engaged in repulsing raids by Indians and Spanish pirates. There were frequent alarms, the sound of gunfire, and at night the sky glowed with the fires of his enemies. This would not normally have perturbed a hardened campaigner, but he had also the civil administration of the colony, and unfortunately he swallowed every rag of gossip.

Frederica was little more than a place on the map, a wretched outpost of Empire, as yet poorly organized, consisting of a fort, huts and tents, with only its storeroom for a church and no other facilities for pastoral work. The surrounding territory was a wilderness of wood, swamp and prairie, of prowling and thieving Indians and wild life. Georgia itself was a small strip of country between South Carolina and Florida, as yet unparcelled out, with a sea coast of sixty or seventy miles. Savannah was a town of frame-work houses. And beyond stretched the vast American hinterland, as yet wild and undeveloped.

In such surroundings Charles looked wistfully back to the life he had left, to Oxford common rooms and to those bright Cotswold days with quoits and dancing on the Rectory lawn.

Here he was confined to an office, dealing with Oglethorpe's correspondence, with Spanish traders and other business of the Colony, snatching what time he could for pastoral work. What strange fate had brought him to this? There was no "noble savage", not even a field ripe for harvest, only rough living (and that he would not have minded), office chores, and a pack of angry women. Rarely was a man more pestered by malicious talk and petty intrigue, or less fitted to meet it. On March 16 he records: "I was wholly spent in writing letters for Mr. Oglethorpe. I would not spend six days more in the same manner for all Georgia."

The initial troubles, minor in themselves, led to a train of intrigue. The first was over the baptism of a child by immersion. Then Mrs. Hawkins' maid came to him in distress, having been struck by her mistress in a temper, and she refused to go back. He pacified her and quite properly persuaded her to return, himself going with her, only to be bitterly reviled for his pains. This was followed by a shooting incident. Oglethorpe had prohibited Sunday sport, and Dr. Hawkins, disregarding the order, had been found shooting in the woods and had been placed under arrest, whereat his wife went berserk, firing a gun like a mad woman; and, fixing the blame on Charles, vowed that she would expose his "d——d hypocrisy". She had already nearly murdered two constables by breaking a bottle on their heads. Oglethorpe, when these annoyances were brought to his notice, acted with singular indiscretion, listening too readily to unfounded complaints and charging Charles with disloyalty.

But the matter became serious when Charles was persuaded by one of her friends that Mrs. Hawkins had been seduced by Oglethorpe. In all innocence he believed it and was horrified. He little knew that others were slandering him to Oglethorpe, imputing the same offence to himself.

The confusing cross-currents of malice which followed are hardly worth pursuing. Oglethorpe, driven to distraction, declared it was much easier to govern an army than a handful, and blamed Charles for not keeping the peace. Charles, meanwhile, ignored the complainants, took to prayer, and preached to a faithful minority. His living-quarters were uncomfortable —he was often sleeping on the ground, Oglethorpe having refused him either a house or a bed. Charles had brought little equipment from England, having expected furnished accom-

53

modation, but Oglethorpe denied him even the loan of a kettle. "Knowing I was to live with Mr. Oglethorpe, I had brought nothing with me from England, except my clothes and books; but this morning, asking a servant for something I wanted (I think a tea-kettle), I was told Mr. Oglethorpe had given orders that no one should use any of his things. I answered that that order, I supposed, did not extend to me. 'Yes, Sir,' says she, 'you were excepted by name.' Thanks be to God, that it is not yet made capital to give me a morsel of bread. . . . Having laid hitherto on the ground, in a corner of Mr. Reed's hut, and hearing some boards were to be disposed of, I attempted in vain to get some of them to lie upon. They were given to all besides."

He was now in public disfavour. Even his well-wishers were afraid to speak to him. "Some have turned out of the way to avoid me. Others desired I would not take it ill, if they seemed not to know me when we should meet. The servant that used to wash my linen sent it back unwashed."

At this point Charles fell ill with dysentery and was obliged to take to his bed. A friendly fever, he called it, welcoming this uncomfortable opportunity to relax, though it was a severe attack, and he would have been uncared for, but for the kindly ministrations of two sympathetic women. He dragged himself from bed to attend a dying man and perform other duties. There was a night of gunfire, when from his hut he watched the settlers fly in a panic into the fort. And there were other troubles: "Sunday, April 5th. At one this morning the sandflies forced me to rise, and smoke them out of the hut. The whole town was employed in the same manner. My congregation in the evening consisted of two Presbyterians and a Papist. I went home in great pain, my distemper being much increased with the little duty I could discharge."

The following day he records: "Mr. Oglethorpe gave away my bedstead from under me, and refused to spare one of the carpenters to mend me up another." But it was not the deprivations that he minded, so much as Oglethorpe's unexpected bitterness—the one man he had wished to please.

By now news of his condition had reached his brother in Savannah, who came at once with Delamotte to his relief. John, who stood high in the opinion of the General, whose respect for him amounted almost to veneration, took a firm

54

grasp of the situation, interviewing the troublemakers and dissuading Charles from his resolve to starve rather than ask further favours of the General. He stayed a week, at the end of which Charles had seen Oglethorpe and a reconciliation had followed. It was a patched-up affair, without recriminations, with Charles speaking his mind and with the General playing the part of a romantic hero—he was about to leave on a dangerous expedition from which, he said, he might not return, adding, "But death is to me nothing." And calling for his favourite sword, which had been his father's, said, "With this sword I was never yet unsuccessful."

Charles returned his cordiality, though with less melodrama, protesting his innocence, declaring that they had both been deceived, and "taking myself to be now at liberty to tell you what I thought never to have uttered". The General was palpably uneasy in having offended John Wesley and in not having fully allayed his suspicions. Charles continues: "When I had finished this relation, he seemed entirely changed, full of his old love and confidence in me. After some expressions of kindness, I asked him: 'Are you satisfied?' He replied: 'Yes, entirely.' 'Why, then, Sir, I desire nothing more upon earth; and care not how soon I follow you.' " Oglethorpe then embraced him with cordial affection.

The great man was escorted to the boat, Charles along with others running by the shore through the woods to see the last of him. "God be with you," he cried, "Go forth, *Christo duce, et auspice Christo*!" The boat stopped for a moment in acknowledgment, and the General replied: "God bless you all!"

Easter Sunday was a day of alarms, with fires on both sides of the settlement. That night the watch was doubled, the settlers were alerted, and news was expected every hour of Oglethorpe's death. But on the following Thursday, to Charles' relief, he returned safely, seven enemy ships having been dispersed. And now deeply moved by his deliverance, he could not do enough for Charles and condemned himself for his former attitude which he imputed to his want of time for consideration. "He ordered me," says Charles, "whatever he could think I wanted; promised to have me an house built immediately; and was just the same to me [as] he had formerly been."

But Charles' resolution to return to England remained unchanged. In less than three weeks he left for Savannah, taking

55

his brother by surprise and there for two months more he served Oglethorpe, while his brother took over his pastoral work in Frederica.

His health mended. There were more attacks from Spanish pirates. His days were spent in drawing up trading bonds and contracts and attending the magistrate's court, and his evenings with Oglethorpe in correspondence. He seldom retired before 1 a.m., rising again at 4. He swam at dawn in the river and met with alligators. He became friendly with a young Dutchman called Appee, to whom he confided his intention of resigning, proposing that he should take over his post as secretary, and only later discovered that he was a plausible rogue who had deceived both his brother and Oglethorpe who were warmly attached to him.

On July 25 he wrote his letter of resignation to Oglethorpe, who can hardly have been surprised and who, to his credit, made possible Charles' honourable return to England, by making him the bearer of dispatches to the Trustees of the Colony. At the same time he requested him not to inform them of his resignation, hoping that Charles might reconsider his decision, and in any case not wanting a successor to be appointed before he himself arrived back in England, "There are," he said, "many hungry fellows ready to catch at the office; and in my absence I cannot put in one of my own choosing." And his parting advice to Charles was: "On many accounts I should recommend to you marriage, rather than celibacy. You are of a social temper, and would find in a married state the difficulties of working out your salvation exceedingly lessened, and your helps so much increased."

A week later, John, who had arrived back from Frederica, accompanied his brother as far as Charleston, where they encountered the ambivalent Appee who was awaiting the English boat, and Charles, still unaware of his false nature, welcomed the prospect of his company on the voyage. During his ten days in Charleston he was appalled by the cruelty of the slave owners and his *Journal* recalls shocking incidents. There were thirty thousand negro slaves at the time in Georgia.

His next stage was by boat to Boston—an unpleasant voyage under a drunken captain who nearly stranded the vessel, and with Appee now throwing off his mask and displaying, to Charles' astonishment, his dishonest and licentious character.

Charles was delighted with Boston and met with great kindness from its citizens. He records his impression as the town came into view on a fine September morning: "A prospect entirely new and beautiful beyond all I had ever seen." The boat moved smoothly between innumerable small islands and green hills in endless variety. "We had a full view of the town stretched out a mile and a half upon the shore, in a semi-circle. We landed at Long Wharf . . . I lodged in a public house, went to bed at eleven. Appee followed me, drunk, between one and two in the morning."

The next day he became the guest of Mr. Price, the Commissary, remaining with him for nearly a month, until the next boat to England, and happy and crowded days followed—a welcome contrast after the shacks of Frederica. He preached in Boston churches, called on the Governor, made excursions including a visit to Cambridge, frequently dined out, conferred with the clergy, and spent pleasant hours with leading citizens. Everything, he said, was the reverse of Georgia.

Unfortunately, however, his illness returned, preventing his full enjoyment of Boston hospitality. Physically weak, his mind again filled with uncertainty regarding the future and, in a confused mood, he wrote to his brother John. The letter is in shorthand, intermixed with Greek and Latin, to ensure secrecy, as some of their letters had been tampered with. He had been offered and had declined a comfortable living in Boston. He harks back to "the fatal hour when I left Oxford". He wonders how to dispose of the remainder of his life. "I can either live at Oxford or with my brother (Samuel), who before I left England had provided for me without my asking. He will labour all he can to settle me. But I trust God will not suffer me to set up my rest there." In his confusion he even hankers after Georgia. "But Georgia alone can give me the solitude I seek after. I cannot look for a long life there, but neither do I count that a blessing."

He is too ill now to keep up with his Boston activities. "I am wearied by this hospitable people, they so vex and tease me with their civilities. They do not suffer me to be alone. The clergy who come from the country on a visit, drag me along with them when they return . . . My disorder, once removed by this most salubrious air, has again returned." But his dry humour is never long absent. "All my friends advise me to

57

consult a physician, but I cannot afford so expensive a funeral."
The doctors of Boston generously gave him their services, and
Dr. Graves made the long journey from Charleston to attend
him without fee. Every remedy was tried. "I vomited, purged,
bled, sweated, and took laudanum, which entirely drained me
of the little strength I had left."

The depression of his later years is already casting its
shadow, though not wholly pessimistic, nor to be taken too
literally, for Charles, alternating between high and low spirits,
in times of weakness was apt to brood sombrely on death, but
the mood was never sustained and activity invariably restored
his high spirits. We must not attach too much importance to
his depressive tendencies (or to his later "Funeral Hymns").
Melancholia was a contemporary characteristic, and hardly
a writer of the day failed to give it popular expression, as in
Blair's *Grave*, Hervey's *Meditations among the Tombs*, Thomson's
Sickness, Gray's *Elegy*, Warton's *Pleasures of Melancholy* and,
earlier, Burton's *Anatomy of Melancholy*. Addison, Young, Par-
nell, Dr. Johnson and Cowper, also among others, were no less
prone than Charles Wesley to gloomy moods and morbid
themes, and he was no more unusual in this respect than his
contemporaries. This must be remembered in any evaluation
of his character and work.

Three further letters to John before he left Boston are revealing. "It is fine talking while we have youth and health on our
side, but sickness would spoil your boasting as well as mine . . .
I am just now much worse than ever; but nothing less than
death shall hinder me from embarking." He was so ill that his
Boston friends tried to dissuade him from sailing. "I am wearied
on all sides by the solicitations of my friends to defer my winter
voyage till I have recovered a little strength." But he resisted
their kindness. "I am therefore determined to be carried on
board tomorrow, and leave the event to God." The following
day he was driven to the wharf, his friends waved farewell, and
the long journey to England began.

It was a wretched voyage. After two days he began prayers
in the main cabin, but this was almost beyond his strength.
He suffered from colic. A storm struck the ship and most of the
livestock (sheep, hogs and poultry) were swept overboard. The
boat had a bad reputation and he had been warned in Boston
against sailing in one so overladen and unseaworthy. The leaks

were such that it kept four men continually at the pumps. In the threatened ship, he found it hard even to pray. "I prayed," he says, "for power to pray." Then, reinforced in the height of the storm, he rose from his bunk to comfort the stricken passengers.

Meanwhile a pump failed, and all hands were called to stop the leaks. But his mind was now at rest. "In this dreadful moment, I bless God, I found the comfort of hope; and such joy in finding I could hope"—a conviction, he says, of the power of God that overruled all that he was by nature and that surpassed all rational evidence. It marked a significant stage in his spiritual development and without delay he followed it up by making his way to Appee's cabin and imploring him to seek God and His mercy. As we follow the tortuous process of Charles' experience let us hold in mind this incident when in the storm he knelt in the lamplit cabin and wrestled for the soul of the faithless Appee. Henceforth he would wrestle with many tortured spirits, but never under such wild conditions or with a more hardened cynic.

The storm abated, only to return three days later, the sea breaking into the main cabin. They were delayed by a ship bound for Boston which called for help, having lost most of its provisions, and they gave it a barrel of beef and a keg of rum. So the weary voyage continued until, mercifully preserved, after forty-four days, they landed at Dover.

Appee throughout had behaved abominably, and Charles, who had lent him £24 (which he never saw again), was only too anxious to be rid of him. The other passengers had found him equally objectionable. Not until afterwards did Charles learn that he had been obliged to flee from Holland for having robbed his father and had gambled away a plantation. He wondered how he had managed to impose on John and on the wary Oglethorpe, and resolved that never again would he be so easily taken in. "I could not help reflecting on the profound sagacity and spiritual discernment of my brother and myself, particularly *his*, who was born for the benefit of knaves!"—a shrewd judgment, for no one could be more naïve or gullible than John Wesley. Charles, who was a far better judge of character, benefited from the experience and never trusted a rogue again.

But he was not yet quit of Appee, who clung to him like a

leech and, plausible to the end, protested his innocence. They were together in the coach to Canterbury, where Charles deliberately shared a bed with him to "hinder him having a different sort of bedfellow". Charles, however, was no fool, and could be as firm as any when he wished. "Appee was so very grievous to us, that not only I, but all the passengers, resolved that this should be the last day of our acquaintance. At six in the evening we came up to London. I immediately took coach for Charles Rivington's, leaving my friend Appee, who promised to come next day, and pay me what he owed me." But the next day Appee was in Newgate, having been arrested for having cheated the captain out of the cost of his passage to England. Years afterwards Charles encountered him in a ragged red tunic, hardly recognizing the former swaggering adventurer, and shortly afterwards he visited him in the Tower where he was awaiting transportation.

Chapter Four

WRESTLING JACOB 1736–1738

CHAPTER FOUR

FOR CHARLES it was a happy homecoming. He spent his first night with Charles Rivington, the bookseller in St. Paul's Churchyard, and the following morning attended Communion at St. Paul's. His friends flocked to see him. Sir John Philips brought him good news of the Holy Club, and James Hutton carried him off in triumph to stay with his parents in College Street, Westminster, where they took in Westminster scholars as boarders and which became for a time his London home. His return had stirred public interest—Atlantic travellers in those days were rare and the Wesleys' American adventure was hot news. The journals of John Wesley and Benjamin Ingham had already reached London and the publication of the former was eagerly awaited. Charles, the first of the adventurers to return, though hardly a conquering hero, was a figure of popular curiosity and welcomed as one returned from the dead, for rumour had spread that he had been drowned at sea.

He lost no time in reporting to the Trustees of the Colony, but his days were so crowded with visits and interviews that his fever returned and when he consulted his doctor he was packed off to bed and bluntly told that if he had not had a constitution of iron he could not have survived. But bed was no place for a lively enthusiast of twenty-eight with a story to tell and people eager to listen, and within two days, defying doctor's orders, he resumed his engagements.

He visited the Bishop of London on two successive days and waited on the Bishop of Oxford, who told him to call without ceremony whenever he wished. He saw influential supporters of the Colony, among them Lord Carpenter, Lord Fitzwalter, Lord Egmont, Colonel Bladen and Dr. Hales. He presented his dispatches to the Trustees, though, having lost his voice, he was unable to address them. He dined with Uncle Matthew who, blunt as ever, commented dryly that the French, if they had any remarkably dull fellow, sent him to convert the Indians!

In this way Charles spent two agreeable months, unable to

63

preach, but otherwise active, particularly when Oglethorpe arrived, when there was fresh business to attend to. Oglethorpe had been reading Charles' journal and was none too pleased. It was written, he said, with great spirit, to which Charles tartly replied that "it was writ with a great deal of truth". He was still considering returning to Georgia but, as he carefully informed Oglethorpe, only on the distinct understanding that he went out as a missionary. Under no circumstances would he go out again as secretary, though Oglethorpe asked him to reconsider this.

Family reunions followed. His mother was then living at Tiverton with Samuel, and on his way to her Charles stayed in Oxford to record his vote in a University election and to see old friends. He paid his respects to the Dean of his College and to the Rector of Lincoln, and found time to preach to the prisoners in the Castle. He stayed a week with his brother-in-law, Westley Hall, who was curate of Wootton, near Marlborough, where he saw his sisters Patty and Kezzy. A second week followed at Tiverton where, on arrival, he raced excitedly up the stairs to be greeted warmly by other members of the family, though his mother unfortunately was indisposed in bed.

On returning to London he called on his old friend, Mrs. Pendarves, and the following week was at Mickleton in Gloucestershire and rode over to Stanton, where the Granvilles and Kirkhams were overjoyed to see him, especially "my first friend, Varanese".

Meanwhile, in London, he gave evidence before the Board of Trade regarding Georgia. Questions had arisen over trading problems in the Colony and Charles was repeatedly called before the Board to testify as to its future. He called on Lady Betty Hastings, sister-in-law of the Countess of Huntingdon, and accompanied his brother Samuel, who had arrived from Tiverton, to see the Archbishop. He dined at Lord Oxford's, and on hearing that Uncle Matthew had been taken ill, he was with him before the end and, after attending his funeral, hurried off to Wootton to comfort his mother, who had lately removed there.

An interesting occasion followed when he had the honour of presenting an Address on behalf of the University of Oxford to the King at Hampton Court, accompanied by Archbishop

Potter who had nominated him for the purpose. He kissed hands, was invited to dinner, and the following day dined with the Prince of Wales at St. James's Palace.

Charles was certainly not letting the grass grow under his feet, but though caught up in this whirl of activity—enough to turn a young cleric's head—he had not yet overcome his inner unrest. Three people profoundly influenced him at this period. He took pains to cultivate their acquaintance, and their influence had a marked and lasting effect upon Methodism.

The first was William Law, whose book *A Serious Call* was in wide circulation and, along with Scougal's *The Life of God in the Soul of Man*, had deeply impressed him. Law was a Non-juror who, after being deprived of his living, had acted as tutor in the home of Edward Gibbon, father of the historian, and then had established a religious and philanthropic community on the lines of Little Gidding. For a time he became the spiritual director of John and Charles Wesley—for he influenced John no less than Charles, although, later, both were to part painfully from him on account of his extreme mysticism. But at the moment Charles, seeking a deeper religious experience, was ripe for his guidance and spent long sessions with him discussing the power of God in the soul and the nature of conversion. The sum of Law's advice was "Renounce yourself, and be not impatient". We are nearing the time of Charles' evangelical conversion and have reached a significant point in his development.

The second influence was that of Count Zinzendorf, an Austrian nobleman, who was the leader of the Moravians and had established a remarkable settlement at Herrnhut in Germany. He was now in London and Charles was frequently in his company. The Moravian missionaries on board the *Simmonds* had made such a deep impression on both the Wesleys that they were eager to see more of them and to learn the secret of their confident faith and fine character. Charles, therefore, seized every opportunity of consulting Zinzendorf.

Thirdly, there was Peter Böhler—a name familiar in early Methodism—a young Moravian missionary of twenty-five, who had lately arrived in London on his way to Georgia. Charles welcomed the opportunity of teaching him English and gained much from their association.

CW—E

About this time Charles was paying frequent visits to his friend, John Gambold, who was now Vicar of Stanton Harcourt. The old vicarage is still there, known as Wesley's Cottage —scene of memorable conferences of the early Methodist leaders, before Gambold had resigned the living to become a Moravian bishop. Charles' *Journal* has a significant record of one of his visits. His sister Kezzy was staying there at the time. "Calling accidentally in the evening at my sister Kezia's room, she fell upon my neck, and in a flood of tears begged me to pray for her. Seeing her so softened, I did not know but that this might be her time, and sat down. She anticipated me, by saying she had felt here what she never felt before, and believed now there was such a thing as the new creature. She was full of earnest wishes for divine love; owned there was a depth of religion she had never fathomed; that she was not, but longed to be converted; would give up all to obtain the love of God. . . . I prayed over her, and blessed God from my heart; then used Pascal's prayer for conversion, with which she was much affected, and begged me to write it out for her. After supper (at which I could not eat for joy), I read Mr. Law's account of Redemption. She was greatly moved, full of tears and sighs, and eagerness for more." And the following day: "I prayed with Kez, still in the same temper; convinced all her misery had proceeded from her not loving God."

His sister's mood quite evidently matched his own and there were others of their circle undergoing a similar experience. Such earnest and prolonged seeking could hardly fail in the end, and Kezia's spiritual crisis anticipated by some months that of her two brothers, which in each case followed much the same course. No words could express its meaning better, or the aim of the early Methodists, than those which she herself used, in wishing earnestly for divine love and in owning that "there was a depth in religion which she had never fathomed". This was pre-eminently the mark of the Methodist vision and the theme of its devotional song. In one of Charles Wesley's greatest hymns is an echo of Kezia's prayer:

> Love divine, all loves excelling
> Joy of Heaven, to earth come down,
> Fix in us Thy humble dwelling,
> All Thy faithful mercies crown . . .

Come, Almighty to deliver,
Let us all Thy grace receive . . .

Finish then Thy new creation,
Pure and spotless let us be[1]

How often, when singing the well-known words, never hack-
neyed or irrelevant, do we realize that they breathe the essence
of Methodism! In no other popular devotional form do we
find at this period mystical thought expressed so clearly. By a
miracle of compression, in two dozen lines in which language,
metre and meaning combine in rare harmony and lucidity,
Charles sets forth the doctrines of Assurance and Perfect Love.

Jesu, Thou art all compassion,
Pure, unbounded Love Thou art . . .

Never was poet or mystic more divinely inspired than when (at
a later date) he composed this memorable hymn (see Plate 7).
No wonder Methodism with such high themes borne on such
wings of song compelled the attention of the age!

But all that was yet to come. Charles' spiritual evolution was
as yet incomplete. We have seen only the threads that lead to
the final pattern, the ragged ends and pieces. Not at this stage
could he have written "Love Divine" or have sung it with such
confidence. His sensitive conscience must still face unrest, his
buoyant spirit be cast down by despair; but Charles never trod
an even course like his more predictable brother. He was either
on the heights or in the depths. He was more deeply moved
than John, more perceptive, more compassionate. John had a
spirit of iron. He could be obstinate, insistent, peremptory; he
would have made a good field commander, a Napoleon, a
Wellington. Charles was of a gentler breed. He was of the stuff
of which, not heroes, but artists and mystics are made, of the
company of Pascal, George Herbert and William Blake.

He had now resumed his preaching and moved frequently
between London and Oxford—on one journey being attacked
by a highwayman. Despite his earlier decision, his mind was
still set on Georgia. He even made sailing arrangements and
began to take leave of his friends, making the long journey

[1] In the original: Let us all Thy Life receive,
Pure and sinless let us be

67

again to Tiverton and calling at Salisbury to say good-bye to his mother, who protested against his returning to the Colony. Then, to Oglethorpe's displeasure, John Wesley arrived back from Georgia.

Renewed ill-health at this juncture obliged Charles to change his plans. Böhler was in constant attendance on him, and the doctors hardly thought Charles could live. He smoked tobacco to relieve a violent and persistent toothache, but, unlike his father who had enjoyed his pipe, found it "an abominable remedy". His condition worsened, pleurisy developed, and he remained critically ill. He wrote afterwards to Samuel: "They bled me three times, and poured down draughts, oils and apozems without end. For four days the balance was even. Then, as Spenser says, 'I over-wrestled my strong enemy.' Ever since I have been slowly gathering strength, and yesterday took my first journey to my sister's room, who has been with me from the beginning, and no small comfort to me. One consequence of my sickness you will not be sorry for,—its stopping my sudden return to Georgia. For the doctor tells me to undertake a voyage now would be certain death."

His resignation had been held over at Oglethorpe's request, for he still wished to retain him and offered to supply a temporary deputy. But Charles was advised to remain at College, since he might, as senior Master, expect offices and preferment, and on April 3, 1738, he finally resigned his secretaryship.

His recovery, however, was short-lived, for within ten days he was prostrate again with pleurisy and weakened more than ever by drastic remedies. We are hardly surprised that he was utterly depressed. He was frustrated, disappointed, and physically disabled. And, unlike Kezzy, his inner conflict was not yet resolved.

Each day he received the sacrament and each day he longed for a greater awareness of God. Böhler was constantly at his bedside and Charles painfully reconsidered his doctrine of faith. Like Pascal, in physical agony, he wrestled for victory. Böhler prayed that Charles might see God's intention for him in this illness. The Moravians taught that a man cannot have peace without assurance of God's pardon. "But," argued Charles, "I now have peace, but cannot say of a surety that my sins are forgiven."

The final stages of his deliverance were prolonged and, but for his utter sincerity, might seem at times morbidly theatrical. It was a generation predisposed to sentiment; paradoxically an age of reason and of dramatized emotion. Charles certainly kept himself and his friends in a high state of feeling. The latter came and went, offered prayers and advice and brought in reinforcements. Or, like Mr. Broughton,[1] came in blustering, adopting a hearty attitude, suggesting that a good man has no need to fret after a faith he cannot *feel*: "God help you, poor man, if I could think you have not faith, I am sure it would drive me to despair." But Charles was in no mood for bluster and was consumed with a desperate hunger for God.

"God," he says, "still kept up the little spark of desire, which he himself had enkindled within me; and I seemed determined to speak of, and wish for, nothing but faith in Christ. Yet could not this preserve me from sin; which I this day ran into with my eyes open; so that after ten years' vain struggling, I own and feel it absolutely unconquerable."

Meanwhile his condition remained the anxious concern of his friends, who with clinical thoroughness took his spiritual temperature which varied with his mood. And finally, perhaps in desperation, they introduced, of all people, a pious brazier of Little Britain. Charles was on the point of removing to the house of Mrs. Hutton, with whose son he had been staying, "when God sent Mr. Bray to me, a poor ignorant mechanic, who knows nothing but Christ, yet by knowing him, knows and discerns all things . . . Mr. Bray is now to supply Böhler's place. We prayed together for faith. I was quite overpowered and melted into tears, and hereby induced to think it was God's will that I should go to his house and not to Mr. Hutton's. He was of the same judgment. Accordingly I was carried thither in a chair."

It was a strange arrangement—to leave his Westminster lodgings for a room above a shop in Little Britain, and to exchange the company of congenial friends for that of working people. Mrs. Hutton was naturally displeased and wrote off to Samuel at Tiverton: "Mr. Charles went from my son's where he lay ill for some time and would not come to our house, where I offered the choice of my two best rooms, but chose to go to a poor brazier's in Little Britain, that the brazier might help him

[1] Secretary of the S.P.C.K., 1743–77.

forward with his conversion." The site of Bray's shop (No. 12) is marked today by a plaque. When we stand before it we are on historic ground.

Bray, a man of deep insight and enlightenment, showed great kindness to Charles, who was resolved to remain there. The sick-room audiences continued. "I longed to find Christ," he says, "that I might show him to all mankind." Whether he had found Him or not, he was already actively commending Him and from his sick bed was converting others. "From this time I endeavoured to ground as many of my friends as came in this fundamental truth, salvation by faith alone; not an idle, dead faith, but a faith which works by love, and necessarily productive of all good works and all holiness."

Bray's sister, Mrs. Turner, a simple, kindly woman, had just been converted under Bray's guidance, while Charles remained in such heaviness of spirit that even Bray grew discouraged. Mrs. Turner pitied the sick man's obvious distress and longed to help him, but held back, not presuming to teach a clergyman his business. Her brother, however, persuaded her and, shy and trembling, her eyes bright with happiness, she related her experience to Charles who was deeply impressed by her simple testimony.

It was the eve of Pentecost, and on Whitsunday, May 21, 1738, he records: "I waked in hope and expectation of His coming." At nine that morning his brother arrived with friends and sang a Pentecostal hymn before going on to St. Paul's. When they left, Charles prayed for the gift of the Comforter and afterwards, composing himself for sleep, heard a voice which said: "In the name of Jesus of Nazareth, arise and believe, and thou shalt be healed of all thy infirmities." He mistook it for the voice of a Mrs. Musgrave; but what, he thought, if it should be Him, and this the day of His coming?

Later he learned that Mrs. Turner, constrained by a vivid dream, had climbed the stairs and had quietly spoken the words outside his door. "Speak you the words," Bray had told her, "Christ will do the work." And to Charles she confessed: "It was I, a weak, sinful creature, spoke; but the words were Christ's; he commanded me to say them, and so constrained me that I could not forbear." This proved the turning point in Charles' career. The voice of the woman was as the voice of

God. He found and felt, while she was speaking, the assurance that he sought.

That day the house in Little Britain was full of Christ; a strange sense of His presence pervaded its dark corners and filled every hour. And Charles, taking his Bible, opened it at words singularly prophetic: "He hath put a new song in my mouth, even a thanksgiving unto our God. Many shall see it, and fear, and shall put their trust in the Lord." God had "chased away" the darkness of his unbelief, and that night he recorded in his journal: "I now found myself at peace with God, and rejoiced in hope of loving Christ . . . I saw that by faith I stood; by the continual support of faith, which kept me from falling, though of myself I am ever sinking into sin . . . yet confident of Christ's protection."

And now the poet broke within him. Two days later, while the experience was fresh upon him, he composed the hymn:

> Where shall my wond'ring soul begin?
> How shall I All to Heaven aspire?

It is not among his greatest hymns—there is immaturity in its unevenness and it fails to sustain its fine opening, but it reflects the emotion under which it was written.

His next concern was for his brother. If only John could receive the same assurance! He had not long to wait, for within three days, on the night of May 24, the miracle was repeated. "Towards ten, my brother was brought in triumph by a troop of our friends, and declared: 'I believe'. We sang the hymn with great joy, and parted with prayer. At midnight I gave myself up to Christ; assured I was safe, waking or sleeping. Had continual experience of His power to overrule all temptation; and confessed with joy and surprise, that He was able to do exceeding abundantly for me, above what I can ask or think."

It was some four years later that he composed his more famous poem "Wrestling Jacob", incomparably superior to his conversion hymn and among the finest lines he ever wrote. Watts, the hymn-writer, said it was worth all the verses that he himself had written. With unerring genius Charles makes dramatic use of the story of Jacob, adapting it to his own experience:

71

Come, O Thou Traveller unknown,
  Whom still I hold, but cannot see,
My company before is gone,
  And I am left alone with Thee;
With Thee all night I mean to stay,
  And wrestle till the break of day . . .

In vain Thou strugglest to get free,
  I never will unloose my hold:
Art Thou the Man that died for me?
  The Secret of Thy Love unfold:
Wrestling, I will not let Thee go,
  Till I Thy Name, Thy Nature know . . .

'Tis Love, 'tis Love! Thou died'st for Me
  I hear Thy whisper in my heart!
The morning breaks, the shadows flee:
  Pure universal Love Thou art . . .

Another early conversion hymn, hardly less dramatic is "And can it be, that I should gain". There are others equally reminiscent of his experience. In hymn after hymn we learn its meaning and why he struggled so long: "I cannot rest till pure within", and

'Tis not a bare release of sin
  The guilt and pain my soul requires,
I want a spirit of power within,
  Thee, Jesus, Thee my heart desires.

Most popular of all (in this group) is the hymn "For the anniversary day of one's conversion":

O for a thousand tongues to sing
  My dear Redeemer's praise!
The glories of my God and King,
  The triumphs of his grace!

In the original it begins: "Glory to God, and Praise, and Love", and runs to eighteen verses, some of which are of poor quality.

Once again Charles had anticipated his brother. John might command, Charles was only too willing that he should, but Charles was the forerunner. As in the formation of the Holy

Club, so here in their evangelical conversion, he preceded John. He was the herald, the pioneer, the first of the Methodists.

And now he was rapturously upheld by the excitement of his mystical experience. Where John spoke in measured terms of a heart strangely warmed, he poured out his soul in song. He had heard God's whisper in his heart. He was enthralled, caught up into heavenly places. Always with rapture he recalled his experience.

There was also, as we have seen, a strong mystical element. Like Traherne, he looked out upon a transfigured world. He saw God in the lives of the poor, in the homely faces of Bray's associates—of cobblers, coachmen and wig-makers, of simple seeking souls who crowded into the brazier's home; and in the dark cells of Newgate and the Marshalsea. At St. Paul's he found new meaning in the sacrament: "In the prayer of consecration I saw, by the eye of faith, or rather, had a glimpse of, Christ's broken, mangled body, as taken down from the cross. Still I could not observe the prayer, but only repeat with tears, 'O love, love!' At the same time I felt great peace and joy."

His experience could hardly have been deeper than his brother's, but he felt it with more intensity. In John it produced a steady and consistent glow, but in him, a devouring and consuming flame. John marched into the future with firm and steady tread, unruffled and restrained, but Charles plunged into it with passionate abandon, with the vision of a saint and the ardour of a crusader. His one desire was for perfect love, his one theme: "O let me commend my Saviour to you".

There were setbacks, for the way of the pilgrim is never smooth and Charles was by nature susceptible to changing moods. There were days when he could not pray and found even the sacrament a burden.

Thursday, June 1st. I was troubled today that I could not pray, being utterly dead at the sacrament.

Friday, June 2nd. I was still unable to pray; still dead in communicating; full of a cowardly desire of death.

Saturday, June 3rd. My deadness continued, and the next day increased. I was exceeding heavy and averse to prayer; so that I almost resolved not to go to church . . . When I did go the prayers and sacrament were exceeding grievous to me; and I could not help asking myself, "Where is the difference between what I am now, and what I was before believing."

But the darkness was not like the former darkness and would be dispersed. Bray told him his deadness could not hinder God, and Charles himself declared that such times are the best "to labour for our neighbour, when we are most cast down, and most unable to help ourselves". And within hours the mood had passed.

The two brothers lost no time in communicating the news of their experience to their acquaintances, many of whom responded, but some were cynical, like an Oxford friend of Charles who thought he was running mad and looked for his halo! Others were puzzled and distressed, including their mother, their brother Samuel, Mrs. Hutton and Mrs. Delamotte. Charles was a close friend of the Delamotte family and often visited them at Blendon Hall. But now he met with coolness. "At Blendon I found Mr. Delamotte not over-cordial, yet civil; met letters from my mother, heavily complaining of my brother's forsaking her, and requiring me to accept of the first preferment that offered, on pain of disobedience. This a little disquieted me."

Even William Delamotte had cooled, and Mrs. Delamotte, not wishing her family to be further involved, rated Charles soundly for a sermon he had preached at the village church, adding, "It is hard people must have their children seduced in their absence. If every one must have your faith, what will become of all the world?" A hot dispute followed and, after complaining that his brother preached an instantaneous faith, she ran angrily out of the house.

But three days later, back in London, Charles rejoiced that God had added seven more under his ministry, and he had hopes of even greater things. Often tactless, always insistent, and never inhibited, Charles passionately pursued his mission. Page after page of his *Journal* at this period records names and stories of his converts—an interesting and mixed assortment, of every age and type, including, as at Bexley and Islington, clergymen and members of their congregations. A month later he speaks of troops of followers. He appears to have exercised strong pressure—his mellower pastoral methods were yet to come, but at this juncture he plunged headlong after every lost sheep and gave no rest to those whom he pursued. As Christ had sought him, so he must seek others, pleading, praying, arguing and caring, eager only to win souls for God. Even on coach journeys he could not be silent and there were embarrassing incidents. Once in the coach to London a lady was so offended that she threatened to beat him, but on another occasion he so impressed a fellow passenger that the coach was halted for prayer and afterwards, he records: "We sang and shouted all the way to Oxford."

In due course he preached again at Bexley and encountered Mrs. Delamotte. No one could be angry with Charles for long. "Well, Mr. Wesley," she asked, "are you still angry with me?" And a happy reconciliation followed. "She carried me in her coach to Blendon, where the poor servants were overjoyed to see me once more. While we were praying for her, she sent for me up to her closet. I found her quite melted."

In contrast to the elegance of Blendon Hall were the noisome cells of Newgate, which Charles was now regularly visiting. In July we find him there on nine days caring for ten malefactors under sentence of death. Charles, who all through his life was unwearied in prison work, gives a vivid account of these visits: "July 12th. I preached at Newgate to the condemned felons, and visited one of them in his cell, sick of the fever; a poor black that had robbed his master. I told him of one who came down from heaven to save lost sinners, and him in particular; described the sufferings of the Son of God, His sorrows, agony and death. He listened with all the signs of eager astonishment. I left him waiting for the salvation of God."

Charles, along with Bray, spent the night before their execution locked with them in their cells until the following morning when he gave them the sacrament. His *Journal* continues: 'At half-hour past nine their irons were knocked off, and their hands tied. I went in a coach with Sparks, Washington, and a friend of Newington's. By half-hour past ten we came to Tyburn, waited till eleven: then were brought the children appointed to die. I got upon the cart with Sparks and Broughton . . . I prayed first, then Sparks and Broughton . . . The black had spied me coming out of the coach, and saluted me with his looks. As often as his eyes met mine, he smiled." Two hymns were sung, one being that by Charles' father, which might have been written for that hour:

Behold the Saviour of mankind
Nailed to the shameful tree!

Charles kissed two of the prisoners. "Mr. Broughton told them not to be surprised when the cart should draw away. They cheerfully replied, they should not; expressed some concern how we should get back to our coach ... When the cart drew off, not one stirred, or struggled for life but meekly gave up their spirits. Exactly at twelve they were turned off. I spoke a few suitable words to the crowd; and returned."

It makes strange reading today, but we cannot fail to be impressed by the selfless compassion of Charles and his associates and by the vigour of their evangelism. These executions at Tyburn (which was near where the Marble Arch now stands) were public spectacles thronged with onlookers, and the fact that children were among the victims shows the contemporary attitude to crime (and to juvenile delinquency), when a simple theft was a capital offence.

During this year (1738) Charles again met Lord Egmont and declared his intention of returning to Georgia if his health permitted. In September he preached in Westminster Abbey and administered Communion, and a month later was in the pulpit of St. Margaret's. At St. Antholin's he preached for the first time without notes; with some nervousness, he says, though the sermon lasted for three-quarters of an hour!

He still kept in touch with the residue of the Holy Club, paying Oxford frequent visits and preaching to the prisoners in the Castle. He arranged with his friend Piers to receive his sister Kezzy as a boarder. And he had two significant interviews with the Bishop of London. On the first occasion he waited on him with his brother, to answer complaints against their preaching the doctrine of Assurance, and having satisfied him on this point, they inquired: "Are the Religious Societies conventicles?" The Bishop hedged: "No, I think not; however, you can read the acts and laws as well as I; I determine nothing," and they parted on good terms, the Bishop adding that they might have free access to him at all times.

76

A month later Charles took him at his word and a spirited interview followed. It began with a dispute over Charles' intention to baptize a woman who had already been baptized by a Dissenter. "He (the Bishop) immediately took fire, and interrupted me: 'I wholly disapprove of it; it is irregular.'" But Charles was obstinate, almost to the point of rudeness. "My Lord, I did not expect your approbation. I only come, in obedience, to give you notice of my intention." This led the Bishop to inquire about his licence.

"Who gave you authority to baptize?"

"Your Lordship; and I shall exercise it in any part of the known world."

"Are you a licensed curate?"

"I have the leave of the proper Minister [Mr. Stonehouse]."

"But don't you know, no man can exercise parochial duty in London, without my leave? . . . I have power to inhibit you."

Charles then pressed him:

"Does your Lordship exert that power? Do you now inhibit me?"

"O, why will you push things to an extreme? I do not inhibit you."

"Why then, my Lord, according to your own concession, you permit or authorize me."

"I have a power to punish, and to forbear punishing."

"That seems to imply, that I have done something worthy of punishment. I should be glad to know, that I may answer. Does your lordship charge me with any crime?"

"No, no! I charge you with no crime."

"Do you then dispense with my giving you notice of any baptisms for the future?"

"I neither dispense, nor not dispense."

And after further argument, the Bishop curtly dismissed him: "Well, Sir, you knew my judgment before, and you know it now. Good morrow to you."

In this attitude of Charles we find an echo of his father's obstinacy. He was acting at the time as curate at St. Mary's, Islington, and the fact that he was unlicensed weakened his argument. This was unfortunate, for it led to antagonism which at this early stage might have been avoided. The interview

77

indicates, however, that the Wesleys moved easily and fearlessly in episcopal circles, and also that the Revival was passing now into a vigorous phase, beyond that of a few scattered groups of enthusiasts, and was already producing disquiet.

Chapter Five

HERALD OF REVIVAL 1738–1739

EIGHTEENTH-CENTURY LONDON—THE REVIVAL UNDER WEIGH—TROUBLE AT FETTER LANE—ISLINGTON CURACY —FIRST FIELD PREACHING—MORE LAMBETH INTERVIEWS— DISLIKE OF PUBLICITY.

CHAPTER FIVE

L ET US look for a moment at the London of those days. Its population was just under 700,000, that of England and Wales amounting to 6,500,000. The high death rate did not decline until the latter part of the century and there was heavy child mortality. According to one estimate based on parish records, from 1730 to 1749 the burials of children under five was 74.5 per cent of those baptized, though this may err on the high side, as the records are incomplete, but even so it was appalling. Among the causes were perennial fevers, bad sanitation, lack of light and air, along with poverty and overcrowding. There was child labour from the age of eight. The poorer inhabitants lived in narrow and congested streets and alleys, for the most part in ruinous tenements, in garrets or cellars with little accessibility to fresh air and sunlight. A family would occupy a single room. Cleanliness was hardly possible.

Dr. R. Willan, writing at the end of the century of this period, found that bed linen was rarely changed, blankets and coverlets were never washed and along with curtains (if any) never renewed until they fell to pieces. From three to eight persons of different ages often shared the same bed, in some cases sleeping cross-wise. Broken windows were stuffed with rags or mended with wood and paper. Dark passages were heavy with the foul air and fetid effluvia from the vault at the bottom of the staircase. The ground floor was often a shop or warehouse.

These tenements proliferated in the first half of the century, due to building restrictions of an earlier period through fear of London becoming too big. One woman—a Mrs. Farrel— owned nearly twenty of such houses in the parish of St. Giles and amassed a fortune of six thousand pounds from letting twopenny lodgings. A cellar let at a shilling or eighteenpence a week housed a family, and in the case of the Irish, more than one.

The scandalous number of deserted children led to the establishment in 1739 of the Foundling Hospital, the doors of which were besieged when first opened, and a vile traffic developed of bringing unwanted children into London by carriers, waggoners and even by vagrants.

The wealthier classes had already moved west, where streets and squares, unlike the east end, were being spaciously laid out with properties on long leases. Cavendish, Hanover and Grosvenor Squares and New Bond Street, with adjacent properties, were built in the first half of the century. Prosperous citizens of the middle classes were spreading into rural suburbs like Marylebone and Islington, and speculative builders were developing new estates in St. Pancras and St. George's Fields. Spitalfields was built over, Stepney and Bethnal Green were still largely agricultural, but the Limehouse and Wapping area was densely populated. Covent Garden, no longer fashionable, was given over to theatres and night cellars. Gay in 1717, wrote of "Drury's mazy courts and dark abodes" and of harlots "who nightly stand where Catherine Street descends into the Strand". Westminster Bridge was not completed until 1750, and Tothill Fields, the last place in London used for regular bull-baiting, was full of rubbish dumps and wandering swine. The New Road from Paddington to Islington, part of which is now Marylebone Road, Euston Road and Pentonville Road, was constructed in 1756 across the outlying fields. Holborn, St. Giles, Fleet Street, Long Acre and Shoe Lane were a labyrinth of courts and alleys, the haunt of thieves and beggars. The Fleet Ditch was a foul stream into which tripe-dressers, sausage-makers and tanners threw their offal. From Lambeth to Rotherhithe the banks of the Thames were intersected with filthy creeks and tide ditches, and the eastern riverside districts were honeycombed with alleys of ill-fame.

London consisted then, even more than now, of separate self-contained communities determined by trade and social class, movement between which was difficult, as there was no cheap transport and the streets were unpaved. Each householder was responsible for the care and repair of his own frontage, which more often than not meant neglect. Street cleaning, drains and sewers came at the end of the century, when the runnels were replaced with side gutters. Until 1762 the only street lighting was that provided by householders, after which parish lamps using cheap oil with cotton wicks were introduced, replaced by gas lamps forty years later.

The outskirts of the city were mostly nondescript areas of smoking brick kilns, market gardens, hog fields, and stagnant pools and marshes, haunted by tramps and footpads, unsafe to traverse except on Sundays when crowds streamed in from the country to the tea and pleasure gardens.

Gin and poverty were the twin evils of the period, devastating in their effects, adding untold misery to their victims. The descriptions by contemporary writers and artists—Fielding, Hogarth, Gay, and by later historians, of the poorer life of this period are not overdrawn. Behind the grotesque caricatures of Beer Lane and Gin Alley were tragic realism and bitter irony reflecting unspeakable misery and degradation. Gin was the poison of the poor. Children of the lower strata were literally conceived in gin. Sold without duty, licence or restriction, it took its ghastly toll. Every fourth house in St. Giles's was a gin shop. Such monstrous excesses obliged Parliament later in the century to impose heavy duties on spirits, along with drastic restrictive legislation.

London, as always, drew to itself a tide of immigrants, good and bad. In addition to labourers (for the new building sites) and weavers, country lads and girls swarmed into the capital, those from the north being especially in demand for domestic service as coachmen, footmen, cooks, housemaids and scullions, though numbers remained unemployed and many on arrival became the victims of sharks and procurers.

Londoners seem to have lived less at home in those days. They used clubs and coffee houses, bought their food at the pie shops and had their meat cooked at the bakers and cookshops. Thus we find that Dr. Johnson, Goldsmith and others, on their first arrival in London each occupied a garret, taking their meals at coffee houses and using them as a good address.

This glance at the life of the period does not take in the whole picture. Elegance and good taste marked other sections of the community. There were prosperous citizens, the solid houses of merchants, tradesmen, apothecaries, the glittering social round of the London season, the masques and balls, the literary coteries, the fashionable clubs; and, outside London, the civilized refinements of Bath and the county towns, and the comfort and leisure of the landed gentry, of the more affluent country rectories, and the homes of the professional classes.

It is true that the worst features of the age were found in

London, where crime and violence for a time gained the upper hand, but similar conditions prevailed elsewhere, as Wesley found among the miners of Kingswood, the mobs of Wednesbury and the squalor of Irish cabins.

The picture changes as the century advanced, when improvements such as sanitation and street lighting—astonishing novelties at the time—lessened crime and disease and were followed by better standards of health and decency, not least in street behaviour. But it is against this more sordid background that we must see the work of the Methodists or we wholly misunderstand it; for while they appealed to all classes, it was upon the submerged and degraded that they made their strongest impact. Fearlessly and deliberately they went to those who needed them most. They penetrated the dark underworld. "Methodism," says a competent critic, Mrs. M. Dorothy George, "doubtless counted for much both as a civilizing influence among the people and as one of the channels of the growing spirit of humanity and the growing knowledge of the poorer sort."

When we read of the unchecked emotion of the crowds which flocked to the open air services of the Methodists—weeping, persecuting, fighting, swearing, some drunk with religion, others with gin—we must remember that they were mostly composed of those who swarmed out of their squalid hovels and tenements, eager for sensation, ripe for excitement, like the crowds which gathered at Tyburn. This accounts in part for the earlier excesses which often embarrassed the preachers and for which they were not primarily responsible; on the contrary, they sought to restrain and channel these wild emotions. Charles, in particular, had little patience with hysterical converts. The mania, ecstasies and like phenomena, which for a short period marked these open air services, were the natural reaction of a rough, superstitious and gin-sodden rabble, and were hardly distinguishable from the wild and brutish excitement of crowded cockfights and public hangings.

These were the people to whom the Wesleys came, laying aside their good name and prospects, and under them the miracle—for it was no less—was achieved. We can understand Charles' reluctance in facing them. It needed courage. No others in all England at that time cared more deeply for those for whom no man cared or went to such lengths to reach and redeem them. And these same wild and impressionable crowds were only too eager, when given the opportunity, to sing Charles Wesley's hymns to the catchiest tunes of the day.

The revival was now under weigh, though neither planned nor premeditated, and with as yet no defined form or, beyond house groups, any organized existence. But nothing could stem the flowing tide.

It soon became evident that the Fetter Lane Society, mainly Moravian, could no longer contain the ordered discipline or ardent activities of the Methodists, who had no inclination either to quietism or schism. Other religious societies with which the Wesleys were associated were being increasingly affected by fanatical and emotional tendencies, from which even the pious Bray was not immune, and which the Wesleys found disagreeable and embarrassing. This led to growing friction, and Charles, always frank, was not slow to speak his mind, adhering strictly to his Anglican upbringing, and strongly supported by his brother. A dispute also arose over lay preaching, of which both Charles and Whitefield at the time disapproved. It was an unhappy phase and Charles was accused of high-handedness. But the Fetter Lane Society had its way, showing blindness and bigotry, listening to fanatics, admitting doubtful converts, refusing to attend St. Paul's for Communion as had been its custom, and finally the Methodists, led by John Wesley, established themselves in a disused foundery near City Road. Charles was thankful to be free of them. "They declared themselves no longer members of the Church of England. Now am I clear of them. By renouncing the Church they have discharged me." It was a providential separation, for only thus could the purity and aim of Methodism be preserved.[1]

Meanwhile John Wesley, after visiting Zinzendorf's settlement in Germany, was forming his first societies—small groups, offshoots of those in Bray's house and Fetter Lane, were springing up in a score of places. And Charles, busy as an evangelist, was meeting with surprising success, though he still planned to return to Georgia. Charles Delamotte had arrived back in England, and Whitefield was preparing to make his third

[1] See page 102 for the final separation over the question of "stillness".

85

Atlantic crossing, having been presented with the living of Savannah.

Whitefield's meteoric success was the talk of London. Crowds assembled wherever he preached—in parish churches, fashionable drawing rooms and in the open. Unlike Whitefield, Charles with his more sensitive nature, shrank from popular success. When the former looked to him to take over his work in Bristol, he replied: "I am continually tempted to leave off preaching, and hide myself . . . Do not reckon on me, my brother, in the work God is doing; for I cannot expect He should long employ one who is ever longing and murmuring to be discharged. I rejoice in your success, and pray for its increase a thousandfold."

Whitefield had never approved of Charles' secretarial work and had written to him two years earlier: "My friend will not take it amiss, if I inquire why he chooses to be secretary to Mr. Oglethorpe, and not rather go where labourers are so much wanted, in the character of a missionary. Did the Bishop ordain us, my dear Sir, to write bonds, receipts, etc. or to preach the Gospel?" And now he was urging him to take to field preaching and to care for his great following of colliers at Kingswood during his absence. At the same time Charles was being pressed to settle in Oxford where the vacant living of Cowley was available, but without regret he saw it filled by another.

The only parochial work of his life was to assist for six months as curate at St. Mary's, Islington, where his friend and convert, George Stonehouse, was Vicar, though, as we have seen, Charles was never actually licensed for the purpose. St. Mary's was an early and strong Methodist centre in what was then a developing and wealthy suburb. When Anglican pulpits were being closed against the Wesleys, the Vicar offered them generous accommodation. Many of the earliest Methodist meetings were held in his vicarage and vestry, and Whitefield preached his first open-air sermon in London in the churchyard.

Difficulties, however, arose, not with Stonehouse, but with the churchwardens who, when Charles arrived one Sunday, gave him a stormy reception in the vestry. They demanded to see his licence and forbade him to preach, one becoming so abusive as to declare that he, along with Stonehouse and Whitefield, had the spirit of the devil. Two prominent members of the congregation, Mr. Justice Elliott and Sir John Gunson, then appeared and rebuked the wardens, and Charles proceeded into the church, but was forcibly prevented by the beadle from entering the pulpit. Stonehouse preached "a thundering sermon", but proved a weak ally, for after a repetition of the incident, he reluctantly dispensed with Charles' services. Charles felt it keenly and recorded: "The last time I had met Mr. Stonehouse and our accusers in the vestry, he astonished me by telling me, 'He had consented that I should preach no more.' I thought to myself, 'What is man? or what is friendship?' and said nothing. Today, in company with my brother and him, I mentioned, without intending it, my exclusion through his consent. He pleaded, the Bishop of London had justified his churchwardens in their forcible expulsion of me; but at last was quite melted down; would do anything to repair the fault; resolved no other should be excluded by him, as I had been." But it was too late, and within five years Stonehouse himself, who was evidently a vacillating type, had joined the Moravians.

Trouble followed in other London churches. "At St. Antholin's the clerk asked me my name, and said, 'Dr. Venn has forbidden any Methodist to preach. Do you call yourself a Methodist?' 'I do not; the world may call me what they please.' 'Well, Sir,' said he, 'it is a pity the people should go away without preaching. You may preach.' I did so, on good works."

Twice in this year of expanding evangelism (1739) Charles had interviews with the Archbishop. On the first occasion he went with his brother and was received with "great affection", the Archbishop mildly advising them to give no more umbrage than was necessary for their defence, to forbear exceptional phrases; and to keep to the doctrines of the Church. They told him they expected persecution and they would abide by the Church, till her Articles and Homilies were repealed. "He assured us he knew of no design in the governors of the Church to innovate; and neither should there be any innovation while he lived; avowed justification by faith only; and his joy to see us as often as we pleased."

They went on from him to the Bishop of London who denied having condemned them or of even having heard much of them, declared Whitefield to be a pious, well-meaning youth, though his *Journal* was "tainted" with enthusiasm, warned them against Antinomianism, and dismissed them kindly.

But the Lambeth interview four months later was very different. Charles was accompanied by Henry Piers, Vicar of Bexley, and his Grace expressly forbade the latter to allow the Methodists to preach in his church, charging them with breach of the canon. Charles mentioned his forcible exclusion from St. Mary's, but the Archbishop refused to discuss it. "He asked me what call I had. I answered, 'A dispensation of the Gospel is committed to me.' " The Archbishop then warned him that he would "not proceed to excommunication YET". It did not help matters when Charles asked his opinion of Whitefield's phenomenal success and recommended Gamaliel's advice. "He dismissed us; Piers, with kind professions; me, with all the marks of his displeasure." But, adds Charles, "I felt nothing in my heart but peace." Singing and prayer followed at Bray's, but later he was depressed with great heaviness and discouragement.

On the following Sunday he accepted Whitefield's advice and joined him in field preaching. He had already preached in the open in the villages of Essex, where churches had been closed to him, and now he overcame his reluctance to face Whitefield's immense congregations in Moorfields and on Blackheath. His *Journal* on Saturday, June 23, reads: "My inward conflict continued. I perceived it was the fear of man; and that, by preaching in the field next Sunday, as George Whitefield urges me, I shall break down the bridge, and become desperate. I retired and prayed for particular direction; offering up my friends, my liberty, my life, for Christ's sake and the Gospel's. I was somewhat less burdened; yet could not be quite easy, till I gave up all."

Sunday dawned—a busy and momentous day; and appropriately, as he records, St. John Baptist's Day. After prayer he found ten thousand waiting for the word in Moorfields. He preached on "Come unto me, all ye that travail, and are heavy-laden, and I will give you rest". "The Lord was with me, even me, his meanest messenger, according to his promise." Afterwards at St. Paul's, the sacrament put fresh life into him. "My load was gone, and all my doubts and scruples. God shone upon my path; and I knew that this was his will concerning me." At Newington he accepted the Rector's invitation to preach and afterwards walked on to the Common and cried to multitudes upon multitudes, "Repent ye, and believe the Gospel."

By way of contrast, the following weekend he was in Oxford, preaching before the University. His theme was Justification, and he was heard with close attention, though his sermon displeased the Heads of Colleges. The Vice-Chancellor received him, to whom he gave a full account of the Methodists, of which the latter approved, but objected to the irregularity of preaching in other men's parishes. The Dean of his own College was less friendly and spoke with unusual severity against field preaching. "He used his utmost address to bring me off from preaching abroad, from expounding in houses, from singing psalms; denied justification by faith only, and all vital religion: promised me, however, to read Law and Pascal." But "all were against my sermon, as liable to be misunderstood".

For the next month he continued preaching in Moorfields and on Kennington Common. Blackheath was another crowded preaching site. The inn, The Green Man, still stands, to which the preachers adjourned, sometimes as many as thirty, for food and lodging.

Always he was conscious of his own unworthiness, and success only provoked further misgivings. Who, he asks, would covet great success? "I live in a continual storm. My soul is alway in my hand. The enemy thrusts sore at me, that I may fall; and a worse enemy than the devil is my own heart." This was no affectation, for no man was ever less pretentious. He was never built for crowds; he neither sought nor desired them, though they thronged to hear him and hung on his words. After preaching to more than ten thousand, he would write to a friend that "was I not forcibly detained, I should fly from every human face. If God does make a way for me to escape, I shall not easily be brought back again. I cannot like advertising. It looks like sounding a trumpet."

But the crowds constrained him and the sheer pressure of the work sustained him. When William Law told him that he would run away and hide rather than endure such notoriety, Charles replied, reflecting his own experience: "You might, but God would bring you back like Jonah." And on the day of one of his greatest triumphs, when many were converted and the crowd would hardly let him go, he wrote: "and before the day was past felt my own sinfulness so great, that I wished I had never been born." His was more than the success of a popular preacher—he made no attempt at popularity, and loathed the very thought of it; the rare quality of his achievement lay in his devotion and humility.

Thus it was that, carried irresistibly forward by the momentum of the rapidly growing Movement, he came at last to Bristol which fixed the pattern of his life for the next thirty-two years.

Chapter Six

A CRITICAL YEAR 1740

CHAPTER SIX

CHARLES' BRISTOL journey was not without incident. At Bengeworth, near Evesham, he found his friend, Benjamin Seward, a well-to-do Baptist, absent from home, and Mrs. Seward refused to receive him. Seward, however, later found him at an inn and took him home, though his wife, "miserably bigoted", would not meet him. Apart from crowded services Charles' three-day visit could hardly have been agreeable; Mrs. Seward was irreconcilably angry with him, her maids were of the same spirit, and so was their Baptist pastor, their complaint being that he offered Christ to all.

At Gloucester he was welcomed by a thronged Society, but when he requested the use of a church, as was his custom before preaching in the open, the clergyman sent a civil message that he would be glad to drink a glass of wine with him, but dared not lend him his pulpit for fifty guineas. While in the city Charles encountered his friend, Mrs. Kirkham, who had so often entertained him at Stanton. He was on his way to preach in a field and she did not disguise her displeasure. "What, Mr. Wesley, is it you that I see? Is it possible that you, who can preach at Christ Church, St. Mary's &c., should come hither after a mob?" He cut her short with: "The work which My Master giveth me, must I not do it?" and went to his mob.

He preached in the street and in an inn at Painswick; and at Runswick, where a church was available, a window was removed to enable his sermon to be heard in the crowded churchyard. It was a memorable occasion. "They appeared greedy to hear." At night an even greater throng gathered and Charles, deeply moved, only with difficulty made his way through what he called "this most loving people" to return to Ebley.

In 1739 his brother had acquired a property in Bristol—the New Room, as it was afterwards known—in the Horsefair. It survives in good preservation, an eighteenth-century gem in the heart of the new shopping centre, and is the oldest Methodist preaching house in the world. Here Charles came in company with his brother and entered upon a two months' ministry.

Bristol, like London, was a scene of violent contrasts, and was the second largest city in the kingdom. Charles found it congenial. Within two days he was among the colliers in the wild mining area of Kingswood, four miles distant. Not even Georgia offered a rougher field for enthusiasts and it was here that Methodism launched its first full-scale enterprise. The need was desperate, but what could a handful of preachers hope to achieve? The epic of Methodism lies in the story of their Kingswood campaign. Kingswood was literally won for Christ. Schools sprang up—Whitefield had started one, and by 1750 John Wesley had four others in the town; a chapel was built and there was a preachers' settlement. Today an illuminated beacon on Hanham Mount, provided by the town, along with a replica of Wesley's pulpit, mark the memory of those days, when the Wesleys built their school in a forest clearing among the cockpits and coal-mines, and ministered to the miners, squatters and roving thieves of the area.

In Bristol Charles preached regularly in the Weavers' Hall, on the Bowling Green, at Baptist Mills, Gloucester Lane, and in the Brickyard. At the latter he marvelled at five thousand people taking it so patiently when he called them thieves and adulterers! But to the colliers he offered the heartening themes of the prophet: "The blind receive their sight and the lame walk." "The wilderness and solitary place shall be glad for them, and the desert shall rejoice and blossom as the rose." "I triumphed," he says, "in God's mercy on these poor outcasts . . . O how gladly do the poor receive the Gospel! We hardly knew how to part."

Despite his success he still had sombre reactions. When confronted with disloyalty, discovering drunkenness or disorder among those whom he trusted, he was painfully discouraged and confessed: "I am a poor creature on such occasions, being soon cast down." After administering the sacrament to nearly forty colliers, he declared that he found no comfort in it himself. "I always find strength for the work of the ministry, but when my work is over, my strength, both bodily and spiritually, leaves me. I can pray for others, not for myself. God by me strengthens the weak hands, and confirms the feeble knees; yet am I myself as a man in whom is no strength. I am weary and faint in my mind, longing to be discharged." Yet he could go out again the same day to face an even bigger multitude, endure a noisy opposition, and say afterwards, "I never felt such a power before, and promised the people that they should feel it too; for I saw that God has a great work to do among us by Satan's opposition. I lifted up my voice like a trumpet, and in a few moments drove him out of the field. For above an hour I preached the Gospel with extraordinary power, from Blind Bartimaeus." The following day the experience was repeated, but "after preaching, a messenger of Satan came. He seldom fails me after success."

A lifeless atmosphere had the same effect. "Weak, dead, speechless, among the men bands. I wanted to get away without speaking or praying because they were all as dead, it seemed, as I. I was overruled to stay and pray, and had the spirit of prayer as never before. We were all in a flame; I prayed again and again not knowing how to part." He never failed in finding power among the colliers. After preaching, he enjoyed taking meals with them and was constantly in and out of their homes.

There were other times, however, when the sacrament refreshed him, as at St. Philip's where, after receiving it, he gained reassurance. "I first earnestly asked that God would not send me empty away. I returned to my pew, and was immediately overpowered, in a manner inexpressible . . . I asked, with all enthusiasm, some token from his word. I hardly remember to have read the passage: 'Thou art my battle-axe, and weapons of war.' "

All this time the stream of converts grew, and name after name fills his *Journal*, showing his deep pastoral interest and care. Quakers, drunkards, miners, housewives—a mixed assortment of both the educated and the poor, he enumerates by the score, describing their condition and giving the time and circumstances of their relief. He baptized a convert in the river at Baptist Mills, and gave notice in a letter to the Bishop of Bristol of seven others who desired baptism by immersion at his hands.

He preached regularly on Hanham Mount and once a week in Bradford-on-Avon, journeying to both places by coach, and hurrying back, often late, to face his city congregation. He devoted the midday hour to interviews, but found that more came than he could cope with, "all seeking what many have found". Nor was his activity confined to this regular routine, for in a spare hour he would go out into the lanes and streets and call men to repentance.

The work proceeded against a rising tide of opposition. He was called a Papist, a Jesuit, a seducer and a Jacobite. The clergy complained openly of the increased numbers attending their parish Communions through his activities and threatened to repel them. One vicar, angered at finding an extra hundred communicants in his church, afterwards declared that because they had no communion of their own, it was not for him to accommodate them. One would have thought, especially in that age of small congregations, that such an influx would have been welcome. Charles offered his assistance to lessen his trouble, but it was declined.

There were difficulties also with Dissenters. He received a letter from Bearfield asking him never to return to that place, whereupon he set out for it at once with his brother and faced the trouble-makers—two thousand of them clamouring against his gospel of universal love. He begged them not to lose their charity, and for an hour and a half called all sinners to the Saviour of the world. This, of course, was the theme of the Revival: "For all, for all, my Saviour died," and it was this which had provoked their bitterness.

A typical irritation was a writ served on him for alleged trespass, at an earlier date, when walking over an open field to preach on Kennington Common in London. He was charged with damages of £10 and costs, £9 16s. 8d. But the writ arrived late and rather than return to London he met the demand, the receipted account for which is preserved, bearing his endorsement: "I paid them the things I never took. To be rejudged IN THAT DAY."

In November he was called to Oxford to respond in divinity disputations, after which we find him again in trouble with the Seward family, one of whom—Henry, a brother of Benjamin, was particularly abusive, threatening to strip his gown over his ears. To prevent his brother from seeing Charles he attempted to remove him to Badsey on the ground of insanity, and a pretty story follows of how this scheme was foiled by a child who watched in the lane outside Seward's house and slipped a note into his hand as he entered his coach, unseen by Henry, who was on the box. The upshot was that Benjamin, on learning that Charles was in the neighbourhood, directed the coach to his door. A warm meeting followed and we find Charles breakfasting and preaching in his house. Never, said Charles, had he met a man of so little sense as Henry Seward. There were two other brothers: William, a convert of Charles, who after serving at the Treasury, joined Whitefield in America, where he purchased five hundred acres of land for a school, and on returning to England accompanied Howell Harris on his preaching tours. His story has a sad ending, for he was fatally stoned by a mob when preaching at Hay—the first Methodist martyr. A lost fragment of his diary has recently come to light in the Chetham Library, Manchester. Thomas, a fourth brother, was an Anglican clergyman.

Charles had a pleasant encounter with another Dissenter, Joseph Williams of Kidderminster, who, after inviting him to that town, went specially to Bristol to hear him, and was so impressed that he wrote a letter intended for the *Gentleman's Magazine*, but, on showing it to Charles, the latter modestly objected to its publication, and it was found among his papers after his death.

The letter gives a clear picture of Charles at this period.

Hearing that Mr. Charles Wesley would preach in the afternoon, just out of the city, I got a guide and went to hear him. I found him standing upon a table, in an erect posture, with his hands and eyes lifted up to heaven in prayer, surrounded with, I guess, more than a thousand people; some few of them persons of fashion, both men and women, but most of them of the lower rank of mankind . . . He then preached about an hour, from 2 Corin. V. 17–21, in such a manner as I have seldom, if ever, heard any Minister preach; that is, though I have heard many a finer sermon, according to the common taste, yet I have scarcely ever heard any Minister discover such evident signs of a most vehement desire, or labour so earnestly, to convince his hearers that they were all by nature in a state of enmity against God, consequently in a damnable state, and needed reconciliation to God . . . These points he supported all along, as he went on, with many texts of Scripture, which he explained and illustrated . . . and used a great variety of the most moving arguments and expostulations, in order to persuade, allure, instigate, and, if possible, compel all to come to Christ and believe in him for pardon and salvation. Nor did he fail to inform them thoroughly, how ineffectual their faith would be to justify them in the sight of God, unless it wrought by love, purified their hearts, and

CW—G

reformed their lives . . . Afterwards I waited on Mr. Wesley, asked him many questions, and received much satisfaction from his answers.

Williams accompanied Charles the same evening to an indoor meeting and found the room so full that they could hardly get in. His letter proceeds:

> Never did I hear such praying, or such singing, never did I see or hear such evident marks of fervency of spirit in the service of God, as in that Society. At the close of every single petition, a serious Amen, like a rushing sound of waters, ran through the whole society . . . They seemed to sing with melody in their hearts . . . Such evident marks of a lively, genuine devotion, in any part of religious worship, I never was witness to in any place, or on any occasion . . . I do not remember my heart to have been so elevated in prayer or praise, either in collegiate, parochial or private worship, as it was there and then . . . I found, upon inquiry, that great numbers in Bristol . . . have been reformed from a vicious course, who, now without neglecting their necessary employments (as has been invidiously suggested) make religion their principle concern; and particularly, that the case is remarkably thus with many of the colliers in Kingswood, whose wickedness, a few years ago, was notorious.

In April 1740 Charles was back in London, taking over his brother's work at the Foundery, where he found many of his old friends were deserting to the Moravians, including the Brays, the younger Huttons, even the faithful Charles Delamotte, and Stonehouse was on the point of resigning his Islington parish and joining the Moravians in Germany. On Easter Day Charles unburdened his heart at the Foundery: "Who hath bewitched you, that you should let go your Saviour? that you should cast away your shield and your confidence, and deny you ever knew Him?" The congregation, deeply moved, were in tears as he called them back to the Saviour.

He had good reason to challenge them, and only by the plainest speaking and by exerting all his energy and authority did he hold his London following. The fanatics had gone so far as to declare that the comfort of the sacrament was that of the Devil, and this was typical of the nonsense which he had to contend with, and of how far they exasperated him. It was incredible that his one-time friends remained unmoved by his

Bristol success and by the daily evidence of the London crowds which thronged to hear him, and that they deliberately and maliciously set out to undo both his own and his brother's work. But Charles was a born fighter and he opposed them with the same passion as when at Westminster he had defended Andrew Murray against the bullies of the school. He referred to them as "dogs of hell", though he added the wry comment: "The old man rose in me, but my God kept me within bounds."

His brazier friend, Bray, still in charge of the bands, as the inner groups were called, which he had miserably misled during Charles' absence, was badly ruffled, and Charles deliberately challenged him, for it was no time for evasion. "I declared I would not give place to him by subjection, no not for an hour; but whoever cast off the ordinances, I would cast him off, although it was my own brother." But although his temper was sorely tried by these prolonged disputes, he was thankful that he had returned from Bristol in time to deal with them and prevent further confusion. "The true light shone in our darkness. Several saw His glory."

Two rules were now firmly agreed upon by his own followers: 1. that no order shall be valid, unless the Minister be present at the making of it, and 2. that whoever denies the ordinances to be commands, shall be expelled the Society. Thus, clearly and on Charles' initiative, Methodism was finding a sensible and solid foundation and wholly in line with the tradition of the Church; and it was at this date and under these circumstances that he wrote his hymn on "The Means of Grace", of Cowper-like wistfulness, with pointed emphasis on the need of constant renewal of the inner life:

> Still for thy loving-kindness, Lord,
> I in thy temple wait;
> I look to find thee in thy word,
> Or at thy table meet.

> Here, in thine own appointed ways,
> I wait to learn thy will . . .

Charles matched every crisis with a song which invariably reflected his mood, and these lines make crystal clear his attitude:

I do the thing thy love enjoins,
And then the strife give o'er.

As we have seen, the *Journal* makes bleak reading here. "I attended my brother to Fetter-lane. The first hour passed in dumb show, as usual; the next in trifles not worth naming . . . We parted as we met, with little or no singing, less of prayer, and nothing of love. However, they carried their point, which was to divert my brother from speaking." And after another such meeting: "We parted as we met, without either prayer or singing. The time for these poor exercises is past."

The Wesleys remained adamant regarding the place and significance of the ordinances as both means of grace and commands of God. "I talked in the evening with James Hutton, concerning the division which must soon come." The simple souls, as Charles called them, "say they are *to be still*; that is, not to search the Scriptures, not to pray, not to communicate, not to do good, not to endeavour, not to desire. . . . Lazy and proud themselves, bitter and censorious toward others, they trample upon the ordinances, and despise the commands of Christ. I see no middle point wherein we can meet."

Meanwhile he pursued his mission. He heard his brother preach on the Common to a multitude of ten thousand. He preached at Wapping to the poor. He continued to record the names of his converts; Cordelia Critchett, a Papist, Bridget Armstead, desiring baptism, and many others including an unnamed correspondent who wrote: "My friend, there are many teachers, but few fathers; but you are my father, and begat me by the Gospel, and, I trust, many more." One name stands out, that of Grace Murray, who later became John Wesley's housekeeper at Newcastle and whom he would have married but for Charles' abrupt intervention. "I received," says Charles, "the following simple letter," and he little dreamt of the storm of gossip and emotion his correspondent would one day provoke in Methodist circles. Her soul, she wrote, was like a troubled sea. She saw her own evil heart, her cursed, devilish nature, and felt such helplessness that she could not so much as think a good thought. And she ended with pious phrases of conviction that God had redeemed her. "Dear Sir, I have spoke the state of my heart, as before the Lord. I beg your prayers, that I may go on from strength to strength."

During this period Charles found a stalwart ally in Howell Harris, and despite their strong difference of opinion over Calvinism they became lifelong friends. Harris, a young Welsh schoolmaster, who was already showing unusual gifts as a preacher, had "blundered in" to the Foundery one night by mistake during one of Charles' services and, though a Calvinist, at once sided with him against the Moravians, and for a time assisted him. Charles declared that he had been sent by God to help him. "We took sweet counsel together, and went to the altar of God as friends." He was indeed a man of thunder and of consolation. And he drew the fire of the enemy by declaring in all plainness that it was through the sacrament that he had found forgiveness at the altar in Talgarth church. The Moravians, who had hoped for his support, were infuriated. Charles meanwhile pressed him into the front line of attack, rejoicing in the flame he kindled, and paying him generous tribute. How closely Howell Harris was associated with Charles at this period can be seen from a writ served on the Foundery congregation on the grounds that it was a seditious assembly, the persons named being: Charles Wesley, Clerk, J. Hutton, bookseller, Timothy Lewis, printer, and Howell Harris, *alias* the Welsh Apostle. Sir John Gunson, however, intervened and the writ was quashed.

To Charles' sorrow there was a final breach with his old friends, the Delamottes of Blendon Hall. "No longer Blendon to me," he records. "They could hardly force themselves to be barely civil. I took an hasty leave, and with an heavy heart, weighed down by their ingratitude, returned to Bexley." On the following day, however, he made a last effort to repair this broken friendship, revisiting the Hall and speaking with great plainness: " 'Do you, therefore, at this time, in the presence of Jesus Christ, acquit, release, and discharge me from any further care, concern, or regard for your souls? Do you desire I would never more speak unto you in His name?' Betty frankly answered; 'Yes'; Mrs. Delamotte assented by her silence. 'Then here,' said I, 'I take my leave of you, till we meet at the judgement-seat.' With these words I rendered up my charge to God. . . . With Blendon I give up all expectation of gratitude upon earth."

A reorganization of the Wesleys' London Societies followed, with a severe pruning of membership, leaving a bare remnant of the faithful. "We gathered up our wreck. Nine out of ten are swallowed up in the dead sea of stillness. O why was not this done six months ago? How fatal was our delay and false moderation! . . . I tremble at the consequence . . . I told them plainly I SHOULD ONLY CONTINUE WITH THEM SO LONG AS THEY CONTINUED IN THE CHURCH OF ENGLAND. My every word was grievous to them. I am a thorn in their sides, and they cannot bear me." It was a painful task, and marked the final breach with the Society at Fetter Lane.

In the summer of 1740 Charles returned to Bristol. Outside Wycombe he found the body of a man shot through the head by a highwayman and afterwards went out of his way to visit the murderer who had been apprehended. At Kingswood he met with a warm welcome from the colliers. Here the seed had fallen on good ground. He describes a memorable Sunday with them: "I went to learn Christ among our colliers, and drank into their spirit . . . O that our London brethren would come to school to Kingswood. . . . God knows their poverty but they are rich. . . . Some thousands waited for me at Rose-Green." Others might reject his testimony, but these received it gladly. And on the Tuesday he preached to a thousand children. They were days of glowing triumph, of crowded Communions and expanding membership, though care was taken to remove the unfaithful. "I was forced to cut off a rotten member. . . . I reproved one who had fallen asleep again." There was no room for slackness or disloyalty.

But the clergy for the most part remained hostile and in the Temple Church he was refused Communion, the clerk informing him after the sermon that he must leave, as the Vicar would not give him the sacrament. Charles immediately went to the vestry and quietly desired admittance. "Are you of this parish?" asked the Vicar. To which Charles replied: "Sir, you *see* I am a clergyman." The Vicar then rudely charged him with rebellion in expounding the Scriptures without authority, and said, "I repel you from the sacrament." He then ordered Charles' removal and sent for constables, afraid lest the infuriated miners who were present might attack him.

A serious illness at this point laid Charles aside for six weeks and for some days it was thought that he would not recover and was even reported dead. He was nursed, however, by a good Methodist and was attended by Dr. Middleton who, though a complete stranger, showed him great kindness, refused payment, and always afterwards attended the poorer Methodists of the city without fee. Moved by his kindness, Charles wrote his "Physician's Hymn"—"Physician, Friend of human kind." He had hardly recovered when he was called upon to face a riot at Kingswood, where the colliers were demonstrating against the high price of corn. He met the main body as he entered the town. They were in an ugly mood, but welcomed him with affection, not having seen him since his illness. But it was a perilous moment; sticks and stones were flying and there was a good deal of violence. Charles with great patience, after listening to their complaint, succeeded in calming them, and though threats of rioting continued for some hours, the affair ended with the more moderate among them taking their complaint to the Mayor. "Then they all returned as they came, without noise or disturbance. All who saw were amazed; for the leopards were laid down. Nothing could have more shown the change wrought in them than this rising."

Following his first journey into Wales in November, he returned to Bristol and on Christmas Eve he set out at five in the morning for London. There Charles found a crowded audience awaiting him at the Foundery, where he preached on the great Christmas themes and gave God thanks. It was the end of a memorable year. "He hath done great things for us already, but we shall see greater things than these."

Nor had his sense of humour deserted him, for among his visitors was a plausible beggar who offered to teach him "the grand arcanum" for five shillings. Charles gave him sixpence, telling him that as he had the art of transmutation, it was the same as if he had given him half a guinea!

Chapter Seven

TRAVEL AND PERSECUTION
1739–1747

FONMON CASTLE—WALSALL RIOTS—APOSTLE OF THE NORTH
—CORNISH WELCOME—AND OPPOSITION—SEPARATION FROM
WHITEFIELD—DEATH OF SUSANNA—BAD ROADS—ASSAULTED
AT DEVIZES—WEST STREET—COVENT GARDEN.

CHAPTER SEVEN

THROUGHOUT 1740 the future of Methodism had remained precarious and Charles had played a considerable part in rescuing it from disruption, not least by his firmness in preserving orthodox principles within the widening context of the Revival. We must not underestimate this substantial contribution to the consolidation of his brother's work, without which Methodism would have been severely weakened and 1740 could have been a year of disaster.

South Wales was easily accessible from Bristol and he now paid several visits there in quick succession, staying with Robert Jones at Fonmon Castle, near Barry—a mansion still occupied by descendants of the same family. The young Squire had been an Oxford contemporary of Charles and was a convert of Howell Harris, but, reluctant to accept Calvinism, had responded to Charles' more liberal influence, accompanying him back to Bristol to see for himself the activities at Kingswood which greatly impressed him. And at Fonmon Castle he formed the second Methodist Society to meet in Wales. Charles often preached in its courtyard, and in the dining-room which served as a chapel, as well as in the neighbouring churches of Wenvoe and Porthkerry.

He also made frequent journeys to London, where he ministered at the Foundery and resumed his visits to the felons in Newgate, where, on one occasion, he was locked in the prison yard by an unfriendly jailor, and took the opportunity of mounting a bench and preaching to the prisoners who climbed to the windows of their cells to listen.

It was at this point that Methodism underwent its fiercest persecution, and Charles, along with his brother, was involved in violent scenes in the Walsall and Wednesbury area. This was the time when John Wesley, who bore the full brunt of the attack, was dragged by the hair from the steps of the Cross down the main street of Walsall, and when their lives were imperilled. Charles, when preaching from the market steps, was violently attacked.

He met with similar hostility in Sheffield. "As soon as I was at the desk with David Taylor, the floods began to lift up their voice. An officer (Ensign Garden) contradicted and blasphemed. I took no notice of him, and sang on. The stones flew thick, hitting the desk and people." To avoid harm to the congregation he resumed the service out of doors, but stones continued to strike him, and an army captain ran at him with a sword and held him at its point. He had boasted that he would frighten the life out of the preacher. Charles shamed him, however, by baring his breast, and the man quietly put up his sword and slunk away.

The mob later destroyed the preaching house. The constable was sent for and Charles was asked to leave the town, but he thanked him for his advice and said he would not leave a moment the sooner for the uproar, telling him, "I knew my business, as I supposed he did his." The din continued throughout the night, but Charles calmly went to bed and slept. At five the next morning he was up and preaching, and, with the crowd at his back, walked through the open street, passing the wrecked preaching house where not one stone had been left upon another. Yet he records that it was a glorious time and many had the Spirit of glory resting on them.

Later the same fate threatened the house where he was lodging. Its windows were smashed and we are not surprised that his host was ready to surrender. He had been to a Justice and been refused a warrant, and his home was on the point of destruction. Charles was quietly writing within the threatened building and only the cries of his host called him out. He then dispersed the rabble by reading the Riot Act.

Two days later he moved on to Barley Hall, a farmhouse (still standing) which for generations was to serve as a strong Methodist centre. In the lane to the farm he was waylaid by an ambush and violently assaulted. His horse swerved from side to side, till he forced his way through, and his companion, David Taylor, was copiously bleeding from a wound in the forehead. Finally Charles' horse bolted with him down the steep hill, but he escaped unhurt, though bespattered with eggs and dirt, with torn clothes, and an arm stiff and painful from a blow received in Sheffield.

He met with a kinder reception in Leeds. Where on his previous visit he had walked the streets and no man stood by him, he now found a following. A barber, William Shent, was among his first supporters and Charles stood outside his shop and preached. Even the clergy went out of their way to do him honour. At the parish church he was shown into the Minister's pew and assisted at Communion, but he says that he dreaded their favour more than the stones in Sheffield.

In 1744 Charles published his *Hymns for Times of Trouble and Persecution* which bear direct reference to the brutal antagonism to which the Methodists were exposed. Familiar among them is "Ye Servants of God, your Master proclaim"—a lusty hymn sung today by congregations oblivious of its origin:

> The waves of the sea have lift up their voice,
> Sore troubled that we in Jesus rejoice;
> The floods they are roaring, but Jesus is here,
> While we are adoring, He always is near . . .
>
> Their fury shall never our steadfastness shock,
> The weakest believer is built on a Rock.

There is an echo of the period in the hymn "And are we yet alive?" which is sung always at the opening of the Methodist Conference, though hardly with the same relevance:

> What troubles have we seen,
> What mighty conflicts passed!

Such hymns came out of a furnace of suffering. In this high hour Charles led no flagging army, but a band of hard campaigners, and when all seemed lost rallied them like a cavalry leader, himself in the forefront, urging them on with militant songs: 'Come on, my Partners in distress', 'Our Captain leads us on', "Surrounded by a Host of Foes",

> Only have faith in God,
> In faith your foes assail . . .
>
> But shall believers fear?
> But shall believers fly?

and, like the call of a bugle, "Soldiers of Christ, arise".
While in Newcastle he met with hysterical outbreaks,

common at that period in Methodism, which he called, "the fits". "Many, no doubt, were, at our first preaching, struck down, both soul and body, into the depth of distress. Their *outward affections* were easy to be imitated. Many counterfeits I have already detected . . . Today, one who came from the ale-house, drunk, was pleased to fall into a fit for my entertainment, and beat himself heartily. I thought it a pity to hinder him; so, instead of singing over him, as had been often done, we left him to recover at his leisure. Another, a girl, as she began her cry, I ordered to be carried out. Her convulsion was so violent, as to take away the use of her limbs, till they laid and left her without the door. Then immediately she found her legs and walked off."

Similar exhibitions had already caused embarrassment in Bristol, where John Wesley had failed to discourage them and had even been deceived by them, but Charles put a stop to them. Under no circumstances would he tolerate them and plainly admonished his hearers: "Last night, before I began, I gave public notice, that whosoever cried so as to drown my voice, should without any man's hurting or judging them, be gently carried to the farthest corner of the room." This had the desired effect; there were no more "fits".

He was strict also in admitting new members. "We have certainly been too rash and easy in allowing persons for believers on their own testimony; nay, and even persuading them into a false opinion of themselves. Some souls, it is doubtless necessary to encourage; but it should be done with the utmost caution." His strong sense of order and discipline had a marked effect on the qualitative development of Methodism. John Wesley could be ruthless, but Charles, exercising even greater strictness, had the heart of a shepherd.

He might almost be called the Apostle of the North, for both now and later he spent much time there—once, ten weeks, lodging in a thatched house in Horsley—evangelizing the area, where Methodism became firmly established. Premises were acquired in Newcastle, known as the Orphan House (though it never held orphans) which served, like the Foundery, as a hostel and preaching centre.

Returning south he paused at Selby where, dining in mixed company, he was asked if there was any good in confirmation. He replied: "No, nor in baptism, nor in the Lord's supper, or any outward thing, unless you are in Christ a new creature," and confounded his hearers by relating his religious experience.

He stopped also in Epworth, scene of many memories, where all who met him saluted him heartily, and he preached in Edward Smith's yard. At Nottingham he found his brother preaching in the market place, and received a full account of the Wednesbury riots. That night he began a Society there of nine members. Three days later he formed the first Birmingham Society, numbering thirteen. They were still days of small beginnings, but the brothers cast their net wide. Societies rapidly grew and the number of them multiplied.

After returning to London and encouraging the Foundery membership, which was still suffering from the shock of the Moravian controversy, he set out in hard rain for Cornwall, enjoying his brother's company as far as Exeter, getting lost, like most travellers in those days, on Bodmin Moor, and arrived at St. Ives too weary almost for words. It was not surprising, for he had ridden from Newcastle in just over three weeks, with many intervening halts.

In Cornwall he found a simple and warmhearted people, but also considerable opposition, not least from the clergy. In Wednock church he stood within two yards of the pulpit and heard such a "hodge-potch" of railing, foolish lies as Satan himself might have been ashamed of. He did not hesitate afterwards to "mildly" reprove the preacher by calling him a liar! But the worst outbreak of antagonism was at St. Ives where, led by a drum, the mob followed him like ramping and roaring lions.

Knowing his sensitive temperament, we cannot but wonder how he endured such frequent and bitter hostility. He was obliged often to break off in the middle of a prayer to silence a noisy demonstrator, as at Pool, where a drunkard was so persistent that the warmhearted tinners finally set upon him. Or as at Hexham when he was preaching in a cockpit and two cocks were brought in and set fighting.

At St. Ives he had just announced his text when rioters entered, threatening murder, breaking sconces and windows, scattering benches, and leaving nothing but the bare walls. "I stood silently looking on," is Charles' simple comment. They swore he should never preach there again, which he immediately disproved by proceeding with his sermon. Led by the son of the Mayor, they then attacked the women present, at which Charles strongly protested. They next fell to quarrelling among themselves and broke the head of the Town Clerk. But the longer they raged, the more power Charles felt from above. "I bade the people stand still and see the salvation of God, resolving to continue with them, and see the end . . . Having kept the field, we gave thanks for the victory."

Further rioting followed when he and his fellow preachers were stoned as Popish incendiaries. Eggs were thrown in at the windows, followed by large stones, and so great was the violence that he was obliged to dismiss the congregation. The following day the Mayor intervened by confiscating the rioters' drum and threatening to swear twenty new constables and suppress the disturbance by force.

A pleasanter picture is of Charles' visit to Land's End, where on the extreme point of the rocks facing the Atlantic he wrote the hymn, "Come, divine Immanuel, come".

> Carry on thy victory,
> Spread thy rule from sea to sea.

The weather had evidently been unkind, for after a fortnight's fog (in midsummer) he makes the dry comment: "I saw a strange sight, the sun shining in Cornwall." But despite the weather and the opposition he appears to have enjoyed Cornwall, and like his brother, to have progressed through it triumphantly. The tin miners accompanied him by the hundred from village to village singing Methodist hymns, to the displeasure of many of the clergy who by no means welcomed such vigorous disturbance of their placid (and often stagnant) parish life.

It was with regret that he left the area, despite a last-minute outrage at St. Ives, where the drunken Town Clerk led his tipsy followers to Charles' lodging, threatened to pull it down and were so violent that Charles' friends begged him to leave by a back way, which he refused to do. Accompanied by about twenty followers on horseback he rode slowly through the open street, leaving, as he said, the lions' den.

A summons from his brother to a conference recalled him to London and he had nearly three hundred miles to ride in five days. But he did not hesitate to preach to about a thousand, mostly gentry, in Exeter, and, missing his way at Bridport, found "a poor creature ready for the Gospel". He stopped also in Salisbury to visit his sister Martha, who had been deserted by her husband, Westley Hall, an unstable cleric, who, after turning Moravian, had fallen into serious delusions and licentious ways. Charles tells us that he gathered up a few more scattered sheep between there and London, and by nine at night on the fifth day he reached the Foundery.

After the Moravian controversy, when many "left the ship", there remained the deep rift with the Calvinists. In 1741 Whitefield had separated from the Wesleys, and Charles, less forgiving on this issue than his brother, preached more vehemently against Calvinism. It was with sorrow that he parted with the convert of his Oxford days. In spirited lines he had eulogized him:

> From strength to strength our young Apostle goes,
> Pours like a torrent, and the land o'erflows.
> To distant climes his healing doctrine brings,
>   And joins the morning's with the eagle's wings.

But "O had he kept the post by Heaven assign'd!" and the poem degenerates into fierce invective against "the hellish, blasphemous, exploded lie".

The breach, happily, was not final, and nobler sentiments follow:

> Come on, my Whitefield! since the strife is past,
> And friends at first are friends again at last.

Charles, fighter though he was, was a great peacemaker, and never more so than with his alienated friends. The poem is full of autobiographical reference and reflects a generous spirit. Their friendship survived and Whitefield graciously conceded that Charles first projected his Savannah orphanage. "It was first proposed to me by my friend, Mr. Charles Wesley, who with General Oglethorpe had concerted a scheme for carrying on such a design, before I had any thoughts of going abroad myself."

Charles' relations with Howell Harris never reached the same point of estrangement, though he was obliged to rebuke him openly for preaching Calvinism at Kingswood. But when ill-disposed persons tries to sow discord between them he at once brushed them side and publicly declared his admiration of Harris's work, afterwards sending him the following cordial letter: "My dearest Friend and Brother,—In the name of Jesus Christ I beseech you, if you have His glory and the good of souls at heart, come immediately and meet me here. I trust we shall never be two in time or eternity. O my Brother, I am grieved that Satan should get a moment's advantage over us; and am ready to lay my neck under your feet for Christ's sake. If your heart is as my heart, hasten in the name of our dear Lord to your second self, C. Wesley."

John Cennick, who was in charge of the Kingswood School, on turning Calvinist was less accommodating, and by using his position to oppose the Wesley's teaching of free grace created an intolerable situation ending in his dismissal. "Alas", Charles wrote, "we have set the wolf to keep the sheep! God gave me great moderation toward him, who, for many months, has been undermining our doctrine and authority."

The controversy with the Calvinists was responsible for Charles' numerous hymns on God's Everlasting Love, and a Collection under that title appeared in 1741. "Father whose Everlasting Love" is a notable example, in almost every line of which a word or phrase is italicized to give pointed emphasis to the Arminian view, of free grace for all:

> A *World* He suffer'd to redeem,
> For *All* He hath th'Atonement made.

He could never express too strongly the breadth, the sheer immensity, of God's redemptive love: "For all, for all, my Saviour died."

Susanna, the mother of the Wesleys, had died on July 23, 1742, at the Foundery where her later years were spent. She had watched, at first dubiously, then with growing interest and acceptance, the work of her two sons. In a real sense she was the Mother of Methodism, having schooled her family in methodical piety and opened her home in Epworth for religious services, though she never surrendered her Anglican principles or was swept off her feet by her sons' enthusiasm. The Moravians had tried, and failed, to influence her. And in a revealing and mildly reproving reply to a letter from Charles she appears not to have welcomed his spiritual guidance.

Charles, she says, has no need to worry, and is mistaken in her case, though she believes his letter to her is well-meant. "You ask many questions which I care not to answer; but I refer you to our dear Lord, who will satisfy you in all things necessary for you to know. I cannot conceive why you affirm yourself to be no Christian." That was in 1740. And Susanna remained Susanna to the end—calm, critical, and inflexible.

She had earlier informed Whitefield, who had a great regard for her, that she did not like her sons' way of living, and wished them in some place of their own, where they might regularly preach. Yet she had been the first to remove John Wesley's scruples against employing his first unordained preacher, Thomas Maxfield, stating plainly: "You know what my sentiments have been; but take care what you do with respect to this young man; for he is as surely called of God to preach as you are."

The grave of this remarkable woman is in Bunhill Fields, but Charles' epitaph inscribed upon it is painfully inadequate. How came he to compose such uninspired doggerel or, as in the second of its four verses, to speak of her life of Christian patience and devotion as "a legal night of seventy years":

> True daughter of affliction she,
> Enured to pain and misery,
> Mourn'd a long night of griefs and fears,
> A legal night of seventy years.

If ever a woman deserved a glowing testimony it was his own mother.

There was a recurrence of trouble on his next visit to the Midlands, in 1744. Staffordshire was the seat of war and he set out for Wednesbury, the field of battle. The magistrates again refused to restrain the rioters and even encouraged them, one offering five pounds to be rid of the Methodists, and another, rather than protect one who had been half murdered, delivered him into their hands, throwing his hat in the air and egging them on. Such irresponsibility on the part of the law naturally provoked further disorder, and the suffering of the Methodists in this area was pitiful. They were threatened, blackmailed, robbed, assaulted, and in some cases made homeless. Their windows were smashed, their homes were wrecked. Their doors were watched night and day, and the slightest sound of hymn or prayer resulted in a rough entry followed by theft and destruction. Throughout the district Methodists were beaten up and in Walsall posters invited people to join in destroying them. Opposition in Birmingham was milder, where Charles met only with dirt and stones in the Bull Ring, with the bells of St. Martin's ringing their loudest to drown his discourse.

At Thorne, near the scene of his ambush, he was relieved to find opposition had disappeared. "Where are the wild creatures that were for braining me and my horse, the last time I came this way!" On reaching Newcastle he wrote to his brother, dissuading him from presenting a Humble Address to the King from the Methodist Societies, affirming their loyalty at the time of the threatened French invasion. His objection to it was that it would imply "or at least would seem to allow that we are a body distinct from the national Church, whereas we are only a sound part of the Church. Guard against this." It was Charles' constant care to avoid any appearance of severance from the Church, and John Wesley, on reconsideration, followed his advice.

The worst opposition he encountered was at Devizes, organized by the curate, when the bells were rung backwards, his host's house was ransacked, the preaching house was blocked with a waggon, and the stable of the inn was broken open and the preachers' horses were set loose and found hours afterwards up to their necks in a pond. The outbreak was so malicious that Charles for once was at a loss what to do, until rescued by a friendly Baptist. But the violence was renewed and reached its height on the following day when the boys of the town rang their bells "like the devil's infantry", a mob filled the streets, a fire engine was brought out and water hosed into Charles' lodging until the Mayor forcibly removed "the spout". A larger engine was then produced and flooded the lower rooms, driving the inmates into an attic with no way of escape. A stalwart defender had been thrown into the horse pond, with, it was said, a broken back, and his wife was hysterical. Charles, when begged to escape disguised in women's clothes, refused, and his companion, Meriton, hid his money and watch, resolved that the crowd should have nothing but his carcase. Meanwhile the local gentry plied the mob with pitchers of ale, as much as they could drink.

After a three hours' siege "an old serpent, who sat observing us at an opposite house, in the shape of a lawyer", advised the reading of the Riot Act and the crowd dispersed after setting a guard on the house. But with darkness the mob returned with the fire engine and began to remove the roof. A small girl called through the door: "Mr. Wesley! Mr. Wesley! Creep under the bed. They will murder you. They are pulling down the house." The constable then offered Charles a safe passage if he would undertake never to preach there again, to which Charles replied that he would promise no such thing.

He and his party now planned to escape at midnight and arranged for the recovery of their horses, but fearing the house would be destroyed, they suddenly emerged and were greeted by a wild shout. Fortunately Charles in the confusion was unrecognized, though Meriton was soon on the ground with two bulldogs on him, one of which caught his horse by the nose. He felled it with the butt end of his whip, Charles held his mare while he remounted, and, before further attack, they escaped. Later, having transferred to a coach in Bath, they went singing on their way, but their triumph was short-lived, for the coach overturned and its six occupants were hurt, though not seriously. Out of this experience at Devizes came a memorable hymn, "Worship and Thanks and Blessing", full of gratitude, ringing with victory:

> Thy Glory was our rereward,
> Thine hand our lives did cover.

He still felt the burden of his public work. "I took up my cross," he records, "to oblige my brother, and began examining the classes." And he wrote to encourage a friend, after an unfortunate case of disloyalty which had provoked bitter ill-feeling, "Do not weary of well-doing . . . Pray for me, that I also may endure unto the end; for a thousand times I cry out. 'The burden of this people is more than I am able to bear.' O my good friend, you do not know them. Such depths of ingratitude I did not think was in the devils of hell."

We find him again in Cornwall, staying with Thompson, the hospitable Vicar of St. Gennys, and coming late at night by the pits and shafts of the mines to Gwennap Pit, a natural amphitheatre, scene of countless Methodist assemblies, and still remarkably preserved and used for an annual gathering. The Evangelicals in their enthusiasm were apt to exaggerate their past shortcomings, and a chorus of reckless testimony from three fellow clergymen followed Charles' confession, in a crowded service in St. Gennys church, that he had been dead to God and in a state of damnation for eighteen years. Meriton, his travelling companion, added, "And I for twenty-five." "And I," cried the Vicar, "for thirty-five." "And I," said Mr. Bennett, not to be outdone, "for seventy."

By this time opposition in Cornwall had lessened. "The whole country," Charles records, "is gone forth after the sound of the Gospel." The preachers were in wide demand and preached daily in new places, sometimes five and six times a day. The county was sensible of the change, for at the previous Assizes there was not a felon to be found in its prisons and at the last revel there had not been enough men to make a wrestling match.

Dr. Johnson called Charles "a stationary man", which was true of his later years, but at this period, and from the day he had first left London, to put it no earlier, he was hardly less mobile than his brother, sharing with him the toils and perils of the road. A cross-section of his *Journal*, taken at any point during these years, bears this out. In the five months following this Cornwall visit he covered half the country, from Minehead to Bristol and South Wales, through Wiltshire and the Cotswolds to Oxford and London, and on through the eastern counties and Midlands as far as Newcastle-on-Tyne, returning by the same route to London.

Nor was it easy travelling. In Wiltshire, he blundered on a dark night in a little village and found neither bed nor victuals. He had a "woful journey" to Epworth, and near Durham after much wandering came by night, half-starved, to his inn. At Newcastle he found the roads almost impassable on account of snow and was obliged to walk to Sunderland and back on foot—no small distance, and the hail and snow were so violent that he could hardly stand and was on the point of lying down in sheer exhaustion. The following day he walked knee-deep in snow to Whickham and back to Horsley, his jaw stiffened by the cold.

The ill-conditioned roads—even the main highways in places—were often quagmires and the by-roads little more than cart tracks and pack horse trails, with long desolate stretches between human habitations. Defoe in his *Tour through the Whole Island of Great Britain*, published in 1724, gives reliable details. The roads of the Midlands were clayey and dirty, and as all traffic converged on London—coaches, carriers, waggoners, and droves of cattle, hogs and sheep—these highways were ploughed so deep, and materials for repair were so difficult to come by, that the burden of their upkeep was too great for the local landowners responsible for their maintenance. Until the coming of the turnpikes only the great Roman roads remained, firm and solid, surviving the wear of a thousand years. Otherwise the roads were deep-rutted, undrained, often flooded, and with but few bridges. The two main roads into London, to Islington and Smithfield, were "run to ruin" and a scandal to the city. Travellers from Wales suffered badly on Birdlip Hill, near Gloucester, and Sussex endured the utmost distress through want of good highways. In the course of the century the more rapid extension of turnpikes and bridges brought great improvements.

We cannot stop to follow Charles' many journeys in these years, but always the pattern is the same, of triumphs and setbacks, of waiting multitudes and crowded preaching houses, of fierce though intermittent persecution, of Societies scattered in his absence or showing fruitful increase. The *Journal* is a record of unwearied effort. And not of preaching only, for in every place to which he came he exercised the care of a pastor, identifying himself with the people, visiting the sick and the imprisoned, reasoning with the unreasonable, pleading with the sinful.

A typical Sunday in Bristol (September 23, 1744) began with five a.m. preaching in the Horse Fair, followed by Communion at Kingswood, a baptism and a second sermon, then by horse to Bristol for a third sermon, after which he returned to Kingswood for a love feast, and at midnight went back to Bristol to sleep.

In 1744 Charles listened to the last sermon his brother preached before the University of Oxford. He himself had preached there two years earlier and on a trumpet theme: "Awake thou that sleepest, and arise from the dead, and Christ shall give thee light." His converts were by no means all of the poorer sort. The Revival gathered in people of every class, and

Whitefield, in particular, attracted a distinguished following, though he appealed no less to the illiterate. John Wesley had been quick to note the fashionable westward drift from the city and had followed it by acquiring the lease of a former Huguenot chapel in West Street. Here the Wesley brothers, Whitefield, the saintly Fletcher and other leaders ministered in crowded services, and the narrow street, now so unprepossessing, in the Drury Lane area, was lined regularly with the waiting coaches of their more fashionable followers. The plain building survives, now adapted to other purposes, but though shorn of its glory, it is haunted by old memories. It was the mother Church of West End Methodism until its activities were transferred to Hinde Street Methodist Church and to Kingsway Hall, the thriving centre of the West London Mission.

Among its first worshippers, and a notable convert, was Mrs. Rich, the wife of John Rich, the proprietor of Covent Garden Theatre. Beginning as a waitress at Bret's Coffee House, she became an actress at Covent Garden and after serving Rich as housekeeper became his third wife. Her husband, annoyed by her conversion, insisted on her returning to the stage and only capitulated when she threatened that if she did so she would publicly testify. Both he and his wife were prominent figures in stage circles. He had been connected with Drury Lane and had built the New Theatre in Lincoln's Inn Fields before opening in Covent Garden in 1732. He had also produced Gay's *Beggar's Opera* and with such success that it was popularly said to have made Rich gay and Gay rich.

In time he also was influenced by Methodism, though at first with some reluctance. Charles describes the first time he was his wife's guest: "Dined at Mrs. R.'s. The family concealed their fright tolerably well. Mr. R. behaved with great civility. I foresee the storm my visit will bring on him." And later he records: "Poor Mr. R. has got an hook within him which shall bring him at last to land." But it was hard work on the part of Mrs. Rich, as we see from the following letter which she wrote to Charles in 1746:

"Dear and Rev. Sir,—I am infinitely obliged to you for your kind letter. It gave me great comfort, and at a time I had much need of it; for I have been very ill, both in body and mind. Some part arose from my poor partner, who, I fear, has in a great measure stifled his convictions which God gave him. . . . I gave a copy of the hymn to Mr. Lampe,[1] who at the reading, shed some tears, and said he would write to you; for he loved you as well as if you were his own brother . . . The enclosed is a copy of a song Mr. Rich has sung in a new scene, added to one of his old entertainments, in the character of harlequin-Preacher, to convince the town he is not a Methodist. O, pray for him that he may be a Christian indeed, and then he will be no more concerned about what he is called, and for me,

Your unworthy daughter in Christ."

Rich in the end became such a good friend of the Methodists that Smollett declared that he laboured under the tyranny of a wife and the terrors of hell-fire at the same time. His wife, who on his death was left in affluence, remained a lifelong friend of Charles and his family.[2] Her coach was often at his disposal and she gave Methodist parties at her house in Chelsea. He found pleasure in his association with this circle, which not only gave him (and Methodism) new and agreeable contacts, but proved valuable at a later period when he was launching his musical sons.

[1] J. F. Lampe, the composer, a friend of Handel, and a member of of the Covent Garden Company, who became a Methodist and composed a number of tunes for Charles' hymns.

[2] One of her daughters married Mr. Beard, a musical celebrity of the day, whose first wife had been Lady Edward Herbert, daughter of Earl Waldegrave. Beard gave good help in encouraging the musical gifts of Charles' two sons.

Chapter Eight

THE GWYNNES OF GARTH 1747–1749

CHAPTER EIGHT

IN NOTHING did the brothers differ more than in their approach to marriage. John sailed recklessly into it (after several near shipwrecks), but Charles came to it naturally. John was secretive, where Charles was open. John married a vixen, but Charles had the sense to choose a good wife. He found his bride, Sally, among the mountains of Wales where the rugged hills run down to the green Breconshire valleys. Her father, Marmaduke Gwynne, was Squire of Garth, near Builth Wells, a zealous magistrate and devout churchman, and his mansion, Garth House, can still be seen, overlooking the winding river. In his day it held an impressive household, for in addition to his nine children, there was a chaplain, twenty servants, and often a dozen or more guests.

The Gwynnes were a wealthy and well-established family. An earlier Marmaduke Gwynne, a barrister, had married a London heiress and been appointed a judge in North Wales, from which office he was removed on charges of corruption, but not before he had acquired the manor of Garth and the greater part of Builth.

His grandson, also Marmaduke, was of finer quality. From Jesus College, Oxford, he entered Lincoln's Inn and became Sheriff of Radnorshire. He married Sarah Evans, one of six sisters, each of whom inherited £30,000. His conversion by Howell Harris must have caused no small sensation and none could have been more surprised than he himself. Hearing that Harris was preaching in the neighbourhood, he had set out to hear him, armed with a warrant intending to arrest him. Harris was a layman and Gwynne was determined to put down irregular preaching. But being a fairminded man, he remarked to his wife before leaving the house: "I will hear the man myself, before I commit him," and was so moved by the sermon that he invited the preacher back to Garth House (see Plate 3) as his guest, where Mrs. Gwynne, less susceptible than her husband, refused to meet him, quitting the room in tears. She was even more shocked when she found later that her husband and Sally (see Plate 4) were regularly attending his services.

She was influenced, however, through reading John Wesley's *Appeal to Men of Reason and Religion* and was further impressed by the high regard in which the Wesleys were held by their Oxford contemporaries, some of whom were among her local acquaintances. The upshot was that her home was opened to Methodist preaching. Her husband attended Wesley's second Conference, one of a group of ten, held at Bristol in 1745 and it was there probably that Charles first met him. A month later, when Charles was laid up with a leg injury at Fonmon Castle and preaching on crutches, Gwynne sent his servant to bring him to stay at Garth, but Charles was unfit for the journey. A week later Gwynne came himself, accompanied by Edward Phillips, the Vicar of Maesmynis, and renewed the invitation, but Charles was still unable to accept. His first visit to Garth was not until two years later, in 1747, on his way to Ireland. He stayed first with Phillips at Maesmynis, where he had arranged to meet his brother who was returning from Ireland, and where Gwynne with two of his family lost no time in calling on him. Charles warmed to them at once. He preached on the following day at Llandrindod and returned to Garth.

It was a happy visit and Charles met with the friendliest of welcomes, both in Gwynne's home and among the neighbouring clergy. John went on his way to Bristol and Charles journeyed to Ireland, escorted by Gwynne and Phillips as far as Dolgelly. But it was rough travelling—the seven miles to Rhayader (where he preached in the church) took seven hours. The Minister seemed a man of simple heart, and surely not eager for preferment, or he would not have been content with his stipend of £3 a year. Charles waited two hours in a storm for the ferry beyond Carnarvon and rode in the dark over the heavy sands, pausing only to dry his clothes at a friendly house, and pushing on through the night to Holyhead, having been in the saddle twenty-five hours.

In Holyhead his courteous offer of assistance to the Vicar in his Sunday services was rudely declined, and he arrived in Dublin to find that the preaching house in Marlborough Street had been destroyed by a Popish mob. He lost no time in preaching in the shattered building to the distressed congregation, his text being "Comfort ye, comfort ye, my people", but in the streets he was pursued by insulting crowds who taunted and stoned him. As in England he preached in the open, taking

126

his stand under the wall of the barracks and on St. Stephen's Green. "Woe is me now," he records, "for my soul is wearied because of murderers which this city is full of. The Ormond mob and liberty mob, seldom part, till one or more are killed." That very day a constable had been beaten and killed and then hung up in triumph, with no one arrested for it. The previous week a woman had been beaten to death by the rabble, though, it is true, she had been caught picking a pocket. Another died after having his stomach jumped upon, and the murderer, when brought to justice, was acquitted.

Such was the city as Charles found it, where on the least provocation Irish blood was up, and his arrival was the signal for fresh outbreaks of old feuds and animosities in which Protestants and Papists when not fighting the Methodists were fighting each other, and where the police, apart from making a few perfunctory arrests, allowed themselves to be bribed with drink and money.

Charles, as usual, refused to capitulate and few scenes in his life show more clearly his stature than when he pleaded with throngs of Papists on St. Stephen's Green, urging them from their own liturgy and the authority of Thomas à Kempis to accept the Gospel. They listened with strange attention and many were in tears. As he challenged them with their own tradition they thought he must be a good Catholic, and all the more when, at the close, he advised them to go to their respective places of worship.

This first Irish visit lasted six months during which he secured land and built a chapel in Dublin, collecting subscriptions for it throughout the city, gathering £70 within two days. The Dean showed him courtesy at the Cathedral and noted with pleasure that the bulk of his communicants were the Methodists, whom Charles regularly took there. Outside Dublin he visited Tyrrell's Pass, where he overtook a lad whistling a Methodist tune and where a great transformation followed his visit. The people had been notoriously wicked, but never did he speak to more hungry souls and he gathered in a hundred members.

A very different reception met him on the road to Athlone, where he and his party were violently attacked and outnumbered and rode through a shower of stones. One of his companions was seriously disabled and remained, unconscious, in the hands of the attackers, and they were obliged to return to his rescue, barely in time to prevent him being dispatched with a knife. A woman who had intervened had been killed. This murderous onslaught had been organized by the local priests and the hedges were lined with Papists, who took to their heels when troops arrived on the scene. The Wesleys generally enjoyed excellent relations with members of the forces, many of whom had joined their Societies; some had established Methodism among the army in the Low Countries and one, Captain Webb, helped to form the first Methodist Society in New York. The brothers took every opportunity of preaching in dockyards, camps and barracks, and here in Athlone the soldiers flocked around Charles, and their officers provided a guard for his safety. The market place was thronged for his sermon, and later, with their escort and travelling slowly on account of their wounded comrade, the preachers returned to the scene of the attack, where on the bloodstained road they sang a song of triumph, then dismissed their guard and went singing on their way.

At Tullamore he welcomed more soldiers who waited on him for instruction, and forty dragoons were converted at St. Philip's Town, where he was delighted to meet and pray with an old couple, the man aged ninety-six, his wife ninety-eight, the former an ex-soldier, full of days and scars, who had worked at his loom till his ninety-fourth year, and both retaining full sense and understanding.

Meanwhile he did not neglect the prisoners in Dublin Jail. "Their cries pierced the clouds . . . Near twenty of the poor wretches pressed after me." In answer to prayer, so it seemed, a condemned woman was both reprieved and converted, "saved by a miracle of mercy", and even the Romish executioner was half converted. Daily the Methodists increased in numbers and the exuberance of the converts was such that when one of them was constrained to cry out, "He is come! He is come! I have Him! I have Him now in my heart!" a stranger who stood with his hat on the stairs was so astonished that he exclaimed: "Lord bless me! What is this?" and turned and fled as if the devil were at his heels.

In addition to persecution Charles had an uncomfortable lodging, as we see in a letter to Blackwell: "A family of squabbling children, a landlady just ready to lie in, a maid who has

4a. Portrait of Sarah Wesley, Charles' wife, painted by John Russell at about the time of her marriage in 1749. It hangs in the New Room, Bristol.

4b. Sarah, the widow of Charles Wesley, in her later years. Smallpox had marked her features and robbed her of her good looks.

5. An extract from Sarah Gwynne's letter to Charles, dated January 19, 1749, and written at a time when Mrs. Gwynne was raising difficulties. She starts her letter: "O what a good God do the Christians serve! What a mercy it is that such a poor weak worm as I am enabled to say 'Thy Gifts, if call'd for, I resign, Pleas'd to receive, pleased to restore' Hitherto, hath God helped! This was the language of my Heart in perusing Your Sweet Letters last night, and my prayers were almost swallow'd up in Praises for the unspeakable Blessings the Lord had made me a partaker of already, thro' Your Ministry . . . ."

no time to do the least thing for us, are some of our inconveniences. Our two rooms for four persons (six when J. Healey and J. Haughton come) allow no opportunity for retirement. Charles (Perronet) and I groan for elbow-room. Our diet answers to our lodgings; no one to mend our clothes; no money to buy more."

Three days later he wrote to him again, this time on money matters. Blackwell, a Lombard Street banker of Lewisham, was a close friend and one to whom both the Wesleys turned constantly for advice. From this letter we gather that Charles had little change out of £20 received towards his Irish expenses, after meeting the travelling costs of two persons, keep for their horses, printing, and other items.

In a letter to his brother he refers to his disinclination to give up drinking tea. "However my example may not clash with yours. We are on different sides in the matter." Writing again to Blackwell, whom he keeps well posted, he refers to the growing prospects of Irish Methodism and says the people will not let him return unless his brother is sent in exchange. John arrived in due course, and after this hectic period, in the spring of 1748, Charles came again and with relief to the friendly home of the Gwynnes in its green valley.

For a week he had endured a raging toothache, aggravated by four days' hard riding through the mountains in pouring rain and against a sharp wind, and sleeping one night in a cold hut with the window nailed against the storm. He had ridden from Holyhead until he could ride no more, and for the last hour of his journey was obliged to walk. But at Garth the friendly door stood open and the family ran to meet him. He was put to bed and for five days they nursed him, after which Mrs. Gwynne carried him out in her chair and on his departure drove him to Builth, from where, accompanied for the first hour by Sally and her father, he rode on to Bristol.

By now Charles was showing a lively interest in Sally who, despite disparity of age, for she was only twenty-one, and he was nineteen years older, felt no less drawn towards him. She was one of a large and attractive family, and Garth House was full of young and eager life. A faded paper is preserved, written by Sally in later years, giving family details, from which we learn that Howell, the eldest, was already married to Lady Rudd; Mary became the wife of Captain Edward Baldwyn of

Diddlebury Hall, near Ludlow; Marmaduke married Miss Howell of Glamorgan; Rebecca (Becky), two years older than Sally, remained unmarried (and afterwards lived for many years with Charles and Sally); Joan was two years younger; Elizabeth (Betsy), four years Sally's junior, married James Waller, a London lace merchant; Margaret died in her eighteenth year; and the youngest, Roderick, at the time was a boy of thirteen. The record adds that Mr. Gwynne died in 1769 and his widow in the following year.

Already Charles had written to Sally from Dublin in the previous September: "I shall probably see you sooner than I expected at Garth," and after referring to the violence he had encountered, "My heart is deeply engaged for you." And he wrote warmly after he had been nursed at Garth: "I cannot forbear a line, to my dearest friend, weary as I am with my yesterday's ride of near ninety mile. If the Lord permit, I should rejoice to see you at my return to B[ristol], and so much the rather because I am far from promising myself another safe return from Ireland." The pastoral tone of these letters barely conceals his growing affection and by the time of his second visit to Ireland the relationship had deepened. They had made a pact of prayer: "Remember to meet me always on Monday noon, and every evening at five." And while waiting for the boat at Holyhead he gave lyrical expression to his feelings, in a letter ending with a prayer: "O Eternal Spirit of Love, come down into my heart and into my Friend's heart, and knit us together in the bond of perfectness. Lead us by the waters of comfort. Swallow up our will in Thine. Make ready the bride, and then call us up to the marriage supper of the Lamb."

This letter, written on the eve of yet another uncertain mission, throws strong light on Charles' character. Its lyrical and mystical qualities reflect his ardent nature and instinctive faith. He cannot separate human from divine love or think of marriage apart from the Heavenly Bridegroom. All is set in an eternal context, and perfect love in this life will endure in the life to come. He also addressed her in verse:

> Two are better far than one,
> For counsel or for fight!
> How can man be warm alone
> Or serve his God aright?

Sally, though hardly less pious, touched on more practical matters. Had he changed his linen? Was he keeping good hours? Already her feminine care was asserting itself. He answers that he puts off his clothes every night, and is sleeping "most immoderately" till six every morning. And he hopes that his "Guardian Angel" is also taking good care. "You will take advice, I hope, as well as give it, and follow a good example by regular sleeping and rising. You cannot be so exact as me, but do the best you can. Expect to give a strict account of yourself, if we should meet again," and he adds in a postscript: "Don't forget your shorthand."

In June 1748 Sally and her father joined Charles in Bristol and ten days later set out with him for London. The purpose of this excursion was to show them Methodist activities. He lodged them at the Foundery, and for two and a half weeks he resumed his London ministry. "I took the field," he says, but he found time to introduce them to many of his friends, to escort them to see Mrs. Blackwell at Lewisham and his friend, Vincent Perronet, at Shoreham, before returning with them to Bristol. On their departure they set out at four and arrived at Windsor at eleven, where Charles and his pillion rider (probably Sally) were thrown from their horse (Charles was always having riding accidents). He showed them over Windsor Castle, preached in Reading, and took them round the Colleges in Oxford, where they stayed for three nights before travelling on to Bristol.

By now Sally must have had a foretaste of what awaited her. On the following Sunday he roused her at four a.m. and took her with him to early Communion at Kingswood and the day's round of four sermons; and for a week she and her father accompanied him to his services in the open; at the Hotwells, where they found ladies listening in their coaches; and at the Horse Fair, singing and rejoicing till midnight. For over six weeks Gwynne and his daughter had been Charles' guests and fellow-travellers. In August he returned with them to Garth where, after a week's preaching in the neighbourhood, well supported by the local gentry and clergy, he rode on his way to Ireland. He had received letters urging him to visit Cork. "My heart was at once made willing and I had my commission."

Sally and her father accompanied him to Llanidloes, and Phillips as far as Machynlleth, after which he faced the long lonely stretch to Carnarvon, from three in the morning till eight at night in the saddle. In Anglesey, unable to procure a guide, he lost his way and blundered on through the sands, reaching Holyhead only to find he had missed the Irish boat. With three days to wait for the next, he wished he had lingered longer at Garth, his heart full of Sally. Finding no opportunity for retirement in his lodgings, he climbed Holy Mountain and wandered in a wilderness of rocks.

After meeting his brother in Dublin he went on to Cork and found it ripe for his message. There were two hundred new members (though he had difficulty at first in forming a Society) and thousands waited for hours day after day to hear him. He records his pleasure: "At present we pass through honour and good report. The chief persons of the town favour us. No wonder then that the common people are quiet. We pass and repass the streets, favoured by their blessings only. The same favourable inclination is all round the country. Wherever we go they receive us as angels of God." But, as always, he distrusts their approbation, fearing favour more than opposition, and never overrates his success. "Were this to last, I would escape for my life to America." He knew it was a passing excitement. "As yet the work is very superficial . . . How few will be God's messengers when the stream turns!"

But for the moment Cork was on fire. So great was the pressure that even Society meetings in private houses were impossible. "The people so crowded in, there was no room for me. Their love at present as effectually prevents our assembling, as their hatred will by and by." The churches also had never been so crowded, though often the clergy, faced with such unaccustomed congregations, railed at them against the Methodists, so that Charles ruefully records that he sent hundreds into church for the priests to drive them out again.

He waited on the Bishop and, finding him absent, took the opportunity of converting his housekeeper. The Governor's wife and many of the clergy attended his services. "Here, indeed, is an open door, such as was never set before me before until now. Even at Newcastle the awakening was not so general. The congregation last Sunday was computed above ten thousand. As yet there is no *open* opposition." The Bishop and his family at Riverstown received him with great affability and he remained for dinner. But Charles was rarely happy when in favour. "I do not find it good for me to be countenanced by my superiors. It is a snare and burden to my soul." "The Lord send to them by whom He will send; but hide me still in disguise and obscurity."

At length he was able to meet the infant Society, in an old playhouse, and to instruct it in the nature of Christian fellowship. He had already laboured hard to convince its members of their need for instruction. He had also encountered absurd rumours, one that "that wicked brother of mine" had run away with another man's wife at Athlone; another, that every kind of wickedness was practised in the Society, except the eating of little children. His work proceeded against a background of latent superstition and unbalanced emotion, and the priests opposed him secretly by imposing a curse on those of their flocks who attended his preaching, though some of the priests themselves listened to him by stealth. One who forbade his people to hear him met with short shrift from a magistrate who threatened to "shut up his mass-house" and send him to jail for twelve months if he persisted in his prohibition.

He preached elsewhere—at Bandon, a town full of Protestants, where the people were impatient to have a Society; at Kinsale, where the windows were full of spectators, many wild-looking people, the boys rude and noisy, and he was hit by a stone, where he preached in the rain, marvelling to find such a crowd in such weather, and where even the Romanists owned that none could find fault with him. Some insisted on his being their guest and the Governor gave orders that none should disturb him. One who attempted to do so would have been torn to pieces, had he not fled. The Roman Catholics, Charles was assured, were his firm friends. "It is worth observing that in Kinsale I am of every religion. The Presbyterians say I am Presbyterian; the church-goers, that I am a Minister of theirs; and the Catholics are sure I am a good Catholic in my heart."

He returned to Cork for a final farewell, where he managed to secure a whole morning to himself and "to my beloved friends in Wales". Sally is increasingly in his mind and he wrote to her, expressing his emotion on taking his leave of "this dearest people". He was also greatly refreshed by reading the Bishop of Exeter's charge to his clergy, worthy, he thought, to be written in letters of gold, and he quotes an extract: "My brethren, I beg you will rise up with me against only moral preaching. We have been long attempting the reformation of the nation by discourses of this kind. With what success? Why, with none at all. On the contrary, we have very dexterously preached the people into downright infidelity . . . Let me, therefore, again and again request, may I not add, *let me charge you*, to preach Jesus, and salvation through His name." This was the very essence of Methodism and shows that not every prelate was indifferent.

By now his mind was finally fixed on Sally and on his return to Bristol he unfolded his design to a friend, Mrs. Vigor, and also informed his brother with whom he shared an arrangement that neither would marry without consulting the other. "My brother and I having promised each other (as soon as he came from Georgia), that we would neither of us marry or take any steps towards it, without the other's knowledge and consent, today I fairly and fully communicated every thought of my heart." John, who loved managing other people's lives, had already suggested three likely names, S.P., M.W., and S.G., and entirely approved of the last, who was Sally. "We consulted together about every particular, and were of one mind and heart in all things."

Now all that remained was to make the proposal, and of Sally's answer there could be little doubt. But what of Mrs. Gwynne? That goodhearted but shrewd and managing lady, though well-disposed towards Charles, would naturally raise the question of money. What was Charles' fortune, his income, his prospects? How would she regard a proposal from a penniless parson? And how could a travelling preacher of Franciscan habits maintain a wife accustomed to the scale of Garth House?

Fortunately, just at this time, he was left a legacy by an old friend, Mrs. Sparrow, a relative of Blackwell, £50 of which he was able to collect, and, fortified with this, within six weeks he arrived back in Garth to face the ordeal. He found the family singing and was affectionately received, especially by Mrs. Gwynne. He first discussed tactics with Sally. "I advised with Sally how to proceed. Her judgment was that I should write to her mother." Meanwhile he got some of his flock together, prayed for an hour with Grace Bowen, the family nurse, and preached to the household. He let the weekend pass, taking Sally and Betsy to Maesmynis and on to Builth. There were wandering glances and whispered conferences. Quite frankly he was nervous. "I took further counsel with Sally, quite above all guile or reserve. I was afraid of making the proposal." And he hides his hesitancy under a pious phrase. "The door of prayer was always open."

On Monday he consulted Becky, who was heartily on his side, and that evening he approached Mrs. Gwynne, who answered outright that she would rather give her daughter to Mr. Wesley than to any man in England. "She afterwards spoke to me with great friendliness above all suspicion of under-hand dealing; (the appearance of which I was most afraid of)." Her only concern was over money. "She said she had no manner of objection but 'want of fortune'." Charles proposed £100 a year. She answered that her daughter could expect no more.

The next day, "Mr. Gwynne leaving the whole matter to his wife, I talked the matter fully over, and left it wholly with her to determine. She behaved in a most obliging manner, and *promised her consent*, if I could answer for £100 a year." And two days later: "I talked once more with Mrs. Gwynne, entirely open and friendly. She promised to tell me if any new objection arose, and confessed I had acted like a gentleman in all things."

Only one thing marred his happiness. It seems that the attractive Sally had had other suitors, one of whom was his friend and travelling companion, Phillips, who now in his dis-appointment showed great bitterness. Charles ignored his dis-agreeableness—brutishness, he called it—took a cheerful fare-well of the family, and in company with Phillips, despite their estrangement, returned to Bristol, and then on to London to break the glad news to his brother and to secure his income.

John was delighted, so was Vincent Perronet, who saw the hand of God in it, and Blackwell thought it was the Lord's doing. Charles said they would not allow him to make any doubt of it and chid him when he expressed any fear or diffi-dence. Mrs. Stotesbury, of Newington Green, declared that from the moment of seeing Sally she wished it with all her heart. The news had become public and the two thousand members of the London Society, with hardly an exception, approved Charles' choice. Ned Perronet was disappointed that Charles had not chosen his sister, and a Miss Cart, whom Charles had baptized, had wounded feelings. "Our poor dear S. Cart," he wrote to Sally, "makes my heart ache to see her; she is so above measure dejected. My cheerfulness has murdered hers. She guesses the cause of my joy, as I do of her sorrow: neither is it in my power to comfort her." But a month later she had revived and was more affable and friendly than he had ever known her. Meanwhile, in Wales, Phillips' jealousy continued and, still not without hope, he was writing to Sally.

Blackwell, always generous, offered to assist in securing the necessary income by opening a subscription list among a few influential friends, but John disapproved and suggested that the income should be guaranteed annually out of their book-room profits. Both John's books and Charles' hymns were finding a ready sale, although the latter had not yet appeared in a separate collection, and John wrote to Mrs. Gwynne, suggesting this arrangement. Charles also wrote: "It was with difficulty I refrained from acknowledging the great kindness and generosity you have always shewed me, especially when last at Garth," and he referred to his financial prospects: "Till now I neither knew nor cared what my writings and my brother's were worth. But I ordered my printer at B[ristol] to make an exact estimate. His account of their value . . . is £2,500, exclusive of the book I am now publishing, which will bring in more than £200 clear, besides a new version of the Psalms worth as much or more, and my journals and sermons, which I am daily called upon to publish. What all these copies amount to I will have computed and sent to you, when you have leisure to examine them. I am ashamed to trouble you with this strange kind of writing, however necessary. Permit me only to add one thing more. If after the strictest scrutiny you are satisfied as to a provision, and Mr. Gwynne and you see cause to give your consent, I would desire Miss Sally might secure her fortune in case of her own mortality, that it may return to her own family. I seek not hers, but her; and if the Lord should give and take away I shall want nothing upon earth. I abhor the thought of being a gainer by her in temporals, and could not rest unless secured from this danger. Your regard for me must not here interpose to hinder what would vindicate my character, and be most for the credit of the Gospel."

Meanwhile he awaits the issue, sending a line to Sally:

> "The lot, the fatal lot
> Into the lap is cast,
> But God whose mercy changeth not
> Shall order all at last.

The Bell strikes One! yet cannot I close my eyes till I have assured you of my invincible affection for one with whom I expect to pass a happy eternity."

In the previous December he had put in hand a two-volume edition of his hymns and he was proud that Sally was his first subscriber. The receipt for her subscription reads: "Dec. 24. 1748, Received of Miss Sallie Gwynne the sum of two shillings and sixpence for the subscription of two volumes of hymns which I propose to deliver on the payment of two shillings and sixpence more. C. Wesley." And he added: "The enclosed shows you my first subscriber, whom I set at the head of my list as a good omen. Many have followed your example already, being readier to part with their money than I to take it." The publication of this book excited Sally no less than Charles, and no doubt she had a hand in its final preparation.

Mrs. Gwynne sent a prompt reply to John's proposal, though it came as a bomb-shell. Capital income apart from land had no place in her economy, and books, not to mention hymns, were a dubious asset.

> "Revnd Sir," she wrote to John, "I received the favour of yours and entirely concur with you in every particular mentioned in the first part of your lettr, and wish I could joyn in approving of the Proposals you are pleased to make in the latter part of it. My objection is that nothing can be settled where no money is laid down on land secured from the due payment thereof. If that can be compassed without inconvenience by you and your brother and self I find it would be entirely satisfactory to as many of this family as have been made acquainted with it who also joyn with me in hearty respects to you, being Revnd Sir, your faithful Hum.Sert, Sa. Gwynne."

Charles read this undisturbed, though he did not own a square foot of land in the world, not even a home, and, in terms of property, hymn-books were hardly to be compared with the broad acres of Garth. He wrote immediately to Sally declaring that her dearest Mother's *consenting so far* to be plainly miraculous and what he never expected and that he cannot

137

think that Providence would suffer the matter to proceed so far, were it to stop there. He then hastened to consult Vincent Perronet, who sent the following frank and tactful letter to Mrs. Gwynne, pleading Charles' cause:

January 1749

Madam,—As the trouble of this proceeds from the most sincere friendship, I have reason to believe you will easily excuse it. Give me leave, Madam, to say that if you and worthy Mr. Gwynne are of opinion that the match proposed by the Rev. Mr. Charles Wesley be of God, neither of you will suffer objections, drawn from this world, to break it off . . .

I have a daughter now designed for a pious gentleman, whose fortune is not half that of our friend's; and yet, I would not exchange him for a Star and Garter. I only mention this that I might not appear to offer an opinion which I would not follow myself.

However, I have been hitherto speaking as if Mr. Wesley's circumstances really wanted an apology; but this is not the case. The very writings of the two gentlemen are, *even at this time, a very valuable estate:* and when it shall please God to open the minds of people more, and prejudice is worn off, it will be still much more valuable. I have seen what an able bookseller has valued a great part of their works at, which is £2,500: But I will venture to say, *that this is not half their value.* They are works which will last and sell while any sense of true religion and learning shall remain among us. However, as they are not of the same nature with an estate in land, they cannot be either sold or pledged without the most manifest loss and inconvenience.

I shall trouble you, Madam, no farther, than only to add, that from the time I had the pleasure of seeing Miss Gwynne at my house, I have often had her upon my mind. I then perceived so much grace and good sense in that young lady, that, when this affair was first mentioned to me, I could not help rejoicing at what promised so much happiness to the Church of God.

May that God, in whose hands are the hearts of the children of men, direct all of you in such a manner as may tend to the promoting of His honour, and the kingdom of His dear Son. I am, with great respect to worthy Mr. Gwynne, yourself, and good family, Madam,

Your very sincere and affectionate friend and servant,
Vincent Perronet.

This carefully framed letter brought a favourable reply, and a settlement was now in sight. Charles wrote off at once to

Sally: "Providence (for I can ascribe it to nothing else) has strangely brought me the best gift Heaven could bestow on man in Paradise, at least it *seems*, as it were within my reach." Letters followed frequently during this period between the two, many of which are preserved, and in their faded pages we can trace and feel the now swiftly flowing current of their love. Every post from London, and there were three a week, carried a letter from Charles, and Sally kept pace with him in reply (see Plate 5). They had much to say to each other and were deeply in love. "It is late," he wrote, "but I know not how to leave off. My heart so overflows with love towards you. And what shall I say more? All my words and thoughts are, under God, devoted to your service. I bless you, and pray Him to bless you, above all that I can ask or think. To His everlasting arms I commit you this night." Later, he is fearful lest such supreme happiness should be snatched from him. "How shall I drag the load of remaining life without you?" And again, "Never have I found such a nearness to any fellow-creature as to you." He is anxious lest he should disappoint her. How will he face up to marriage? "Your confidence in me makes me tremble, lest I should prove a broken reed. For God's sake, and for your own, *do not expect too much*! I am a man of like passions—compassed about with infirmities, weak in faith, and wanting in all things. Yet I humbly hope, if God bestows you upon me, He will help me to be helpful, and make all my desires and endeavours for your good *effectual*."

And now came the final stage of the marriage settlement. On a February morning he set out with his brother and Edward Perronet for Garth, falling off his horse in Kensington, dining in Oxford with the Rector of Lincoln College and waiting on the Dean of Christ Church, "all extremely civil", and after, "wandering through the bogs", arrived at Gwynne's house. Here a new difficulty emerged. Sally met Charles in the dark before he entered the house, with the news that her brother Howell had arrived and was against the marriage. Mrs. Gwynne, however, was extremely open and affectionate. "She fought my battles against her own relations, particularly her son, who has behaved very violently towards her. Miss Becky told him, he might think it a great honour done him by my proposal." The two brothers then had a conference with Mrs. Gwynne, during which John repeated his proposal and agreed to put it into effect, with Mr. Gwynne and Vincent Perronet to act as trustees of the settlement. A consultation followed with Sally who promised to let Charles continue his vegetable diet and travelling. Howell Gwynne became more agreeable and declared he had no further objection. John and Perronet left for London and Charles remained for another week, preaching twice a day. Before leaving, Mrs. Gwynne assured him she would not change and talked freely of the marriage, but begged Charles not to go again to Ireland. Sally, however, would not hear of such a promise and said that she herself would be glad to go there with him.

The wedding took place in Llanlleonfel Church on Saturday, April 8, 1749, at eight o'clock in the morning. A last-minute difficulty was, surprisingly, caused by John. Charles, who had returned to London before the wedding, called at Bristol to meet his brother, who was to perform the ceremony, and travel on with him to Garth. But at Bristol, for some unknown reason and to Charles' astonishment, he appeared full of scruples and even refused to go to Garth at all. What was more puzzling, he now refused to sign his own agreement. Charles kept his temper and hoped for the best, though there was evidently some argument between them. He was also surprised and naturally annoyed when he learned that his brother had arranged a full week's preaching on their way to Garth. It was Charles' wedding journey, but for John it was a preaching tour. Charles' attitude was that if John persisted, then he would go on without him, but, though we are not told how, the difficulty was solved.

They set out at daybreak on an April morning, Charles with a heavy heart, in view of their dispute, which was hardly helped by the greeting he received from his friend Hodges, the Vicar of Wenvoe, at Fonmon Castle, who, inspired no doubt by Phillips, Sally's disappointed suitor, asked him: "Why, brother, what are you seeking in this thing? Happiness? Then you will be sadly disappointed", which suggests that Phillips' jealousy still rankled and had caused some feeling.

For four days they travelled, John preaching several times each day and Charles calling at Brecon for the marriage licence, for which the surrogate refused the fees from a fellow-clergyman. They arrived at Garth to find the family at breakfast, and a talk with Mrs. Gwynne appears to have ended John's misgivings. The settlement prepared by the London lawyers was read over—it is still preserved in the Methodist Archives—, a bond was signed and witnessed, and, says Charles, "we crowded as much prayer as we could into the day."

Saturday dawned, a bright spring morning. We can almost breathe its freshness, as we read his *Journal*, with the light on the river and the hawthorn in bud:

> "Sweet day! so cool, so calm, so bright,
> The bridal of the earth and sky.

Not a cloud was to be seen from morning till night. I rose at four; spent three hours and an half in prayer, or singing with my brother, with Sally, with Beck. At eight I led my SALLY to church. Her father, sisters, Lady Rudd, Grace Bowen, Betty Williams, and, I think, Billy Tucker, and Mr. James, were all the persons present." His brother joined their hands, and the register contains the plain entry: "Charles Wesley and Sarah Gwynne were lawfully married, April 8, 1749." They walked back to Garth House, and prayer and thanksgiving filled the rest of the day. A stranger observed that it was more like a funeral than a wedding. He must have caught them in a solemn moment or hankered after a more bibulous celebration or was another disappointed suitor. John entered so heartily into the proceedings that he seemed the happiest person of all.

It is strange that there is no memorial to Charles, or reference of any kind, in Llanlleonfel Church, which, like Maesmynis and Llantisffraid, has been rebuilt since his day. In Gwynne's time this small chapel of ease was a model among the churches of the district, with its well-flagged floor, white-painted seats, and the Gwynne pew lined with green baize. But when later he left the neighbourhood for a time, it fell into disrepair. He restored it in 1770, and it was rebuilt in 1873.

It stands picturesquely on an eminence across the river from Garth House, with no road but a winding field path to its door. The Rev. Francis Kilvert who visited it in 1873, before its final restoration, mentions it in his *Diary*. "Mr. Welby was holding a bazaar for the benefit of poor old Llanlleonfel Church, now in ruins, but which they hope to get restored . . . Passing by the quaint old house of Garth, formerly one of the numberless possessions of the great Gwynne family, I descended by a cart road into the meadows. The ruined church tottered lone upon a hill in desolate silence. The old tombstones stood knee-deep in the long coarse grass, and white and purple flowers nodded over the graves. The door stood open and I went in. The window frames and seats were gone. Nothing was left but the high painted deal pulpit. . . . Latin inscriptions in remembrance of Marmaduke Gwynne and his family were affixed to the East wall. The place was utterly deserted. . . . We had tea as guests of Mrs. Maitland in the old Garth House which with its partly castellated outwalls and buildings reminded us of an ancient German schloss.

In 1771, after Gwynne's death, William Gardner, who had been his butler, opened the Dol-y-Coed Hotel in nearby Llanwrtyd Wells, which was patronized by well-known people who, no doubt, he entertained with lively reminiscences of the days when the neighbourhood was the rendezvous of leading religious figures and recalled how busy he had been on the day of Charles Wesley's wedding.

It was while staying at Garth that Charles composed the hymn "Jesu, Lover of my soul". The legend is that he wrote it during a threatened storm when a bird flew in at the open window for refuge. We can still see the window, enlarged since his day, and the bedroom that he used. The broad sitting-room and the handsome oaken and curved staircase with its great window remain, and the house, although altered, is as gracious to-day as when he knew it.

Chapter Nine

CHARLES TO THE RESCUE 1749

HIS BRISTOL HOME—JOHN IN JEOPARDY—EARTHQUAKE
PANIC—THE GWYNNES IN TROUBLE—JOHN'S RASH MARRIAGE
—NORTHERN JOURNEYS—SIFTING THE PREACHERS—SMALL-
POX—TROUBLE IN NORWICH—AND IN MANCHESTER.

Thurs Morn. 4 o' Clock

What shall I say, in this solemn
Moment, to my most beloved Friend! — I
am setting out again, to seek his Face,
to know his Pleasure, & prove his
Will concerning me, & One infinitely dear-
er to me than myself. — My Heart
(I own) recoils & trembles. I wd impute
it to Bodily weakness. My too careful
Friends dissuade me from a Journey wch
they think I am not fit for. Dear
Mrs V— cried over me last Night, till
she almost broke my Heart. But I
must not now begin to favour myself. Let the Corruptible Body press
down the Soul, till it sinks itself into
the Grave: Her All is safe — all
is well — & GOD shall wipe away

6. A letter from Charles to his wife on their first parting, dated May 4, 1749.

1. Love Divine, all Loves excelling,
     Joy of Heaven, to Earth come down,
   Fix in us thy humble Dwelling,
     All thy faithful Mercies crown;
   Jesu, Thou art all Compassion,
     Pure, unbounded Love Thou art,
   Visit us with thy Salvation,
     Enter every trembling Heart.

2. Breathe, O breathe thy Loving Spirit,
     Into every troubled Breast,
   Let us all in Thee inherit,
     Let us find that second Rest:
   Take away our Power of Sinning,
     Alpha and Omega be,
   End of Faith as its Beginning,
     Set our Hearts at Liberty.

3. Come Almighty to deliver,
     Let us all thy Life receive,
   Suddenly return, and never,
     Never more thy Temples leave:
   Thee we would be always blessing,
     Serve Thee as thy Hosts above,
   Pray and praise Thee without ceasing,
     Glory in thy Perfect Love.

4. Finish then thy New Creation,
     Pure and Sinless let us be,
   Let us see thy great Salvation,
     Perfectly restord in Thee,

(94)

7. A manuscript copy of the hymn "Love Divine", written by Charles Wesley in his own hymn book. The hymn was first published in 1747.

CHAPTER NINE

CHARLES NOW entered upon his most active period. Within two weeks, leaving his wife at Garth, he returned to Bristol and London and was away nearly two months (see Plate 6). The Gwynne family in the meantime had removed to Ludlow, where he rejoined them; Sally with her mother and Betsy drove to Hereford to meet him, and they stayed overnight at The Falcon. He visited Ludlow at least eight times during the next two years, though he made little headway there with his preaching. On this occasion he was refused the pulpit of the parish church, but received Communion, and afterwards preached in the street where the boys of the town pelted him with eggs and stones, and Mr. Gwynne was obliged to send for the Bailiff to disperse them.

Sally returned with him to Bristol, where they went house-hunting, and she now began to accompany him on his journeys and was received everywhere with great respect. "All look upon my Sally with my eyes." He could hardly have found a wife more congenial to his work or more beloved by his followers. Mrs. Gwynne, anxious no doubt for her daughter's comfort and in view of Charles' constant travelling, advised against their setting up housekeeping too quickly, as we learn from a letter Charles wrote to his brother: "Here is a small convenient house, £11 a year, next Mrs. Vigor's. I have written to Garth for counsel; but my Mother [Mrs. Gwynne] is unexpectedly against our keeping house for some time, if not years. You, I think, will not hinder our living as pilgrims. Write your mind, and turn the scale."

In the same letter he refers to the Gwynne's helpful attitude. "Our fears of Mrs. Gwynne were altogether needless. She has assured her daughters, that rather than we should come into any danger of inconvenience by her son, or by any man, Mr. Gwynne should leave us ourselves executors. He made his will, to which I was witness, and even then proposed making me his executor. I declared, as you may well suppose, that he would appoint Mrs. Gwynne, which he did." Charles was obviously in high spirits and ready for work. "More zeal, more life, more power, I have not felt for some years; (I wish my mentioning it may not lessen it;) so that hitherto marriage has been no hindrance. You will hardly believe it sits so light upon me. I forgot my wife (can you think of it?) as soon as I left her." And the Bristol activities were flourishing. "Farley and the school go well. More scholars. Where will you stow them? Come and build . . . What say you to Thomas Maxfield and me taking a journey (when you return) through all the Societies, northern and western?"

The house he had selected was in Stokes Croft (No. 4 Charles Street), a district which has since deteriorated, one of two tall brick dwellings, which is still well preserved, with the original panelling in its hall and front room (see Plate 8). Here Charles proudly brought his bride and this was their home for the next twenty-two years. "I saw my house," he records, "and consecrated it by prayer and thanksgiving." The same day they received their first guests—their good friend, Mrs. Vigor, and her sisters from next door, with whom they had been staying until their home was ready. "Half-past nine. I slept comfortably in my own house." He had a home at last, and he was pleased that two of his sisters-in-law, Betsy and Peggy, were with them to share their pleasure.

They had hardly settled in, however, when news reached them, which at first they could hardly credit, that John was on the point of marrying Grace Murray. She was a youngish and attractive widow of humble origin, who had been in service and had married a sea captain, and was one of Charles' London converts. For some years she had been matron of the Orphan House in Newcastle, and so highly had John regarded her that she had become one of his inner circle. Her closeness to him can be seen from the fact that she had stayed with him and his party at Garth, had accompanied him and other preachers to Ireland, and been with them on their return when they stayed at Ludlow, where John had arranged to meet Charles to sign the final document of the marriage settlement. As nothing had been said or so much as hinted at on that occasion, which was barely a month before Charles learned the news, he was naturally astounded, and Sally was horrified.

It was a strange interlude in John Wesley's life, and the kindest explanation is that he was a sick man at the time. Grace Murray had nursed him during an illness in Newcastle,

146

and, moved by her care, his practical mind had seen in her a first-rate housekeeper, one who as a wife would entail no extra expense ("desiring nothing more than she had before"), for did he not already employ her? As a nurse, too, she would be invaluable—one who was indefatigably patient, quiet, cleanly, and helpful, "and understands my constitution better than most Physicians." What more could he wish? From his sick bed he had more narrowly observed her than ever before, sizing up her good temper, sense and behaviour. He confessed that he slid into it, he knew not how, saying: "If ever I marry, I think you will be the person." And she, though taken aback, did nothing to discourage him. It mattered little that she was already engaged, or supposed to be, to one of his preachers, John Bennet.

Charles rode post-haste to Newcastle to hear the full story and finally to track down his brother at Whitehaven. After a stormy interview he crossed the fells to a lonely farm at Hindley Hill, where he found Grace Murray awaiting John's return. By now the affair was the talk of Methodism and causing unfavourable comment. Charles burst in upon her and found her in a confused state, flattered by John's proposal, but uncertain as to the outcome and haunted by the thought of Bennet. Exhausted by his frenzied travelling, he could only exclaim breathlessly: "Grace Murray, you have broken my heart," and collapsed through sheer weariness. On recovering, he told her plainly that, having promised to marry one man, she could not properly engage herself to another, that by so doing she was endangering the whole work of God, that he had persuaded his brother against the marriage, and that the sooner she was wedded to Bennet the better.

Grace, numbed by the shock, for she venerated the Wesleys, and Charles was her spiritual father, listened in silence, and within the hour he had her riding pillion to Newcastle. Leaving her outside the town, he sought out the reluctant Bennet and persuaded him, at first against his will—for had she not virtually deserted him?—that all was now in his favour, that his brother realized his mistake, and that she wished to meet him and be forgiven. A reconciliation followed, and within a week Charles saw them safely married.

John, meanwhile, finding his brother had left Whitehaven without his knowledge, followed hard after him to Hindley Hill only to discover that he was two hours too late, and felt he had been deceived, by Grace no less than by Charles. On arrival in Leeds he was heartbroken to hear of her marriage and naturally blamed Charles, who arrived the next day, still angry with his brother and unfortunately with no regard for his wounded feelings. In the heat of the moment Charles accosted him unkindly: "I renounce all intercourse with you but what I would have with a heathen and a publican." This to John was the last straw, but Charles still believed that his brother had behaved with extreme impropriety and had caused needless trouble. George Whitefield and John Nelson did their best to calm the storm, but the Wesley blood was up. John showed remarkable patience and finally Charles exonerated him from blame; a reconciliation followed, and with Bennet's arrival—embarrassing at first—and further explanations, a happier relationship was established. But Charles was unduly optimistic when he wrote afterwards: "George Whitefield and my brother and I are at one, a threefold cord that shall no more be broken". John, whose feelings had been deeply wounded, confessed to a friend: "The whole world fought against me, but above all, my own familiar friend [Charles]. Yesterday I saw my friend (that was), and him to whom she is sacrificed. I believe you never saw such a scene." And elsewhere he spoke of the Lord having removed the desire of his eyes.

He had been outwitted, but had laid himself open to grave misunderstanding and had placed himself in a humiliating situation. Charles acted impetuously, but with good reason. The story has been unduly romanticized—there was drama, but little, if any, romance. Charles' attitude has been criticized as interfering and inconsiderate, but he could hardly have stood aside. His deep concern for the welfare of the Church, and never more than when he rode the length of England to save his brother from such a venture.[1]

We can imagine with what relief he returned to Bristol, where in the house at Stokes Croft Sally had been busy making a neat inventory of the furnishings. Domestic trials followed: Sally had a miscarriage, following a violent thunderstorm. And on his next visit to London he found his sister, the brilliant

[1] Tyerman's opinion, after sifting all the relevant material, was that Wesley was a dupe and Grace Murray a flirt, that Grace played her two suitors one against the other, and that the marriage, had it taken place, far from bringing Wesley happiness, would have impaired his influence and brought discredit on his cause.

but ill-fated Hetty, on her death bed, and was able to visit and comfort her and afterwards attend her funeral.

The Lisbon earthquake disaster, in 1750, followed by lesser outbreaks in London and a madman's prophecy of more to come, produced widespread consternation. Churches were crowded, special prayers were offered, and there was a spate of "earthquake" literature from bishops and others, including hymns and a tract by Charles, who sent a vivid account to his mother-in-law. "The late earthquake has found me work. Yesterday I saw the Westminster end of the town full of coaches and crowds flying out of the reach of divine justice, with astonishing precipitation. Their panic was caused by a poor madman's prophecy. Last night they were all to be swallowed up. The vulgar were in almost as great consternation as their betters. Most of them watched all night; multitudes in the fields and open places; several in their coaches. Many removed their goods, London looked like a sacked city . . . Many come all night, knocking at the Foundery door, and begging admittance for God's sake."

In November 1751 the Gwynne family was in trouble, and Charles and Sally were in Ludlow for over a month. Betsy had become engaged to James Waller of Islington, and for some reason the family disapproved. Waller and his sisters were already known to Charles and on this occasion travelled with him to Ludlow. Charles records that he found the household in great distress and that during his stay he was exercised by severe and unexpected trials. A week later, however, Betsy was married to Waller by Charles in Ludlow parish church, and whatever the objections, the union proved a happy one, though even Charles seems to have had misgivings. "December 4th. Mr. W.'s wedding day. How unlike my own! I rose, after a sleepless night, in the spirit of heaviness. I prayed for them and with them. Soon after eight they were married. And 'twas my ministry to deal the blow!" Gwynne's Ludlow residence was probably in Brand Lane, possibly either the present Garth House or Brand House. Three of his married children lived in Ludlow at this period. The younger Marmaduke was a churchwarden of St. Lawrence Church in 1746–7, where three of his children were baptized, one of whom died in the troubled period just referred to.

John meanwhile reacted from his grief over Grace Murray

by marrying a banker's widow, Mrs. Vazeille. It happened so suddenly and the lady was so unsuitable that Charles thought his brother must be mad in his matrimonial ventures. But this time John left no room for interference. "My brother returned from Oxford, sent for and told me, *he was resolved to marry*! I was thunderstruck . . . Trusty Ned Perronet followed, and told me the person was Mrs. Vazeille! one of whom I had never had the least suspicion. I refused his company to the chapel, and retired to mourn with my faithful Sally, I groaned all the day, and several following ones, under my own and the people's burden. I could eat no pleasant food, nor preach, nor rest, either by night or by day."

He had no personal feeling against her; on the contrary, they were on the friendliest terms. He and Sally had taken her with them on a week's visit to the Gwynnes at Ludlow, had shown her over Blenheim Palace and the Oxford Colleges on the return journey, and on reaching town had stayed as guests in her house. She was in comfortable circumstances, living in Threadneedle Street, with a country house in Wandsworth. And she had four children. She had been kind to John Wesley who, after slipping on the ice on London Bridge and injuring his leg, had been carried to her house, where he stayed until his recovery, and had rewarded his nurse by marrying her.

Charles had reason to feel aggrieved and did not hide his feelings, for his brother had broken their agreement to consult each other in the event of marriage. He was surprised at this breach of confidence and that John could lay aside a solemn arrangement so lightly, and all the more after the prolonged consultations and scrupulous care which had preceded his own marriage. "I was one of the last," he says, "that heard of his unhappy marriage."

In addition to his brother's haste and secrecy, there was Charles' concern for its effect on the Societies and on his brother's work. He longed for John to be happily married like himself, but was he a marriageable man? And was domestic life possible to one with so many travelling commitments, who was hardly ever in one place, who bore the burden of a rapidly growing Movement and who was so obviously the Father of his people? John's own temperament was against it, and Mrs. Vazeille, for all her good qualities, was no partner for a travelling evangelist. Charles by now knew only too well her disposition. On first meeting her he had described her as a woman of a sorrowful spirit, meaning spoiled and peevish, and he proved right in foreseeing trouble. But was she a virago, as is often suggested? If she nagged, she had ample provocation. She was headstrong, hot-tempered, suspicious, quick to take offence, accustomed to comfort, to receive attention and indulge every whim, and few women were less fitted for her new role. John Hampson, who knew both her and John, declared there never was a more preposterous union.

This is not the place to enter upon the unhappiness that followed. John paid a heavy price for his rashness in what proved to be the biggest blunder of his life. We are concerned only with Charles' reaction. His relation to his brother was never afterwards quite the same; close though it remained, the old easy confidence had gone. But he was sorry for him and did all within his power to smooth his matrimonial difficulties.

Nine days after the wedding Blackwell dragged him to see his new sister-in-law, whom he kissed, and to be reconciled to his brother. He took courage from reading Marcus Aurelius, resolving not to resent, not to revenge himself, not to let his peace lie at the mercy of every injurious person. And he brought his wife and sister-in-law together, and took every opportunity of showing the latter his sincere respect and love. Two months later, when she was in Bristol, he displayed to her, both in his own home and in the homes of his friends, all the civility in his power. In the following month, finding her in tears and full of complaints against her husband, he took her home to supper, listened to her troubles and sent her away comforted.

Later, however, she quarrelled with him and was so vituperative that for the sake of peace he and his wife were only too thankful to avoid her, and his letters to Sally, in which he refers to her sarcastically as his "dearest friend", reveal a frigid relationship. "I called, two minutes before preaching, on Mrs. Wesley, at the Foundery; and in all that time, had not one quarrel." And again: "I hope Mrs. Wesley keeps her distance." He was amazed at his brother's patience. But a letter Charles received from Vincent Perronet said; "I think the unhappy lady is most to be pitied, though the gentleman's case is mournful enough." John Hampson told his son he could have murdered her, after seeing her foaming with anger, holding her husband by the hair. "I felt as though I could have knocked the soul out of her." Thomas Jackson, a later biographer, considered her a bitter and unmitigated curse and suggested mental instability, but we must not overlook that in the twenty years she lived with her husband she made from time to time brave attempts to travel with him, enduring considerable discomfort, visiting the Societies, and in his long absences, helped with his business affairs.

Meanwhile the work went on. Sally accompanied her husband to the north. At Worcester he was pelted with dust and dirt, covered from head to foot, and a violent crowd, some with blackened faces, some without shirts, cried him down in the preaching house, beat and injured his followers, broke their windows and battered their houses. At Rotherham he found a growing Society. At Barley Hall, where he had been ambushed, he met with a warm Yorkshire welcome and found a Society of seventy. At Leeds there were two hundred and fifty "each of whom could challenge the world". Scotland was less encouraging, where John Nelson had been beating the air for three weeks and spending his strength in vain, preaching to thousands without a single convert; and where he was told by another preacher, "You might as well preach to the stones as to the Scots."

The main object of this journey was, at his brother's request, to investigate the character of the preachers. The conduct of James Wheatley, who had been dismissed for immorality, had given the Wesley's grave concern. Charles records: "It put my brother and me upon a resolution of strictly examining into the life and moral behaviour of every preacher in connexion with us, and the office fell on me. Sat. June 29th (1751) I set out for this purpose." In the previous year John had written to him: "I wish you could talk a little with every preacher and every exhorter that comes in your way."

The northern area had been neglected and their visits there had been delayed, London, Bristol and Ireland having occupied their time. John's plan to go north in 1750 had failed, and Charles, who set out in his place, met with an accident in Islington and had to turn back. The burden of the work was falling heavily on them both at this time and Charles was obliged to reply to a request from John Bennet for a visit from one of them: "We have but one body apiece, which can be in but one place at a time."

152

The Cork Society, which had been left leaderless, had threatened to take care of itself and become a Dissenting congregation. John, like Charles, sickened at the thought, writing to Edward Perronet: "I am weary of these sons of Zeruiah; they are too hard for me. Dear Ted, stand fast, whether I stand or fall." But even Ted Perronet and Charles incurred his displeasure, though he conceded that in general they both had "a right sense of what it is to serve as sons in the gospel". They *behaved* as he wanted them to, but would not preach *where* he desired. "Others can and will preach *where* I desire; but they do not *behave* as I want them to. I have a fine time between one and the other." John's attitude was that of a Napoleon: "I have not one preacher with me, and not six in England, whose wills are broken enough to serve me as sons in the gospel."

He paid a hurried visit to the north in the spring of 1751, which Charles now followed up in the summer of that year, when he began his purge of the preachers, and sent detailed reports to his brother, as in the following extract, in shorthand (quoted by Dr. Frank Baker): "I see every day the wisdom of not limiting myself. Here is such an open door as compels me to stay, and my chief design for coming seems likely to succeed. Mich. Fenwick is here, I keep him with me, that I may fully prove him. I shall do nothing rashly, and believe nothing without full proof." And to John's frequent letters on the matter he replied: "Ought we to admit any man for a preacher till we can trust his invariable attachment to the Church?"

There was also the question of the preachers' maintenance, which greatly exercised him, for they were as yet unorganized and without regular provision. He therefore widened the scope of his inquiry, so that it became an investigation into, (1) morality; (2) suitability; and (3) maintenance. His brother declared that the Societies must be responsible for maintaining the preachers he sent. "The least that I can say to any of these preachers is 'Give yourself wholly to the work, and you shall have food to eat and raiment to put on'. And I cannot see that any preacher is called to any people who will not thus maintain him. Almost everything depends on you and me."

Thus John was as concerned as Charles, but he also cautioned him: "As to the preachers: my counsel is not to check the young ones without strong necessity; if we lay some aside we must have a supply; and of the two I prefer grace before gifts." But Charles, with more logic, required both. "Are not both indispensably necessary? Has not the cause suffered, in Ireland especially, through the insufficiency of the preachers? Should we not first regulate, reform, and bring into discipline the preachers we have before we look for more? Should we not also watch and labour, to prevent the mischiefs which the discarded preachers may occasion?" John was afraid of losing preachers, but Charles showed plain sense. John attributed much of their weakness to bone idleness, "their not being constantly employed. *I see it plainer and plainer.* Therefore I beg you will inquire of each, 'How do you spend your time from morning till evening?' and give him his choice, 'Either follow your trade, or resolve before God to spend the same hours in reading &c. which you used to spend in working.' " In letter after letter he refers to it, agreeing with Charles in dealing severely not only with the disorderly, but also with the triflers, the effeminate and busybodies, at the same time reminding him: "We must have forty itinerant preachers, or drop some of our Societies. You cannot so well judge of this without seeing the letters I receive from all parts." But when one of the preachers pleaded that nothing in this matter should be done without the preachers' consent he exploded. The bare suggestion he found intolerable. "I have sent one more home to his trade. We may trust God to send forth more labourers; only be not unwilling to receive them, where there is reasonable proof that He has sent them."

It is evident that the brothers were extremely worried. Charles poured out his feelings in a long letter to his friend, Lady Huntingdon. "Unless a sudden remedy be found, the preachers will destroy the work of God. What has wellnigh ruined many of them is their being taken from their trades. The miner, barber, and thatcher, in becoming preachers, have lost their employment. Some affect the gentleman; some, unless stopped in time, will do the Devil far more service than ever they did God; some have fallen into grievous crimes and must therefore be put away. What will then become of them?" And supposing they can be quashed now, who can stop them when he and his brother are dead? "It does not satisfy my conscience to say, God look to that. We must look to that now ourselves, or we tempt God."

Clearly the position was getting out of hand and far tighter organization and stricter discipline were needed. This letter made three proposals. (1) That every preacher who had a trade should return to it, earning his own bread and preaching as he has opportunity. This will prove which have grace and which have not. (2) That no future preacher be ever taken from his business or once permitted to preach, till the point is met how he is to be maintained. And (3) That no one be allowed to preach till Charles and his brother have heard him, talked fully with him, and kept him with them for some days. These, Charles informs her Ladyship, are his first rude thoughts on the matter. But he makes the further point, which he tells her he cannot easily mention to his brother, that if the preachers should be no longer dependent on him (John) for maintenance, his hold over them would be weakened and his authority reduced. "It will break his power, their not depending on him for bread." This shows how Charles' mind was working and that he was beginning to distrust his brother's power. He refers to "that rashness and credulity of his, which has kept me in continual awe and bondage for many years", and says he will make this the single condition of his continuing to act in concert with his brother, namely the return of the preachers to their secular work, "because without this I can neither trust them nor him. If he refuses I will give both preachers and society to his sole management, for this ruin shall not be under my hands."

Later from Newcastle he wrote to Bennet: "A friend of ours (without God's counsel) made a preacher of a tailor. I, with God's help, shall make a tailor of him again . . . Pray earnestly for me, that the Lord may guide and direct me in my *most important* concern—to purge the Church, beginning with the labourers." Charles had called a conference in Leeds, of as many preachers as could be got together. "Bring you all you can; and give notice everywhere. I have silenced another scandalous preacher and sent a third back to his trade."

After this tour, which lasted several months, he had no sooner returned to Bristol than he was suddenly called to London, where his brother had been taken seriously ill and was not expected to live. He found him far gone in a "galloping consumption", awaiting death, having composed his own epitaph and called an emergency meeting of the preachers. Charles preached the same night at the Foundery, "confused and overwhelmed with trouble and sorrow", and went so far as to inform his congregation that his brother's hour had come and their only hope was in prayer. The Society was deeply moved, the public was stirred, many strangers slipping into the Foundery or stopping to inquire in the streets. The crisis continued over the weekend. Charles, at a loss for a subject, opened the Bible at random and preached comfort from the Book of the Revelation. No one could have been kinder at this time in his concern for his brother, or for his sister-in-law, whom he supported in every way and accompanied to Dr. Fothergill for reports on his brother's condition. He was not only alarmed by his illness, but also by the prospect of his own position in the event of his death, and of Methodism left leaderless, and he plainly told the Foundery Society that he neither could nor would stand in his brother's place, if God took him, for he had neither a body, nor a mind, nor talents, nor grace for it. He also had a long wished for opportunity of talking with John of all that had passed since his (John's) marriage, and the result was complete harmony.

On returning to the Foundery he found two letters from Lady Huntingdon telling him that his beloved Sally was ill with smallpox and her life in danger. He left at five the next morning, reaching Bristol at four p.m. "I saw her alive, but, O how changed!" Foolishly and against the advice of friends she had not been inoculated and even now blessed God that she had refused it. Charles with equal folly had told his friends that he left everyone to his own conscience and for his part he looked upon it as taking the matter out of God's hands. For three weeks she lay critically ill, nursed by Mrs. Vigor and others, including Lady Huntingdon, who, risking infection, visited her twice a day. Sally mercifully recovered, but with her face so scarred she was hardly recognizable. She had lost her beauty, but Charles declared that this made him love her more than ever for herself.

During this anxious period he was obliged to return to London to supply the pulpits there, preaching comfort to others while in daily expectation of worse news of his wife. Whitefield encouraged and sustained him, writing: "I pray and inquire, inquire and pray again . . . Night and day you are remembered". And on hearing better news: "Talk no more of having no more work to do in the Vineyard. I hope all our work is but just beginning. I am sure it is high time for me . . . Near forty years and such a dwarf! The winter comes already, and so little done."

But worse news followed. Sally was hardly out of bed when Charles heard that their child, Jacky, aged sixteen months, had caught the infection. Becky sent the first news, with a note added by Sally: "My heart yearns for him so, that I wish I could bear the distemper again, instead of him." Eight days later he died, and was buried before Charles could reach Bristol. Sally wrote pathetically: "I shall go to him; but he shall never return to me," and she enclosed a lock of his hair.

Fortunately John's illness was not fatal and after these domestic griefs we find Charles accompanying him to Norwich, travelling leisurely (for once) as John was still convalescent. It was thought that the journey might do him good, and they stayed with a friend, Captain Galatin. Serious trouble awaited them in Norwich, where James Wheatley had gathered a congregation and had built a chapel, but had fallen again into licentious ways and the city rang with his wickedness. Charles succeeded in forming a small Society, but had difficulty in disassociating himself in the public mind from the scandals of Wheatley. John spent the time quietly preparing his *Notes on the New Testament*, helped by his brother, before leaving for treatment at the Bristol Hot Wells. Charles preached in the crowded market, received Communion in the Cathedral, attended St. Peter's and St. John's, secured and repaired a derelict brewhouse for services and, against considerable opposition, re-established the good name of Methodism. There was one violent occasion when he was attacked by butchers, another when the streets were too hot for his safety. He was at a loss for a church, until the brewhouse was ready, and he was compelled at times to preach in the rain and on fair days under the window of The Bull. It was uphill work. Wheatley had poisoned the fountain. "Preaching to this people is indeed threshing the mountains." A tinker came to his help—a huge grisly man who had championed Wheatley, and now offered to fight for Charles.

A two years' gap follows at this point in the *Journal* and we next find him leaving Bristol again for the north, revisiting his former haunts. He called at Donnington Park, preached in Hunslet parish church, received the sacrament in York Minster (where the congregation was trebled by the number of

Methodists he took with him), and called on Lady Ingham at Aberford, where he was joined by William Grimshaw, the Vicar of Haworth. After ten days with him in the Leeds area, he preached in his church, which, though recently enlarged, could hardly contain the congregation and at a second service, with the church full and twice the number outside, he preached from a scaffold against the church wall.

In Manchester he took tea and also dined with Dr. Byrom, and, as everywhere, he exhorted the Methodists to remain in the Church. "I challenged them to show me one Methodist who has ever prospered by turning Dissenter. I asked, What would become of them when my brother should die; whether they would not then be scattered, and broken into twenty sects old and new?" To avoid this he advised them (1) to get grace, or the love and power of God, which alone could keep and stablish their hearts, (2) to continue in all the means of obtaining this, especially the word, and prayer of all kinds, to read the Scriptures daily; to go constantly to church and sacrament.

At this period these were his constant themes. Many of these distant Societies, Manchester in particular, in the absence of himself or his brother, were in danger of disruption, subject to adverse influences, mostly from sectarians and fanatics. But Methodism had no time for spurious sects or false enthusiasm, and he made it his business in every Society to recover the stragglers and to consolidate the membership, imploring them to keep to their Methodist practices and never to separate themselves from the Church. "Of all members of the Church of England the poor Methodists are most exposed because serious, and therefore, worth stealing; and of all the Methodists those of Manchester in the greatest danger, because the most unsettled and unadvisable . . . When we set the wolf to keep the sheep, no wonder that the sheep are scattered." His favourite text in these years was: "I will bring the third part through the fire," for he had long felt that only a third of the Methodists would remain loyal to their Methodist principles and within the Anglican fold, a third would become Dissenters, and the remainder would drift.

By now he was only too well aware of the inadequacy of some of the preachers he had recently encountered and he wrote plainly to his brother: "One thing only occurs to me now, which might prevent in great measure the mischiefs, which will probably come after our death; and that is, *greater, much greater deliberation and care in admitting Preachers*. Consider seriously, if we have not been too easy and too hasty in this matter." This, he suggested, was why so many of them had so lamentably failed, "Ought any new Preacher to be received before we know that he is grounded, not only in the doctrines we teach, but in the discipline also, and particularly in the Communion of the Church of England? Ought we not to try what he can answer a Baptist, a Quaker, a Papist, as well as a Predestinarian or Moravian? . . . Should we not now, at least, shut the stable door?"

The case could hardly have been put more sensibly or at a more opportune time, for whether in the Church or outside, Methodism could neither thrive nor survive if led by untrained and untested men. John saw only too clearly the force of Charles' argument. The latter was critical of the preachers, caustic at times, but had real affection for them and followed them constantly with his letters and prayers. He had no objection to lay preaching; he was jealous only for their honour and that of the Church. In his *Journal* he predicted: "Those of the Methodist preachers who have faith and patience, may, by and by, have all the churches in England open to them."

But still the Manchester Methodists continued unstable. When advised to go to church, they answered: "The preachers do not advise us to go, neither do they go themselves." Some spoke against it, even those they most confided in. "My brother and I must wink very hard not to see the hearts of such men." George Whitefield reinforced his arguments, warning them against apostasy and to stand by the Church, insisting on the necessity of holiness after conversion, and "he beat down the separating spirit, highly commended the prayers and services of the Church, charged our people to meet their bands and classes constantly, and never to leave the Methodists, or God would leave them. In a word: he did his utmost to strengthen our hands, and deserves the thanks of all the churches, for his abundant labour of love."

Charles wrote to Grimshaw a full account in the same strain: "I could not leave this poor shattered Society as soon as I proposed. They have not had fair play from our treacherous sons in the Gospel; but have been scattered by them as sheep upon the mountains. Nothing but grace can keep our children, after our departure, from running into a thousand sects, a thousand errors . . . Especially family and private prayer, and sacrament, will keep them steady. Let us labour, while we continue here, to ground and build them up in the Scriptures, and all the ordinances."

He also wrote "To my beloved brethren in Leeds" commending their loyalty: "I knew beforehand that the Sanballats and Tobiahs would be grieved when they heard there was a man come to seek the welfare of the Church of England. I expected they would pervert my words . . . But let not their slanders move you. Continue in the old ship . . . Let nothing hinder your going constantly to church and sacrament. Read the Scriptures daily in your families, and let there be a church in every house."

This was the foundation on which he built: the Church, the Scriptures—always the Scriptures, and personal and family piety. He never moved from the Biblical formula of continuing steadfastly in the Apostles' doctrine, in fellowship, in the breaking of bread, and the prayers. The strength of his appeal lay not in wild enthusiasm or vague sentiment, but in this firm consistency expressed in restrained but untiring zeal. John could organize and had bold and brilliant strategy; Charles quietly and solidly underpinned his work. And none could question his sincerity. In his own words: "Let all things be done in love."

Chapter Ten

LETTERS TO SALLY 1749-1771

CHAPTER TEN

AFTER AN absence of two months Charles returned to Bristol and at this point, November 4, 1756, his published *Journal* ends. He was now in his forty-ninth year. From the time he had left England for Georgia he had been travelling incessantly, following in the wake of his brother, desperately holding together the scattered Societies and vigorously consolidating the work. His health was none too good. He suffered from frequent ailments—gout, lumbago, pleurisy, dysentery, and he was increasingly concerned for his family. In consequence his more distant travelling was reduced, though not abandoned. He still lived in Bristol, though London claimed much of his time, where there were now four principal chapels, each of which shared his ministry. In 1753 he paid his last visit to Cornwall, the virtues of which he praised in a letter to Sally: "It flows with milk and honey. I scarce believe it to be Cornwall, the accommodations everywhere are so good, and the people so cleanly; not a whit inferior to them in the north." This was very different from the insults and hard beds of his previous visits.

The brothers were growing more apart, though they still held together in the work. There had been much to divide them, and Charles was increasingly suspicious and critical of his brother's designs. No longer did he look to him, as in the old days, for comfort and counsel and there was less consultation. John's wife was partly responsible, for Charles and Sally, though exercising tact and patience, were only too glad to avoid her sharp tongue. But John deplored Charles' detachment, and reproved him: "I give you a dilemma. Either act in connexion with me or never pretend to it. Rather disclaim it. And by acting in connexion with me, I mean take counsel with me once or twice a year as to the places where you will labour. I do not even know when and where you intend going," and he points out that he is a better judge of this than Lady Huntingdon, Sally or even Charles himself.

Similar letters followed which Charles must have read with mixed feelings and which could hardly have helped matters.

"Either leave off *professing* or begin *performing*." He treated him more as a lagging pupil than a colleague; yet Charles can hardly be blamed in view of his brother's dictatorial attitude. John finally pleaded with him: "O brother, *pretend* no longer to the thing that is not. You do not, will not act in concert with me." He complained that for ten years and upwards Charles had no more acted with him than George Whitefield. "I would to God you could begin to do it now; or else talk no more as if you did." But Charles, after all, was bearing the burden of the London and Bristol Societies during John's prolonged absences, making it possible for him to spend weeks, even months, on his distant journeys, including his many visits to Ireland. John hardly seems to have recognized Charles' solid pastoral contribution, without which his own work might have foundered; and Charles could hardly be expected to be always at John's call like a junior curate.

In 1755 Grace Bowen, the Gwynnes' old family nurse, lay dying in Brecon and Charles hurried from London to be with her, Sally being unable to make the long journey. At great inconvenience he went on this errand of mercy, taking Sally's place at her bedside, and wrote to his wife: "I rode hard to see her before her flight. . . . Her last human desire was to see you and me." From Brecon he went on to Garth where the Gwynnes were again residing. "Brother Howell was very civil to me at Garth; Lady Rudd not uncivil. . . . Your cloak I shall remember to bring; but what occasion can you have for pumps?" There was evidently tension in Garth House, for he adds: "Touching this family, I cannot say much. Poor Becky would be glad to escape from among them . . . You may depend upon her, when a tender, faithful nurse is needed."

During his absences Charles kept Sally well posted with news, and his letters, though unfortunately mostly undated, express the warmest affection. His love for Sally increased with the years and always he wrote to her, no matter how busy, a lively account of his activities, full of gossip, with pride in his family and concern for their welfare. It is mainly only through these letters that we can keep track of him during these years. He could never be too grateful for the love she had brought into his life, or for the kindness of her parents. "In reading over the passages of our history, you cannot think what love I feel towards every one of our family. Your mother, sister, father, cousins, nurse,

164

so behaved as to deserve my love and esteem during life. I look back with delight on every step, every circumstance, in that whole design of providential love. I rejoice with grateful joy at our blessed union, and feel my obligations to every person instrumental therein."

Never, he tells her, had he a greater appetite for labour or more life in performing. And always he considers her, "I need not tell you, this shall be just as *you* please," he says, when discussing some future arrangement. He encourages her accomplishments. "Do not neglect your shorthand; do not neglect your music; but, above all, do not neglect your prayers . . . My heart is with you. I want you every day and hour. I should be with you always, or not at all; for no one can supply your place." He tells her that after catching cold he rose at five and washed away his complaints in a bath near the Foundery which he intends to make use of every day. He is thankful she is out of London during the scorching weather and envies her in her cool hall at Ludlow. And they still maintain their prayer tryst: "Remember me at five. I am weary of my own unprofitableness, and ashamed that I have been of so little use to my dearest Sally."

He mentions his brother-in-law, with whom there was evidently coolness: "You will (for only you can) make my love acceptable to your brother and sister". And, anticipating his own homecoming: "Do not you sometimes reckon how many days before we meet again? . . . I shall bring a servant with me; Salthouse, if he can be spared; or honest Giles, if Harry will take pity on him, and lick him a little into shape. He had a wonderful deliverance the other night, when five rogues seized him crossing the fields, and were about to rob, if not murder him. He prayed them, in his simple manner, to let him alone, when one of them held up his lantern to his face, and cried, 'I believe he is a Wesley; he has a very innocent look; let him go; let him go,' which accordingly they did, and he walked quietly home. How many of Lampe's tunes can you play? I am offered an exceeding fine harpsichord for sixteen guineas. What encouragement do you give me to purchase it for you?"

Meanwhile his brother has again been taken ill and he has been called at two in the morning to his bedside. "He told me he was dying, that his feet were dead already; was perfectly sensible; told me, before his wife, how he had settled his affairs; (not enough to her advantage, I think) . . . made me witness of his reconciliation with his wife; and said he expected to die 'at four or five'." Charles prayed with him, but saw no signs of immediate death and, unable to lessen his brother's apprehensions, waited for the doctor who applied blisters.

The letters continue in the same strain of news and affection. Always Sally is "my Dearest of Creatures". "Every hour of every day you are laid upon my heart . . . I cannot doubt that our next will be our happiest meeting." He writes from York suggesting that she should join him there for the winter. "Write me your answer by the first post, and W. Shent shall fly to fetch you. I myself would come to meet you more than half-way, even to Evesham, if need be. Coals are very cheap. We keep excellent fires." And from Hatfield: "Blessed be the day on which my dearest Sally was born."

Regarding the threatened invasion, he says, "My brother tells me the French are expected every hour, by General Hawley, in battle array, etc.; that the Government have not the least doubt of the invasion, but will do their best to repel force by force." And of the Lisbon disaster: "Great things have been done for Lisbon. A ship was immediately sent off with thousands of barrels of flour; another from Falmouth, laden with herrings, pickaxes, etc.; a man of war to guard the port and ruins, etc. On the day of the earthquake, they were to have had 'an act of faith', that is, a bonfire of the poor Jews and heretics."

He now takes his travelling more leisurely and in short stages, as much to save his old mare as himself. "Moderate travelling I find good for me, having never had better health, since you knew me." He is again making his way northwards, and finds many kind inquiries after Sally, too many to name. "I look every post for a good account of my Sally. This evening I expect to find my brother at Birstal. I pity his poor wife, if now upon the road. There she is likely to stick till the warm weather comes. The roads are almost impassable for wheels . . . I am going to breakfast with Miss Norton, who is as far from the spirit of my *best friend* [his brother's wife], as east from west. What shall you and I do to love her better?" And he adds that Miss Norton flew from the house before the face of Mrs. John Wesley, who retreated to Wakefield before the Conference.

Sally had evidently been chaffing Charles about his horse. "My sure-footed mare gave me no fall, notwithstanding your malicious supposition. You would do well, instead of affronting her, to find me a better; but that I neither expect nor desire. Only I would exchange her for one or two, good chaise-horses."

He fretted because a letter had not reached him, thinking she had neglected to write, "till John was pleased to remember it lay in his pocket, since two in the afternoon." There are frequent references to his children. "Charley you *need* not chastise too severely, if he is indeed so easy to be managed; but I a little doubt a son of mine. You will find by and by he has a will of his own. Persuade him, and you need never compel him. If he will lead, 'tis pity he should drive. Yet I doubt our skill in discerning their tempers so soon." And later: "One, and another, and another, give me presents for Charley; but nobody takes any notice of poor Sally [his daughter]. Even her godmother seems to slight her." He looks forward to meeting his wife and her father shortly at the Hundred House near Ludlow, and, weather permitting, as many of the family who can come. In letter after letter he counts the days to their next meeting, and always he is torn between his duties in London and his family in Bristol. "One letter in a week does not half satisfy me, under your absence. I count the days since we parted and those still between us and our next meeting." He keeps her informed of his work. "Our churches are crowded as at the beginning." The French Chapel in Spitalfields was thronged with poor weavers; "I met near two thousand of the Society at the Foundery . . . I picked up a stray sheep, and delivered him into the hands of his old Leader." Breakfasting at Colonel Gumley's, he was offered the living of Drayton in Oxfordshire, the drunken incumbent being near death. "I neither refused nor accepted it; for I had not consulted you." Then he turns again to family matters. "Not a word of your music! That is a bad sign; a sign of idleness, I fear. When you would have me look out after a harpsichord for you, you will tell me so."

He is concerned about family prayers in his home during his absence. "How does your *Rector* perform? If he will not be your Chaplain at night, I must desire and insist on you, Beck, and Suky's praying together, both morning and evening." And still he journeys: "I crept on, singing or making hymns, till I got unawares to Canterbury." He has seen the King, who looks quite hearty. He includes a note for a friend about it being a bad year for hops. Always he is persuaded that Sally will out-live him [which she did], and more than once refers to it. Elec-trifying, he believes is good, but doubts if it would cure old age.

Another time, Becky is with him singing to her guitar, and, "I should tell you, my brother preached, and won all our hearts. I never liked him better, and was never more united to him, since his unhappy marriage."

In 1758 he visited his niece (Samuel's daughter), who was married to Mr. Earle, a chemist, in Barnstaple. Charles had taken cold on the way—he was now more susceptible to rough weather—and was glad to use a flannel plaster which Sally had luckily packed in his bag. He found his niece in bed, having three days earlier had a still-born child. He had not seen her for seventeen years, just after his brother's death, when she was twelve years old. "I knew her by him. She perfectly remem-bered me, and was overjoyed at the sight of me. . . . She has borne eight children, all dead but one girl." He spent some time in the neighbourhood, enjoying her company and finding her inquisitive after her aunt (Charles' wife) and small cousin, and appreciative of Sally's invitation to visit them. "Next summer, if we live so long, I have half promised to *fetch* her to you. This country is worse than Wales for posts." He found this family visit so enjoyable that he could hardly tear himself away. "I am got into a conjurer's circle, or enchanted castle, and can find no way out. The stronger my niece grows, the more conversible, and harder to be left." Part of the time he spent in copying her father's poems, and Barnstaple people he found agreeable.

A controversy now came to a head over the administration of Communion, and its regular provision for the rapidly in-creasing Methodist membership, and this provoked the further question of the status of the preachers. Hitherto administration had been confined to the clergy associated with Wesley and, in general, the Methodists went regularly to their parish churches, but there was growing dissatisfaction. They naturally objected to receiving it at the hands of indifferent, antagonistic, some-times even tipsy clergymen; in some cases (as of Charles him-self) they were refused it. There was increasing resentment that they could not receive it in their own chapels and from their own preachers, and the latter, conscious of their anomalous position, were becoming restive, pressing their claims and in some cases administering irregularly. From every angle the situation was becoming intolerable, and, short of episcopal recognition, the Wesleys were compelled to make their own arrangements. They had no wish to weaken, much less to break, their ties with the mother Church, and, indeed, were careful to the end of their days to preserve every possible link and, proud of their orders, to remain Anglican priests. But for not much longer could they tolerate a situation in which many of their members rarely, if ever, received Communion, and which became even more aggravated later in America, where, with the withdrawal of Anglican clergy during the War of Independence, not only the Methodists but the population in general were left without adequate pastoral provision. Those who blame Wesley must face the problem which confronted him. What alternative remained? He had more adherents than any man in England, led by a devoted apostolate, but no effort was made to enable him to regulate and adjust his organization within the economy of the English Church. The remarkable thing is the sacramental devotion of these early Methodists. The London and Bristol Societies, served by regular clergy, were hardly affected, but elsewhere the situation was acute.

Charles was greatly concerned and wrote at length (in 1754) to a friend, Walter Sellon, Vicar of Smisby, formerly one of the preachers and a master at Kingswood School, begging him to write at once and discourage his brother from hasty or injudicious action, and imploring him to attend the next Conference where the matter would be fully discussed. He was wrong, however, in suspecting that his brother had already taken steps to separate from the Church, and wrote a further letter to Sellon: "Write again, and spare not. My brother took no notice to me of your letter. Since the Melchizedekians[1] have been taken in, I have been excluded his cabinet council. They know me too well to trust him with me. He is come so far as to believe separation quite lawful, only not yet expedient. They are indefatigable in urging him to go so far that he may not be able to retreat. He may lay on hands, say they, without separating. I charge you to keep it to yourself that I stand in doubt of him, which I tell you . . . that you may write to him the more plainly."

[1] Charles' nickname for the unordained preachers.

Clearly Charles was hoping and working for episcopal recognition of the accredited preachers. "In May our Conference is. You must be there, if alive. We can hold it no longer, (the Methodist preachers, I mean) but must quickly divide to the right or left, the Church or Meeting. I know none fitter for training up our young men than yourself, or John Jones. We must, among us, get the sound preachers qualified for orders." Two months later he wrote again, his earlier letters having had some effect. "I shall at the Conference speak and spare not. . . . He [John] has spoken as strongly of late in behalf of the Church of England as I could wish; and everywhere declares he never intends to leave her."

At the Leeds Conference in 1755, attended by sixty-three preachers, it was resolved, after statements by both the Wesleys, that whether lawful or not, separation from the Church was inexpedient; and those preachers who had begun to administer Communion agreed in future to desist. John Wesley was satisfied and waited on events; Charles, however, felt that many were still unconvinced, and he left the next day for London without warning his brother. He told Sally that he would plead in every Society that they continue steadfastly in the Church of England, adding, "But my heart is more closely united to the true Methodists than ever," and a family note: "Beck must recover her music; most positively, or not look me in the face. It lies upon you to drag her to the harpsichord, and tie her down in her chair."

He then published an open letter in verse, in the manner of the day, addressed to his brother, appealing for loyalty to the Church:

My first and last unalienable Friend,
A Brother's Thoughts with due regard attend . . .

I tell Thee, wise and faithful as Thou art,
The Fears and Sorrows of a burthen'd Heart,
The Workings of (a blind or heav'nly) Zeal,
And all my *Fondness for the Church* I tell
The Church whose Cause I serve, whose Faith approve,
Whose Altars reverence, and whose Name I love.

He will not defend her blemishes,

Or force my Brethren in her Forms to join,
As every Jot and Tittle were divine . . .
Let Others for the Shape and Colour fight
Of Garments short or long, or black or white;
Or fairly match'd, in furious Battle join
For and against the Sponsors and the Sign;
Copes, Hoods, and Surplices *the Church* miscall,
And fiercely run their Heads against the Wall;
Far different Care is mine; o'er Earth to see
Diffus'd her true essential Piety . . .
Wash'd by the Spirit and the Word from Sin,
Fair without Spot, and glorious all within,

and concludes with a direct appeal:

Wilt Thou with me in the Old Church remain,
And share her Weal or Woe, her Loss or Gain? . . .

When first sent forth to minister the Word,
Say, did we preach ourselves, or Christ the Lord?
Was it our Aim Disciples to collect,
To raise a Party, or to found a Sect?

John Wesley could hardly have liked it, though there was little in it to which he could reasonably object, but Charles' reference at one point to "a Pope—a Count—and Leader of a Sect" must have stung him, the Count being Zinzendorf, and the Pope presumably John himself. This *Epistle* was read to crowded congregations, not, we may suppose, without creating excitement, and was dispatched by carrier throughout the country.

Charles also expressed his opinions to the Reverend Samuel Walker of Truro: "My brother ought, in my judgment, to declare in the strongest and most explicit manner, his resolution to live and die in the communion of the Church of England. 1. To take all proper pains to instruct and ground his preachers and his flock in the same—a treatise is much wanting on this subject, which he might write and spread through all his societies. 2. To wait with me on the archbishop, who has desired to see him, and tell him our whole design. 3. To advise, as far as they think proper, with such of our brethren, the clergy as know the truth and do nothing without their approbation." He allowed that lay preaching, of which he fully approved, was a partial separation, but need not be a total one, and that he remained in Methodism, not so much to do as to prevent evil. "I stand in the way of my brother's violent counsellors, the object both of their fear and hate. . . . The restless pains of bad men to thrust me out from the Methodists seems a plain argument for my continuing with them."

At the Bristol conference in 1756 which Charles attended, though he had vowed he would never attend another, there was again no dissenting voice, and John undertook to write a treatise to confirm the Methodists in the Church. Charles, in a shorthand note, declared that for the rest of his life he would follow the preachers with buckets of water to quench the flame of strife and division which they had kindled or might kindle. John's treatise duly appeared (in 1758) *Reasons against a Separation from the Church of England,* to which Charles added a footnote: "I think myself bound in duty to add my testimony to my brother's. His twelve reasons against our ever separating from the Church of England are mine also. I subscribe to them with all my heart. . . . My affection for the Church is as strong as ever: and I clearly see my calling, which is to live and die in her communion. This, therefore, I am determined to do, the Lord being my helper." Thus both the Wesleys at this stage, and John no less than Charles, were doing their utmost not to withdraw from the Church.

The threat of invasion recurred in 1759. "All expect the French," he writes to Sally. "Admiral Rodney is gone to burn their broad-bottomed boats, or die in the attempt. . . . Each carries three hundred men, and is contrived as to land their men on horse-back. In five hours they may reach the Sussex coast." A day of National Prayer had been proclaimed and Charles was kept busy with prayer meetings in Lady Huntingdon's drawing room and crowded services elsewhere. And in preaching he was so full of matter he scarce knew what he said. "We have good times here, that is certain, and the better for the nearness of the French." But he cannot guess what he will do if the enemy land. There were wild rumours. The latest dispatch had thrown the Government into the utmost alarm. "It is supposed that news is come of the embarkation of the French. At present the wind is against them. But the matter will not be determined by numbers. We shall keep them off by prayer as long as we can." Further news to Sally is of the destruction of the French boats, of the arrival of the first prisoners, of a second embarkation, and of panic in Canterbury through a false alarm.

Next came the sensational trial (in 1760) of Earl Ferrars—a cousin of Lady Huntingdon and a brother of the Reverend Walter Shirley, for the murder of his steward. The accused man had been removed from Leicester jail to the Tower and was tried before his fellow peers in the House of Lords. Charles remained in almost hourly touch with the stricken Huntingdon family and visited the prisoner. He attended the trial with George Whitefield and his wife, and wrote a vivid description to Sally. At eleven-thirty the peers entered in state led by the barons and including most of the Royal family, the Bishops, the peeresses and chief gentry of the kingdom, and the foreign ambassadors—a glittering though grim assembly. Ferrars was brought in by the Deputy-Governor of the Tower preceded by the axe. The proceedings ended on the first day at 7 p.m., and Charles, weary but thankful to have kept off the gout, was glad to be in bed soon after eight. He was in court again by six o'clock the following morning when further witnesses were called, including the prisoner's brothers. At five o'clock sentence was deferred until the following day. Charles had been sitting in court for nearly twelve hours.

Ferrars was sentenced to be hanged and his body delivered to the Surgeons' Hall for anatomy. He spent his last night playing piquet with his warders, and rode to Tyburn in his own six-horse landau wearing his wedding clothes and chewing pigtail tobacco. His mistress threw a letter into his carriage, and a mourning coach and his hearse, also drawn by six horses, followed him in procession through the crowded streets from the Tower to Tyburn. Walter Shirley wrote afterwards to John Wesley thanking him for the kindness shown to him and his family in their distress by the Methodists and heartily welcoming him to his church whenever he cared to make use of it.

Charles' letters also give Sally more personal news. He has just buried his brother-in-law, Ellison. The crowds continue at the Foundery. He is frequently at Lady Huntingdon's and Lady Piers, with the Gumleys and the Galatins, at Blackwell's in Lewisham, at Sir Charles and Lady Hotham's, with Lord and Lady Dartmouth, and at the house of Sally's cousin, Lloyd. With some of these Sally was a frequent guest and they, no less than he, were concerned at her lonely life in Bristol. His growing ambition was to have a home in London. "I dined at Lady Piers, who laments her not having an house to accommodate you. . . . But you would rather sit still in Charles Street, I believe, than come to the best house in London." Sally is evidently happier at home with her children. If she comes she must bring young Charles and she will find everywhere a double welcome. But "you would not visit London to sit still in the house all the time, and not visit your friends. Were this the case, you might as well be at Bristol for them. I should be very uneasy at your coming, if you came with mistrust and reluctance."

Mr. Judd invites Charles and his wife to be his guests in Hoxton—"a pretty, quiet country house, in a garden," but Charles does not recommend it: there are too many disturbances: a dog that barks most of the night and scuttling rats. A glass of wine, he tells her, helps him in his indispositions and he always carries his own madeira with him on his journeys. Dr. Fothergill has ordered him to sleep out of town as much as possible and to drink the waters at Bath. Lady Huntingdon, like himself, has been medically advised to return to Bath. "She must go to Bath soon or to paradise." But what of Sally herself? "You say nothing of your own health, and I fill whole letters with mine."

He tells her to look out for a good servant. He worries because she is in a low state and that his own health is not good. After having blamed Mr. Venn for a long sermon, he confesses ruefully that he himself had been guilty of preaching for an hour and a half! He urges her to send his son Charles out on horseback every day, and his daughter also, as soon as she is old enough. And she must look to Charles' practising. He will bring him fresh music when he comes and a present for Sally. But he foolishly cautions her not to let Charles make acquaintance with other boys, to avoid his being corrupted—strange advice in view of his own schooldays, and which reacted unfavourably in his son's development. He refers to John, whose energy at sixty-three amazes him: "He is an astonishing youth." He and his wife will be calling on Sally on their way to Cornwall. "She continues quite placid and tame. You can be courteous without trusting her."

In these letters are references to shortage of money. Family illnesses and frequent journeys between Bristol and London put him to considerable expense. He was generous to his family. He did not send his sons to Kingswood, but provided private tuition in addition to riding and music, and musical instruments were costly. There was a servant for Sally, who had been accustomed to an affluent home. There was no extravagance; on the contrary there was thrift and economy, at times even stringency. Quite early Charles had written: "Money we must get by some lawful means, or debt will stare me in the face."

Both brothers lived under financial strain, but were scrupulous in never taking money for their services, apart from bare expenses and their modest preacher's allowances. Charles, with the upkeep of a family, felt the strain most, despite the annuity settled on his wife from the sale of his hymns. As far back as 1751 he had voiced his concern to his brother, who replied tartly: "There is another tender point which I would just touch on. The quarterly contribution of classes (something more than two hundred a year) is to keep the preachers and to defray all the expenses of the house [the Foundery]. But for this it did never yet suffice. For you, therefore (who have an hundred and fifty pounds a year to maintain only two persons), to take any part of this seems to me utterly unreasonable. I *could not* do it, if it were my own case. I should account it robbery. I have often wondered how either your conscience or your sense of honour could bear it; especially as you know I am almost continually distressed for money, and am expected to make up the deficiencies of this as well as all the other funds. I am willing (if our judgments differ) to refer this, or anything else, to Mr. Perronet or Mr. Blackwell. I desire only to spend and be spent in the work which God has given me to do." This was all very well for John, who was a born ascetic, and who, in any case, had a wealthy wife, but cold comfort for Charles with his more normal family needs. And we must remember that he also agitated for better provision for the preachers. He knew far more than John the cost and cares of domestic life.

Later he wrote to Sally: "Our first thing temporal, is to get out of debt, which is impracticable if we kept house the approaching winter." In 1755 he asks: "Have you paid our landlord?" And in 1759: "How does your money hold out? As for me, I spend none, and have none to spend." A generous fee of ten guineas for officiating at the wedding of his friend, George Stonehouse, came at an opportune time. And in another letter

(1754), we find him promising Sally a fresh supply of money before her own runs out. In the meantime he has been forced to bespeak a coat; and is in need of a hat and shoes, but his creditors must wait for their money.

Following Whitefield's death in 1770, relations with the Calvinists, which during his lifetime he had helped to pacify, again became strained. Since 1743 there had been an agreement to avoid open controversy. At the Conference of 1770, however, John Wesley, in protest against antinomianism, reasserted in strong terms, for the benefit of his members, the doctrine of Justification. This provoked a violent attack from Lady Huntingdon who wrote to Charles in scathing terms about his brother: "As you have no part in this matter, I find it difficult to blame your brother to you, while, as an honest man, I must pity and not less regard you, as you must suffer equal disgrace and universal distrust from the supposed union with him." Charles treated this with contempt, simply endorsing it: "Lady Huntingdon's last. UNANSWERED BY JOHN WESLEY'S BROTHER."

He was now finding that his ministry was more effective in London than in Bristol and is thinking of removal. Along with Beck he is looking for a suitable house and inspects one in Hornsey and another in Newington. "If Beck and I are of the same judgment, we shall take it. My brother himself is quite pleased with our having an house near London." But things are not going too well with Sally, who, ill herself, is coping with family measles and whooping cough, and news follows that her seven months old baby, John James, is seriously ill. Charles tried to catch the next Bristol coach, but failed to get a seat on it and, when next he heard, she had buried yet another of her babes without him. They had eight children, only three of whom survived: Charles (1757), Sally (1759), and Samuel (1766). Jacky (1752) died at the age of sixteen months; Martha Maria (1755), when a month old; Susanna (1761) aged eleven months; Selina (1764), aged five weeks; and John James (1768), aged seven months. The baptismal entry of their first child, in the register of St. James's Church, Bristol, reads: "John Wesley, of Charles & of Sarah a Precher in the Horsfaier."

Charles, saddened by this latest bereavement, was never busier, and never better than when he was busy. At the time he was moving on the crest of a wave. The thought of Sally

8. 4 Charles Street, Bristol, where the Wesleys lived for 22 years.

9*a*. In John Wesley's house in City Road many personal possessions of the Wesleys are preserved including (*left*) Charles Wesley's bureau of veneered walnut dating from about 1710.

9*b*. A chair that once belonged to Charles is now preserved at the New Room in Bristol. Richmond College also possesses a large collection of manuscript hymns, annotated books from Charles Wesley's library and family items.

haunts him, but God's work must go on. Perhaps he under-estimated her trials. "Your critical illness perplexes me greatly. I should never have come hither, had I not depended upon you to follow me. I cannot think of staying here without you. . . . Yet God prospers my labours as at the beginning of my course. Perhaps it is a blaze before death."

He turns to other news. Their friend, Lady Hotham, has died. A preacher has been premature in giving up his business—"a proud, idle, mischievous fool. . . . My brother has wrote, through me, to forbid him. If therefore he does not return to his shop immediately, I will turn him out of the society." Strong words, these, from Charles!

His liveliness in these letters never fails and the depression of his earlier years is moderated. "Encourage Charles in writing, riding, and music. As to the last, he needs no spur, but attention only." He himself is in better health. Beck is in London and keeps a watchful eye on him. He is going to print his *Hymns for Children*. Sally's friends, by the hundred, inquire after her. He has slept at the chapel-house, where an old woman's cough obliged him to keep a watchnight against his will. At Brentford he was more unfortunate—in a bed full of fleas. "I lodged at a sister's, who made over her bed and *companions* to me. They put me in mind of Cornwall. . . . The lops [fleas] forbad my sleeping."

Does Sally have good nights? Do the children disturb her? She must learn to sleep with a deaf ear. Could she bring young Charles to London? If so Mr. Rich will take him to all the oratorios. Charles has a surprise present for his daughter and is arranging for an acquaintance to bring Sally some tea. His friends are wanting to purchase him a house, by subscription, but whether in London or Bristol is undecided. Six years earlier he had told Sally that he was too old for flitting, but now he is eager. It was ten years since he wrote to her: "As I shall pro-bably take much more public care upon me than I have ever done heretofore, my office will require me to spend more time in town, *perhaps to settle here*." And now at last the time had come. "My business here is to get you an house", though he appears to object to securing it by subscription. He hopes to be home within three weeks and looks forward to seeing Sammy's first teeth and listening to Charles' music. "What shall I bring you from London within my power?"

The house problem was finally solved, in 1771, by the generous offer by Mrs. Gumley of the lease of her London house, and Charles wrote off to Sally for her decision. "M. Gumley has left this house quite complete. I want nothing but money to *keep* it." He was fortunate, for the house, Number 1, Great Chesterfield Street, in Marylebone—then a country suburb, was fully furnished, even with a well-stocked cellar, and his only liability was its maintenance and ground rent. Young Charles, aged thirteen, was already in London with his father who was now actively furthering his musical education. Charles was also busy preparing the house, having it aired and cleaned. The person who has been caretaking will make a good servant. "We shall keep her to keep up the fires, to keep the windows open, and to lie in the beds. When you come you will do as you like." As to the removal, he is concerned for the harpsichord and the care of the cat. Sally and the furniture in due course arrived, and for the rest of his life Great Chesterfield Street was his home.

Chapter Eleven

THE SETTLED YEARS 1771–1788

CHAPTER ELEVEN

C HARLES NOW entered upon the happiest period of his
family life. The long journeys were over, though he still
visited Bristol. He was able to pursue his work more
leisurely and on most days rode on his little mare to his duties
at West Street or the Foundery, composing poetry as he went,
on more than one occasion calling for pen and paper on arrival
before the muse escaped him.

The commodious four-storied Georgian house was well
suited to his needs. Its site to-day is marked by a tablet on The
King's Head on the corner of Wheatley Street, opposite the
National Heart Hospital, and Great Chesterfield Street is now
Wesley Street. In those days Marylebone was a village with field
paths and country lanes, with a turnstile where Portland Street
Station now stands. There were tea gardens and skittle alleys.
The M.C.C.'s cricket ground was opened there in 1787. In its
former parish church (demolished in 1949) Charles' parents had
been married. The graveyard, which shows its foundations, is
now a garden of rest and holds the grave of Charles and Sally
with an obelisk to their memory.

Charles welcomed the country air of the neighbourhood and
its detached, though not inconvenient, situation. But his
brother regarded it with mixed feelings. It was too far out for
his liking, and how Charles could spare the time to travel three
miles every day to his work passed his comprehension. "Com-
monly when I am in London, I am so taken up that I cannot
often spare time to go three miles backward and forward." He
would have preferred his brother to be more under his eye.
That was the mistake, he declared, "the getting you an house
so far from me as well as far from both the chapels."

But Charles by no means settled down to a life of ease. He
renewed his visits to Newgate, and prepared his last publication, *Prayers for Condemned Malefactors* (1778). In this same year
he was greatly troubled by the tragedy of Dr. Dodd who had
been convicted, and was later hanged, for forgery, in attempting
to obtain the lucrative living of St. George's, Hanover Square.
His trial was as sensational as that of Lord Ferrars. Thirty

years earlier Dodd had opposed the Methodists, but Charles, forgetting past injuries, gave him comfort in prison and wrote a hymn pleading for clemency.

In 1775 Charles had had a fresh scare when his brother was taken seriously ill in Ireland. Public sympathy was excited, and as the Societies were still in an unsettled state, with no clear arrangement for their future in the event of his death, there was widespread apprehension. Charles was in Bristol at the time, when at one point the press actually reported his brother's death. Fletcher wrote to him at once, urging prompt action. "The Methodists will not expect from you your brother's labours; but they have, I think, a right to expect that you will preside over them while God spares you in the land of the living. A committee of the ablest and steadiest preachers may help you to bear the burden, and to keep up a proper discipline, both among the people and the rest of the preachers; and if at any time you should want my mite of assistance, I hope I shall throw it into the treasury. . . . God and the prayers of the people will give you strength." No wonder Charles was scared! Fletcher himself, of delicate health, had already declined the succession, and Charles had always made it clear that he had neither ability nor strength to replace his brother. Fletcher acknowledged that John had been wonderfully preserved and that the labours he had undergone would have killed both him and Charles ten times over. But in the event of John's removal, Charles must fill the gap, according to his strength. Fortunately John recovered, to Charles' relief, and in the end outlived them both.

Even this crisis did not hurry John to determine the future, though it provoked his constant anxiety. He still halted on the horns of a dilemma, refused to act precipitately, and as late as 1786 could write: "Indeed I love the Church as sincerely as ever I did; and I tell my Societies everywhere, 'The Methodists will not leave the Church, at least while I live'." Two years earlier, however, he had executed his Deed of Declaration, giving the Conference a legal constitution, nominating a group of preachers, known as the Legal Hundred, to act after the death of himself and his brother. Not until they had both passed on would he relinquish or delegate control, thus shelving the final (and crucial) decision and leaving the outcome to posterity.

Following the opening of City Road Chapel in 1778, Charles ministered there regularly with the aid of four ordained clergy, and Matins were read every Sunday. Both the brothers were careful to preserve liturgical forms during Church hours, and it was largely because of their concentration in London and Bristol that the Anglican tradition lingered longer among the Methodists of both cities than elsewhere, and that City Road is among those chapels where it survives.

In the same year Charles visited Bristol and there are more letters to his wife. "My dear Sally is, I suppose, by this time looking for my return; and I have nothing against it, although many press me to continue longer here. This people think they cannot do enough for me. Yesterday my barber put a new wig on my head, ordered by I know not who. My brother wishes to take me to London with him in October, through Portsmouth, Sarum, Winchester, etc.; but I cannot keep pace with him, and have therefore refused his kindness." John was now using a coach and had offered his brother a lift.

In the following year he travelled with his brother and Dr. Coke to Devizes, scene of unhappy memories, and again was in Bristol. "On Wednesday my youthful brother sets out for Cornwall. He seems as active and zealous as ever. Lizzy Ellison [a niece] he is sending to keep school in Yorkshire. N. Lambert [another relative], I doubt not will be soon provided for. She is a serious, solid, deserving girl. How unlike her cousin?" And he asks Sally to write to a friend to find employment for the latter, also to arrange for his "little horse" to be brought to Great Chesterfield Street. He tells her that his journey from Newbury by chaise cost twelve shillings, his fellow passengers paying the rest. He hopes that one of the family will write to him by every post, and that they are keeping up a good routine at home. "Assure me Sam rides every day, Charles rises at six, Sally at seven, her mother before eight; and that my scholars go on with their Latin, at least do not stand still."

Later, his tone has changed. "I creep along the streets, tottering on the grave. My strength seems to abate daily; perhaps through my long walks", and he quotes the poet: "tired in the field of life" and soon to be "safe in the grave, and free among the dead". He has had a narrow escape through being nearly crushed to death by a waggon against a wall, and blames the waggoner. "Had I beat him down, he knew he deserved it; for he plainly designed to run over me." He reproaches Sally for not having written. "I did suppose you had not time to answer my last packet. Your only way is to begin in time, and send me, without scruple, as many single letters as you please." And in reply to some suggestion of hers: "You do not consider that my brother's motions direct mine." There is also an unexplained reference to a case of law. "You forget that I did not expect an end of your Chancery suit till the days of your children's children."

During the riots associated with Lord George Gordon in 1780, the house of his old school friend, Lord Mansfield, in Bloomsbury Square, was destroyed, and he broke into indignant verse. While the mob, out of hand, roamed the streets committing outrages, he gathered the preachers for prayer at City Road, where the chapel itself seemed threatened. Perhaps he feared for his own house, for he prefaced one of his hymns: "Upon Notice sent One that his House was Marked." Altogether it was an anxious period, of war and misery, stagnant trade and intolerable taxation. But he pursued his quiet way, growing older, but growing older graciously, feeling increasingly the weight of the years, and mourning one by one his friends as they passed on.

Blackwell, the banker, staunch supporter and well-loved counsellor, died in 1782, followed three years later by the Vicar of Shoreham, old Mr. Perronet, in his ninetieth year, known as the Archbishop of the Methodists, who had given two sons as preachers and a daughter to be a preacher's wife. And within three months the saintly Fletcher of Madeley had gone. The ship's company was breaking up. Few now remained of those eager Oxford pioneers who, like the followers of St. Francis advancing on Rome and those of St. Bernard marching in the dawn to Cîteaux, ventured all for love of Christ. Charles had rich memories as his mind travelled back through the years. And as the ranks thinned he saluted with an elegy each departed comrade.

But there were new friends and the recovery of old friendships, and there were new interests. Once a week Lord Mornington, father of the Duke of Wellington, came to breakfast and to practise with Charles' sons, carrying his violin under his arm. It was his father, who (as Richard Colley) had accepted

184

the heirship to the Irish estate which Charles had declined. He
equipped the younger boy, Samuel, with a court suit of scarlet,
and wrote to Charles in reply to "my dear and worthy friend's
kind letter": "I entirely agree with you, that there was something very singular and uncommon in the manner by which we
were made acquainted with each other; and the more I consider it, the more I am persuaded that there was the inter-
position of a superior power to that of man in it. I can say with
truth that I esteem the commencement of your acquaintance
as one of the happiest moments of my life." He then referred
to Charles' sons. "Though you have been called out of your
retirement back into a world you wished to keep clear of, yet
you have the satisfaction of finding that the world is obliged to
come to you, and not you go to them. I hope I need not take
any pains to assure you how much I am interested in their
success in life, and how truly happy I shall be to render my
young friends those services they so justly merit. I look upon
myself, in the contracted state I am in, as doing a kind of
penance." It was a gracious acknowledgement of the man who
by standing aside had made possible his father's adoption.
Three years later the boys lost by death this generous patron.

Among old associates was the aged General Oglethorpe,
still hale and hearty, and new acquaintances included Johnson,
Garrick, Burney and Wilberforce. The latter, a rising young
statesman, first met Charles at the house of Hannah More, and
afterwards recorded: "When I came into the room Charles
Wesley arose from the table, around which a numerous party
sat at tea, and coming towards me, gave me solemnly his
blessing. I was scarcely ever more affected. Such was the effect
of his manner and appearance that it altogether overset me,
and I burst into tears, unable to restrain myself." In his
biography is a reference to "that great and good man, Mr.
Charles Wesley. I many years ago prevailed on two friends to
join in allowing his widow an annuity, which she still receives. I
often, I own, thought it a great reflection on the Methodists,
that they suffered such a person to be in real want, as she was
when I undertook her cause." It was an annuity of sixty pounds
which began in 1792 and continued for thirty years. But it was
not entirely true that she had been neglected. Her marriage
annuity of £100 plus her husband's modest salary were continued after his death, but when John Wesley died and the

future of Methodism seemed uncertain, she asked for the principal, relinquished further claims, and her capital became exhausted. She survived her husband, it must be remembered, by thirty-four years.

It was through his sister, Mrs. Hall, that Charles became friendly with Dr. Johnson, who came to hear his sons playing and dozed through the performance. "I understand, sir," he had said, "your boys are skilled in music. Pray let me hear them." And when they had done he thanked them: "Young gentlemen, I am much obliged to you," and departed.

He preferred Charles to his brother—John had no time to sit and talk—and he took a liking to young Sally who often visited him with her aunt. Two letters of invitation survive, one to Charles: "Sir,—I beg that you, and Mrs. Wesley and Miss Wesley, will dine with your brother and Mrs. Hall, at my house in Bolt Court, Fleet Street, tomorrow. That I have not sent sooner, if you knew the disordered state of my health, you would easily forgive me. I am, sir, your most humble servant, Sam. Johnson." The other is addressed to twenty-four year old Sally. "Madam,—I will have the first day that you mention, my dear, on Saturday next; and, if you can, bring your aunt with you, to Your most humble servant, Sam. Johnson."

Sally was short of stature like her parents and brothers, a bright and well-informed girl, who moved in literary circles and was devoted to her father. Once he was impatient with her during a Latin lesson, saying, "Sarah, you are as stupid as an ass." She looked up at him meekly, then burst into tears, and he added quickly, "And as patient." She exercised a strong influence over her brother Charles, with whom she lived, each unmarried, to the end of her days (see Plate 11*a*).

The father has left a full account of his two sons, both musical prodigies, who achieved an all too brief notoriety (see Plate 11*b*). He had no thought of training them as musicians and when it became inevitable had no idea how he could meet the cost; but young Charles' playing attracted attention and generous offers of help were forthcoming. Kelway, organist of St. Martin-in-the-Fields, and a foremost exponent of Handel, was so impressed that he taught him for two years without charge. Charles was delighted. "Such a master for my son was the height of my ambition." Mr. Worgan, no less celebrated, also offered him lessons without fee. Dr. Boyce, composer of *Cathedral Music*, and Dr. Arnold were equally helpful.

Kelway was exuberant over his pupil. "Was you my own son," he told him, "I could not love you better. . . . You have a divine gift," and declared that he had the very spirit of Handel. "The King would eat up this boy . . . I must carry him some morning to St. James's. I have no trouble in teaching him. It is pure pleasure." He played, he said, like Handel himself. And he advised him, "My dear, let not the world debauch you." To his father he said: "You must have great delight in this boy. I am sure he is of a sweet disposition. His very soul is in harmony." To which Charles replied: "All I can say is, that you have him uncorrupted." "Uncorrupted," answered Kelway. "He is purity itself, he is a miracle."

Samuel was hardly less gifted than his brother, composing music even before he could write, second only to him at the organ, before his feet could barely reach the pedals, and gained equal attention. Boyce declared: "He is come among us, dropped down from heaven," and Dr. Burney was as warm in his praise. With the utmost ease the child could play, compose and improvise. He was only eleven years old when his *Eight Lessons for the Harpsichord* was published and an engraving of his portrait was in circulation. An account of both the boys by the Honourable Daines Barrington appeared in *The Philosophical Transactions of the year 1781*. Meanwhile Charles paid forty-five guineas for a fine harpsichord for his younger son and Uncle John presented him with Boyce's three volumes of *Cathedral Music*. Barrington tells us that the boy's invention in varying passages was inexhaustible, that he had remarkable fingering and a tenacious memory, and that his improvisations were so bold that his brother often trembled for him. When Barrington took him to the Horse Guards when a march Samuel had composed for a Guards' Regiment was played, the conductor was amazed to find that its author was only a boy.

The two boys differed in temperament. Charles had less spirit, was dreamy and absent-minded. He had ease and elegance, but we are told that it is doubtful whether through the entire course of his life he was able to dress himself without assistance. If left to himself he was apt to appear with his wig on one side, his waistcoat buttoned awry or the knot of his cravat opposite one of his shoulders. His morals were correct, his respect for his parents tender and affectionate, but in early life he was not deeply impressed by religion. Music occupied all his thought. About the age of twenty-five he became attached to a girl, and his mother consulted John Wesley, who said, "I hear the girl is good, but of no family." "No fortune either," she was quick to add, evidently with the business instinct of her mother. John's response was to send his nephew fifty pounds towards the wedding, but Charles' parents had other objections and the marriage never took place. But young Charles, lost in his music, was hardly cut out for marriage and also was perhaps put off by his father's warning that marriage was either a heaven or hell, adding: "You do not take the way to be happy in a married state."

Six years later, when his father lay dying, he was pressed to apply for the post of organist at the Chapel Royal at Windsor, with good prospects of securing it, but his father, fearing the influence of the Court on his character, discouraged it, and Charles, rather than grieve him in his last hours, did not put in for it. Unfortunately he failed to secure most of the better posts he applied for, including St. Paul's Cathedral, Westminster Abbey, the Charterhouse, Gresham's College, and St. George's, Hanover Square. In every case the name of Wesley prejudiced him. "We want no Wesleys here," he was rudely told at St. Paul's, and the King, hearing of it, sent for him to Windsor, expressed his regret and said, "Never mind. The name of Wesley is always welcome to me." He afterwards sent him £100 by way of consolation and had intended to transfer to him the deceased Kelway's annual pension of £200, but unfortunately his madness intervened and Charles never received it.

He had first been introduced to George III, who was fond of Handel's music, by Mr. Shepherd; and George IV, when Prince of Wales, made him his private organist. On his accession he showed him continued kindness, inviting him often to Windsor, and Charles became the music teacher of his daughter, Princess Charlotte. After the King lost his sight, when Charles was alone with him, he asked, "Is there anybody in the room but you and me?" "No, your Majesty." Then the blind King said, "It is my judgment, Mr. Wesley, that your uncle and your father, and George Whitefield and Lady Huntingdon, have done more to promote true religion in the country than all the dignified clergy put together, who are so apt to despise their labours."

These royal favours gave concern to the young musician's father and uncle. The former wrote: "Be content with your station, and seek not great things," warning his son against any great expectations from Windsor and to be on his guard. "I cannot wish you to play any more at Windsor. It will only stir up a nest of hornets, and set them upon contriving mischief." And to Sally: "I am not sanguine in my expectations of good from Windsor. If Charles has received no evil by it, it is a miracle, and I am satisfied." And Uncle John wrote, commending his nephew for having followed his advice. Charles became organist of the Lock Chapel, in Grosvenor Place, and afterwards of Marylebone parish church.

His brother, far more lively and acute, had broader interests, and his waywardness at times caused anxiety. He was more like his Wesley forebears—independent and unpredictable. Impatient of his father's objection to the theatre, wearied no doubt as a child, possibly humiliated, by his public appearances, or seduced by the flattery of the social circle into which he was far too early introduced by Martin Madan, his godfather, he diverged from his upbringing. For a short time he became a Roman Catholic, the knowledge of which he concealed from his parents, and, when the news could no longer be withheld, the Duchess of Norfolk undertook the painful task of waiting upon his father in Chesterfield Street to inform him. It was a distressing occasion. He received her with dignity, fully robed. She came with deep understanding, for her own son had turned Protestant and she could enter into Charles' feelings. She tried to console him by suggesting that it was possibly the result of grace, but Charles would have none of it and replied testily: "Say, the loaves and fishes, Madam, the loaves and fishes!" The boy had been flattered, and a high mass which he had composed for the papal chapel brought him the thanks of the Pope. Charles, crushed by the news, unburdened himself in verse, but John wrote sensibly and tolerantly to his nephew, refusing to be heartbroken or even appalled, telling him plainly that he cared not what Church he belonged to as long as he was converted, and that whether Protestant or Roman, he could be saved or damned in either. But Samuel made a poor convert and a few years later recanted, declaring that he did not care a straw for any excommunications that the Roman priesthood could utter.

But all that came later. The concerts which the boys gave in their home were of a private nature and continued for some years. The first was held in 1779, when Charles was twenty-one and Samuel twelve. A large room was set apart and suitably equipped. The ticket for a series was three guineas and regular subscribers numbered from thirty to fifty. We can still read in Charles Wesley's handwriting the lists he kept of guests and expenses (see Plate 12). Items of the latter for a concert in 1786 amounted to £1.11.6 and included: apples 4/6, organ 3/–, wine 4/2, tea 3/–, sugar 3/–, cream, 1/–, lemons 1/–. On these occasions, which were well patronized and yielded a small profit, young Charles played on the organ and his brother the violoncello. Among those present were the Lord Mayor and the Bishop of London, and on one occasion Uncle John himself, somewhat reluctantly and, as he confessed, a little out of his element, though he spent an agreeable hour, but preferred plain music and plain company. He came in gown and bands, accompanied by his wife, and who should he meet but his old friend, General Oglethorpe, who, delighted to see him, came forward, bowed and kissed his hand in respect. He always venerated John.

These activities were not without criticism in Methodist circles. Earlier, in Bristol, the boy's precosity had provoked jealousy, and in 1775 Fletcher had warned Charles: "You have your enemies, as well as your brother. They complain of your love for music, company, fine people, great folks, and of the want of your former zeal and frugality. I need not put you in mind to cut off all sinful appearances." But Fletcher, with his links with the narrower Evangelicals, moved in a different world.

John Wesley, whatever his thoughts, withheld criticism and, indeed, from a distance, showed affection and encouragement to his nephews, though with mixed feelings. His brother had written to him after the first concert: "I am clear without a doubt, that my sons' concert is after the will and order of Providence. It has established them as musicians, and the safe and honourable way. The Bishop [of London] has since sent me word, that he has never heard any music he liked so well, and promises Charles five scholars next winter. Here is a musical child from Norwich, whom Sam cherished and recommends. He has sent him many customers so that his mother gets ten pounds a day by them. He has played before their Majesties. We neither envy his gains nor his honours. We do not repent that we did not make a show or advantage of our swans. They may still make their fortune, if I would venture them into the world; but I never wish them rich. You also agree with me in this. Our good old father neglected every opportunity of selling our souls to the devil." John printed this in his periodical, *The Armenian Magazine*, with the dry comment that the concerts were hardly in the order of Providence, that he was of another mind and thought they increased spiritual dangers.

Charles also wrote to his brother (in 1779): "My reasons for letting my sons have a concert at home are:

i.   To keep them out of harm's way; the way, (I mean) of bad music and bad musicians, who by a free communication with them might corrupt both their taste and their morals.
ii.   That my sons may have a safe and honourable opportunity of availing themselves of their musical abilities, which have cost me several hundred pounds.
iii.   That they may enjoy their full right of private judgment, and likewise their independency, both of which must be given up if they swim with the stream and follow the multitude.
iv.   To improve their play and their skill in composing; as they must themselves furnish the principal music of every concert.

Cowper the poet, who frowned on such occasions, satirized musical parsons and Sunday concerts in his poem *The Progress of Error*! "Accomplishments have taken virtue's place" and "Layman have leave to dance, if parsons play." But it was his cousin, Martin Madan, and not Charles, whom he depicted as Occiduus—"a pastor of renown", who "plays the fool on Sundays" and "serves his golden god", and, with Sabbath duties done, "with wire and catgut he concludes the day". But Charles and his sons could have been no less in the poet's mind, especially Samuel who was so closely associated with Madan as his godson and protégé, though the occasional Sunday performances of himself and his brother were confined exclusively to sacred music.

The boys derived their talent from their Welsh mother, who played the harpsichord and had a fine, though not strong, singing voice. Once, when travelling with her husband and resting at an inn at Stone, she was overheard singing in its garden which adjoined that of the Vicarage. The Vicar and his family were drawn to the hedge by the sweetness of her voice and afterwards complimented her and invited her to sing in the church choir on the following Sunday. Sally agreed on condition that her husband preached, which the Vicar declined. And there is a charming incident of her old age recorded in a private diary, when she was present with her son Charles at an evening party. "We were much delighted at hearing Mr. Wesley play upon the harpsichord. He is one of the best performers in England . . . Mrs. Wesley, his mother, who is upwards of eighty years of age, sung, to our great astonishment, two of Handel's songs most delightfully,—'He shall feed his flock' etc. and 'If God be with us', etc. A part of the company staid supper, and we did not return till near 2."

Her husband was less musical, but had a fine ear, and a passion for old church music, and for Handel whom it is probable he had met at the house of Mrs. Rich. But apart from flute-playing in his Oxford days there is no evidence of his talent with any other instrument, though his sweet-toned organ is preserved at City Road Chapel and it is difficult not to think that he played on it. Three of his hymns were set to music by Handel, the manuscripts of which, in Handel's writing, are in the Fitzwilliam Museum, Cambridge.

Sally, who survived her husband by nearly thirty-five years, continued to worship at West Street until her death in 1822 at the age of ninety-six. Her younger son Samuel in 1793 married Charlotte Martin. He remained universally popular and in wide demand as a musician, though a serious head injury caused by an accident produced long periods of mental depression. He kept in touch with the Methodists and gave valuable help in the production of Methodist tunes and in editing his father's hymns. He was warmly received at the annual breakfast of the children of the preachers at City Road in 1827. Describing the occasion to his sister, he wrote: "The preachers prayed lustily for the three of us." He had a numerous family and among his children were the Rev. Charles Wesley, D.D., Sub-Dean of the Chapels Royal and Chaplain to the Queen; John Wesley, who served for a time as a lay secretary at the Wesleyan Mission House; and Samuel Sebastian Wesley, Mus. Doc., the ablest composer of Church music of his day, organist at Gloucester Cathedral, and two of whose five sons became clergymen.

10. Portrait of Charles Wesley, at the age of 64, painted in 1771 by John Russell, R.A. and later exhibited at the Royal Academy. It now hangs at the headquarters of the Methodist Missionary Society. At one time it was described as a copy, but research now indicates that it is the original.

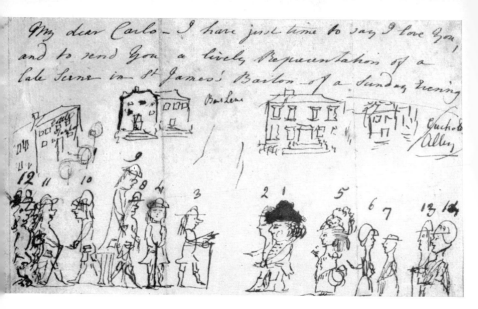

My dear Carlo—I have just time to say I love you, and to send you a lively Representation of a late Scene in St James's Barton of a Sunday Evening.

Barton

Cuckold Alley

11a. An amusing drawing by Sally, Wesley's daughter, in a letter to her brother Charles. Her description of those depicted includes: "No. 1—The Rev'd C.W. coming from square preaching. The painter had not time to take a stronger likeness. No. 5—The Rev'd C.W. Daughter; she has a sweet smile upon her Face, and stands patiently whilst her Papa shakes hands with *all* the colliers, not knowing that she must do so too. a perfect Pattern! *dear Lady!* No. 6—a Methodist sister; lamenting the Vanity of Dress in Miss W."

11b. A portrait, now in the New Room, Bristol, of Charles Wesley's elder son, Charles, who like his brother was a brilliant musician. He was often at Windsor Castle, a favourite with George III, where Princess Charlotte was his pupil and he was for many years organist of Marylebone Parish Church.

Chapter Twelve

FINAL CONTROVERSY 1782–1786

Secret ordinations—Charles' distress—An autobiographical letter—"So easily are bishops made!"—His last Conference—Churchman and Methodist.

CHAPTER TWELVE

FROM THESE family interests Charles turned to face his final controversy with his brother and, in his seventy-ninth year, to attend his last Conference. Southey, who is not always sympathetic or reliable in his *Life of Wesley*, rightly points out that the house which Wesley had raised was divided within itself. There had been the early break with the Moravians, then with the Calvinists, with the Huttons, Zinzendorf, Whitefield and Lady Huntingdon. And friction and tension over the years had marked the growing divergence between "church" and "dissenting" sympathies within the Movement, which could hardly have been otherwise, for Methodism was never confined to a single type. As the Movement grew, the greater these strains became. The wonder is that, while embracing such diversity, it preserved such firm cohesion, and that at Wesley's death, instead of the feared disintegration, it swept on with tidal force for thirty years without a break doubling and trebling its numbers, and thereafter, with continuing momentum, establishing itself as a world Church. In Southey's words, Wesley had raised up a spirit which he could not suppress and to which he could only give useful direction. His original aim was to give new impulse to the English Church, his hope was that his Societies would find a place within its parochial order, his desire was to do what the monastic orders had wished to do, but over a wider field and to a nobler purpose.

In 1784, out of sheer desperation, he took events into his own hands by ordaining in semi-secrecy—for it was in a private house and at four o'clock in the morning—three preachers for America. One of them—Dr. Thomas Coke (who was already in priest's orders) he ordained as Superintendent of his American work, and the other two, Whatcoat and Vasey, as deacons, and the following day as elders or presbyters. It must be remembered that America had by now separated from England and most of the clergy there had left their posts. Four years earlier John had begged Bishop Lowth to ordain "a pious man" for America and been refused on the ground that there were already three clergymen there! John retorted that threescore would not suffice, if they were without piety and knew no more of saving souls than catching whales.

His justification was that in America "for hundreds of miles together there is none either to baptize or to administer the Lord's Supper. Here, therefore, my scruples are at an end." There were fifteen thousand Methodists without proper pastoral care, and as he could not go himself he sent Coke, giving him power to act in his place, but never giving him the title of bishop; it was Coke himself who assumed it. In the circumstances, under pressure of such necessity and from the highest motives—for Wesley acted in good faith and with no thought of schism—his action cannot be judged harshly. And in the light of history, when we consider the phenomenal development of American Methodism, his irregularity providentially matched the need and challenge of the hour. Nonetheless it was a breach of Church order. Charles was shocked when he heard of it from a Bristol layman, Henry Durbin, to whom he replied: "I am thunderstruck. I cannot believe it." Stunned and confused, he called on Durbin to witness that he had no hand in "this infamous *ordination*". And he poured out his feelings to a fellow clergyman, Dr. Chandler (April 28, 1785):

At eight years old, 1716, I was sent by my father to Westminster School, and placed under the care of my eldest brother Samuel, a strict Churchman, who brought me up in his own principles . . . . My first year at College I lost in diversions . . . I took my Master's degree, and only thought of spending all my days at Oxford. But my brother, who always had the ascendant over me, persuaded me to accompany him and Mr. Oglethorpe to Georgia. I exceedingly dreaded entering into holy orders; but he over ruled me, and I was ordained . . . .

Our only design was to do all the good we could, as Ministers of the Church of England to which we were firmly attached, both by education and by principle. My brother still thinks her the best-constituted Church in the world. . . .

Our eldest brother Samuel was alarmed at our going on, and strongly expressed his fears of its ending in a separation from the Church. All our enemies prophesied the same . . . I never lost my dread of separation or ceased to guard our Societies against it. I frequently told them: "I am your servant as long as you remain in the Church of England; but no longer. Should you forsake her, you would renounce me."

196

Some of the preachers very early discovered an inclination to separate, which induced my brother to print his "Reasons against Separation". As often as it appeared, we beat down the schismatical spirit. If any one did leave the Church, at the same time he left our Society. For near fifty years we kept the sheep in the fold . . .

I can scarcely yet believe it, that, in his eighty-second year, my old, intimate friend and companion, should have assumed the episcopal character, ordained Elders, consecrated a Bishop, and sent him to ordain lay-preachers in America! I was, then, at Bristol, at his elbow; yet he never gave me the least hint of his intention. How was he surprised into so rash an action! He certainly persuaded himself that he was right.

Lord Mansfield told me last year, that ordination was separation. That my brother does not, and will not, see; or that he has renounced the principles and practice of his whole life; that he has acted contrary to all his declamations, protestations, and writings, robbed his friends of their boasting, and left an indelible blot on his name, as long as it shall be remembered.

Thus our partnership here is dissolved, but not our friendship. I have taken him for better, for worse, till death us do part, or rather, re-united us in love inseparable. I have lived on earth a little too long, who have lived to see this evil day.

Charles had good grounds for his attitude, which, with complete loyalty to his Methodist principles, he had maintained throughout his career. It was no unyielding prejudice on his part, nor the blind obstinacy of a man without vision clinging to an irrelevant past, but a natural and lifelong consistency. At the same time his worst forebodings were not realized, and though Methodism over the years has divided and drawn apart, and come together again, it has preserved a remarkable coherence.

Meanwhile strong letters were exchanged between the two brothers, with an opening broadside from Charles.

April 14, 1785.
"Dear Brother, I have been reading over again your 'Reasons against a Separation', printed in 1758, and your works; and entreat you, in the name of God, and for Christ's sake, to read them again yourself, with previous prayer, and stop and proceed no further. . . . Near thirty years, since then, you have stood against the importunate solicitations of your preachers, who have scarcely at last prevailed. I was your natural ally, and faithful

friend; and while you continued faithful to yourself, we too could chase a thousand. But when once you began ordaining in America, I knew, and you knew, that your preachers here would never rest till you ordained them . . .

Alas! what trouble are you preparing for yourself, as well as for me, and for your oldest, truest, best friends. Before you have quite broken down the bridge, stop and consider! If your sons [the preachers] have no regard for you, have some regard for yourself. Go to your grave in peace: at least, suffer me to go first, before this ruin is under your hand. So much, I think, you owe to my father, to my brother, and to me, as to stay till I am taken from the evil. I am on the brink of the grave. Do not push me in, or embitter my last moments. Let us not leave an indelible blot on our memory, but let us leave behind us the name and character of honest men. This letter is a debt to our parents, and to our brother, as well as to you, and to your faithful friend."

John replied, quoting epithets from Charles' earlier elegies—"heathenish priests" and "mitred infidels", throwing them back in his face, and declaring himself to be a scriptural *episcopos*. His views, he said, in no way interfered with his remaining in the Church of Engand, from which he had no desire to separate. "What, then, are you frighted of? I no more separate from it now than I did in the year 1758." He admitted that he deviated in some points of doctrine and discipline, but not an hair's breadth more than he believed to be meet, right and his bounden duty. "It is not likely that I should. The high-day of my blood is over. If you will go hand in hand with me, do. But do not hinder me if you will not help." And here a wistful phrase escapes him, a reflection of his loneliness and that even Charles has deserted him. "Perhaps if you had kept close to me, I might have done better. However, with or without help, I creep on. And as I have been hitherto, so I trust I shall always be, Your affectionate friend and Brother."

Charles, stung by having his own epigrams quoted against him, replied, "There is no danger of our quarrelling . . . and you are the last man upon earth I could wish to quarrel with" and repudiated the unfortunate quotations. "That juvenile line of mine: 'Heathenish Priests and mitred infidels' I disown, renounce, and with shame recant." He only knew one mitred infidel and him only by hearsay. As to the Bishops: "They have let us alone, and left us to act just as we pleased, for these fifty years. At present some of them are quite friendly toward us, particularly toward you. The churches are all open to you; and never could there be less pretence for a separation." All of which was perfectly true, for despite their unhelpful attitude the Church authorities had shown remarkable patience and tolerance towards Wesley's irregularities.

In this same letter Charles accepted John's claim to be a scriptural *episcopos* or overseer, "and so is every Minister who has the cure of souls. Neither need we dispute whether the uninterrupted succession is fabulous, as you believe, or real, as I believe; or whether Lord King [on whose work, *Account of the Primitive Church,* John based his view] is right or wrong." After referring to Dr. Coke's "ambitious pursuits" to form a new episcopal Church, he took John up on his phrase about their having drawn apart: "When you took that fatal step at Bristol, I kept as close to you as close could be for I was all the time at your elbow. You might certainly have done better, if you had taken me into your counsel." Charles was more than justified in making the point, for ordinations after midnight and without prior consultation were, to say the least, injudicious. Why the concealment? Was John haunted by the ghost of Grace Murray and Charles' swift (and effective) intervention? Charles, when roused, could be annihilating and John was taking no chances. The letter ends, however, on a happier note, showing that no bitterness could quench affection. "I thank you for your intention to remain my friend. Herein my heart is as your heart. Whom God hath joined, let no man put asunder. We have taken each other for better, for worse. . . . Therefore in the love which never faileth, I am your affectionate friend and brother."

This letter produced an equally plain reply, for the Wesleys never hid their feelings. "I see no use of you and me disputing together; for neither of us is likely to convince the other. You say I separate from the Church: I say I do not. Then let it stand." As for mitred infidels and heathenish priests, he sees fifty times more of England than Charles, and finds few exceptions. He praises Coke, excusing his earlier ambitiousness, and ends: "If you will not or cannot help me yourself, do not hinder those that can and will. I must and will save as many souls as I can while I live without being careful about what may *possibly be* when I die. I pray do not confound the intellects of the people in London. You may thereby a little weaken my hands, but you will greatly weaken your own."

But still he had not met his brother's point, that as a priest of the Anglican Church he had acted irregularly. According to Tyerman, in his *Life and Times of Wesley*, James Creighton, a clergyman who had assisted in the ordinations, declared ten years later that Wesley regretted that he had ordained any of his preachers, expressed his sorrow at the Conference of 1789, and said six weeks before he died, "The preachers are now too powerful for me."

Although John's action almost broke his brother's heart, the latter never carried out his threat to dissolve the partnership, and remained at his side until the end. He had expressed his mind; he could do no more. He relieved his feelings in a final epigram:

> So easily are bishops made,
> By man's, or woman's whim.
> Wesley his hands on Coke hath laid,
> But who laid hands on him?

There was no further bitterness and, in Dr. Maldwyn Edwards' words, "In all the history of the Church there is not even a remote parallel to the story of what these two brothers accomplished for the Kingdom of God". Their lives and their work were inextricably bound together. And to the end they strengthened and sustained each other.

Eighty preachers attended the 1786 Conference at Bristol where a warm debate had been anticipated, but it passed off quietly, and with complete unanimity on not separating from the Church. Charles took no part except to cry out a loud and angry "NO" to a suggestion that Methodist services should be held in Church hours, and to preach at its conclusion from his favourite text, its meaning now more pointed than ever: "I will bring the third part through the fire."

To his wife he wrote: "My brother cannot undo what he has done. . . . Surely I am in a dream. Is it possible that J. W. should be turned Presbyterian? J. W. the schismatic grandson of J. W. the regicide!" It was enough to turn his father and brother in their graves. And of the Conference he told her: "My Dearest partner will be pleased to hear the result of our Conference. The Dissenting party made a bold push for separation. .... All agree to let my brother and me remain in the old ship, till we get safe to land." Plainly the powers of the Wesleys were weakening, and, as Southey points out, they had set going a movement which was fast passing from their control.

Charles wrote also to Mr. Latrobe, a Moravian minister: "My brother and I, and the preachers were unanimous for continuing in the old ship. The preachers of a Dissenting spirit will probably, after our death, set up for themselves, and draw away disciples after them. An old Baptist minister, forty years ago, told me, he looked on the Methodists as a seminary for the Dissenters. My desire and design, from the beginning to this day, is to leave them in the lap of their mother. The bishops might, if they pleased, save the largest and soundest part of them back into the Church; perhaps to leaven the whole lump, as Archbishop Potter said to me. *But I fear, betwixt you and me, their lordships care for none of these things.* The great evil, which I have dreaded for near fifty years, is a schism."

It is interesting to note among the minor business of this Conference John's advice to his preachers; namely, not to let their services exceed the hour, never to scream, never to lean upon or beat the Bible, to introduce no new tunes, to see that none sing too slow, to exhort all to stand to sing and to kneel at prayer, and in services held during Church hours to read the psalms and lessons with part of the Church prayers, "to endear the Church service to our brethren, who probably will be prejudiced against it, if they hear none but extemporary prayer."

Other ordinations followed, but Charles, though saddened, let the matter rest. "Stand to your own proposal," he wrote to his brother, "I leave America and Scotland to your latest thoughts and recognitions. ... Keep your authority while you live. ... You cannot settle the succession." And his verses, of varying periods, reflect his genuine sympathy with his brother's dilemma:

> The word, the care, the labouring zeal,
>   He *doth* to others give,
> And laymen now of Jesus tell,
>   And urge us to believe.
>
> Who but the Holy Ghost can make
>   A genuine Minister! . . .

> Not all the hands of all mankind
> Can constitute one Overseer.

and

> Shall we the Spirit's course restrain,
> Or quench the heavenly fire!
> Let God His messengers ordain,
> And whom He will inspire.

These sentiments disprove any idea that his outlook was rigidly conventional. On the contrary it was that of true catholicity. In his horror of sectarianism, in the sense of the fragmentation of the Church, he would embrace all God's people in a living unity, as we learn from his fine hymn, "Christ, from whom all blessings flow".

> Love, like death, hath all destroyed,
> Rendered all distinctions void;
> Names, and sects, and parties fall;
> Thou, O Christ, art all in all.

Thus he preserved his dual fidelity. Writing in 1771 to one of his oldest friends, James Hutton, who had deserted to the Moravians, he said, "Take it for granted that I am *fixed, resolved, determined, sworn* to stand by the Methodists, and my B[rother] right or wrong, through thick and thin. . . . Notwithstanding my incurable bigotry, can and will you love me? If so, I am your man, your first and latest of friends, your faithful old C.W." Charles to the end remained a sound Churchman and a loyal Methodist.

Chapter Thirteen

DIVINE SONGS

A PROLIFIC POET—PRAISE OF CRITICS—COMPARISON WITH
WATTS AND COWPER—THE WESLEY HYMNALS—A DEVO-
TIONAL CLASSIC—JOHN WESLEY'S PREFACE—THE POOR
MAN'S POET—THE HAPPY WARRIOR.

CHAPTER THIRTEEN

ALL THIS time Charles was composing hymns. Poetry was his natural medium. Where John used his *Journal* to set down his activities, Charles recorded his experience in verse. Prolific as a poet, he wrote more than eight thousand hymns and other forms—too many, by far, much of it pedestrian. George Saintsbury said he was guilty of the sin of excess, though others speak of it as God's plenty. But, as a hymn-writer and at his best, Charles is probably unsurpassed. George Sampson in his Warton Lecture commends his fluency, flaming ecstasy and metrical felicity. "There had arisen in England a new religious poet of burning sincerity, of high poetic feeling, of daring force of expression, and of intensely characteristic style, entirely free from the conceits that trouble us sometimes in Herbert. . . . He could express his great themes in forms so numerous that he became the most varied and audacious metrist of his time." And Sampson, like others, finds it extraordinary that the histories of prosody barely mention him and anthologies overlook him. "His poems are dismissed as mere hymns."

Few, if any, would disagree that "Wrestling Jacob" is a great poem, but so is "Jesu, Lover of my soul", "Love Divine, all loves excelling", his great hymn on the Incarnation, "Let earth and heaven combine", and many of his festival and Passiontide hymns. "Gentle Jesus, meek and mild" is comparable with the child songs of Blake. He deliberately restricted his muse to sacred themes which narrowed the range of his genius and limited its appeal. Had he given it free scope, it might have flowered more richly.

George Sampson is not alone in his praise. W. J. Courthope describes him as the most admirable devotional lyric poet in the English language. Saintsbury, Oliver Elton and Edmund Gosse, among others, speak in similar terms. Julian's *Dictionary of Hymnology* names him as, in quantity and quality, "the great hymn-writer of all ages". Mr. Ralph Lawrence in an essay on the English hymn in *Essays and Studies of the English Association*, 1954, is equally eulogistic: "Charles Wesley remains pre-eminent in the scope, number, and consistent excellence of his hymns. . . . We are left with an impression of light, happiness, and vitality—of soaring vitality—as of a strong man rejoicing in his strength. . . . It is an exhilarating experience merely to read Wesley's hymns." He quotes their dynamic openings; "O for a thousand tongues to sing", "Christ whose glory fills the skies", and "Soldiers of Christ arise". Hymn after hymn rings with the same challenging energy.

Cowper, in comparison, was hesitant and obsessive, burdened with Calvinistic fears, lacking Wesley's buoyancy and confidence. Watts had charm and smoothness, but nothing like the same power and range, though he composed two of our greatest hymns, "O God our help", and "When I survey". Later hymn-writers never achieved the same richness and finished technique as those of the eighteenth century. Here we have only to compare Charles Wesley's eucharistic hymns with those of the Tractarians to see how superior are the former in their full and authentic expression of Catholic doctrine. The Tractarians, more self-conscious and sentimental, never gave it the full flavour we find in Wesley.

It would take a volume in itself to do justice to this side of Charles Wesley, and the ground has already been exhaustively covered. I have written elsewhere on the literary qualities of the hymns.[1] Dr. Henry Bett has given them fascinating and extensive treatment in his *The Hymns of Methodism*. Dr. J. E. Rattenbury has dealt in detail with their theology, as well as with metrical and bibliographical points. Dr. Frank Baker's recent *Representative Verse of Charles Wesley* has a valuable critical Introduction, and there is Bernard Manning's *The Hymns of Wesley and Watts* with its generous and discerning tributes. Here we can only briefly summarize.

First, as to the hymn-books issued by the Wesleys. They were published at different periods, in collections, in penny pamphlets, or singly for special occasions, and ran into many editions. The first hymn-book published by John Wesley, in Georgia in 1737, contained none of his brother's hymns, as none had then been written. Two years later a collection of hymns and sacred poems appeared, by both John and Charles Wesley, and the latter issued two volumes under his own name in 1749; other collections followed and there were numerous small editions in

[1] *The Romantic Movement and Methodism*, Epworth Press (1937, reprinted 1954).

pamphlet form such as *Funeral Hymns, Children's Hymns, Hymns for Earthquakes and Tumults*. Charles wrote hymns for everyone, and for every occasion, for doctors, musicians, miners, malefactors, even for a harlot.

The collection that concerns us now is that edited by John Wesley in 1780 under the title: *A Collection of Hymns for the Use of the People called Methodists*, which was in use until 1904 and has served as the basis of the emasculated editions which from time to time have replaced it. Though no longer in use, it remains the classic among Methodist hymnals and indeed is no ordinary hymn-book, but a devotional treasury.

It contains John Wesley's portrait with his clear signature (but no portrait of Charles, of whose work it almost entirely consists!), and also John's delightful Preface, which Bernard Manning regretted was omitted from the 1904 edition, but which was sensibly restored to its original position in the new hymn-book in 1933.

Why, asks John Wesley, is yet another hymn-book needed, when for forty years he and his brother have published so many? "Because the greater part of the people, being poor, are not able to purchase so many books; and those that have purchased them are, as it were, bewildered in the immense variety." A collection is needed, he says, carefully selected from the others, and "comprised in so moderate a compass, as to be neither cumbersome nor expensive. . . . What we want is, a publication not too large, that it may be cheap and portable; not too small, that it may contain a sufficient variety for all ordinary occasions. Such a Hymn Book you have before you now. . . . It is large enough to contain all the important truths of our most holy religion, whether speculative or practical . . . and this is done in a regular manner. The hymns are not carelessly jumbled together but carefully ranged under proper heads, according to the experience of real Christians. So that this book is, in effect, a little body of experimental and practical divinity."

When we turn to the page of contents we find how well-founded is this claim, for unlike the classification in most hymnals, according to times and seasons, the arrangement here is of pure devotion. It is the *Pilgrim's Progress* in verse, and it is this which makes it unique. What other hymn-book can boast such a devotional sequence?—for mourners convinced of sin, for persons convinced of backsliding, for backsliders recovered, for believers rejoicing, fighting, praying, watching, working, suffering, seeking for full redemption, interceding for the world. As in Dante, every step of the path of the penitent is marked.

To return to the Preface, John next pays high tribute to his brother: "As but a small part of these hymns is of my own composing, I do not think it inconsistent with modesty to declare, that I am persuaded, no such hymn-book as this has yet been published in the English language. In what other publication of the kind have you so distinct and full an account of scriptural Christianity? such a declaration of the heights and depths of religion . . . so clear directions for making your calling and election sure?" Next as to literary merit: "May I be permitted to add a few words with regard to the *poetry*? . . . 1. In these hymns there is no doggerel, no botches, nothing put in to patch up the rhyme; no feeble expletives. 2. Here is nothing turgid or bombast, on the one hand, or low and creeping on the other. 3. Here are no *cant* expressions; no words without meaning. Those who impute this to us know not what they say. We talk common sense, both in prose and verse, and use no word but in a fixed and determinate sense. 4. Here are, allow me to say, both the purity, the strength, and the elegance of the English language; and at the same time, the utmost simplicity and plainness, suited to every capacity. Lastly, I desire men of taste to judge (these are the only competent judges), whether there be not in some of the following hymns the true spirit of poetry, such as cannot be acquired by art and labour, but must be the gift of nature. By labour a man may become a tolerable imitator of Spenser, Shakespeare, or Milton; and may heap together pretty compound epithets, as 'pale-eyed', 'meek-eyed', and the like; but unless he be *born* a poet, he will never attain the genuine spirit of poetry."

Even though the hymns are by no means as free of blemishes as he suggests, and he claims too much, we can accept his general principle that they are free of affectation and weak sentiment, that in their clarity and directness they set forth the strength and vigour of the English language, and that poets are born, not made. He is tilting here at the poor quality of the numerous poetasters of the period and at the pedantry of the more sophisticated poets. It was a period of transition between the formal couplets of Dryden and Pope and the richer rhythms of Blake and the Romantics. Charles, with his use of Anglo-

Eighth Subscr.n Concert 1786.
Expences.

Samuel.	3.	3.	0
W. for Gown	1.	1.	0
James Kenton	1.	1.	0
China Plates &c		:9.	0
Sally for Gown	1.	1.	0
Cups & Saucers		?0.	0
Knives & forks		12.	0
Jn. 6. Nich.		10.	6
Cleaning Chandelier &c		2.	6
Carpenter		16.	0
Sally Apron		2.	6
Gloves M. Moon			
Sally's Hair 1 x 1.6 x 1. x 1.6 x 1.6 x 1.6 x			
Sam Eddy D.s	1.		
Kenton	1.	1.	0
Sally's Gown		6.	6
Carp.n Chairs in		14.	6
Bill		1.	6
W. & Gloves		1.	6
Sally's Cap		2.	0
Minding Juitcloth		2.	0
Sally gloves		1.	
Wife		1.	
Green Cloth		1.	0

12. The Wesley family often held Subscription Concerts at which the talented sons performed. This is a note, now among the large collection of Wesley papers and letters in the Methodist Archives, of the expenses of the Eighth Concert of which seven evening performances were given. It may be noted that Sally's expenses feature prominently, including a hairdressing bill for each evening.

Christ, our merciful High-priest
With thy people's grief distrest,
Help us for our Guide to pray
Lost in his mistaken way:

By a show of good misled
Lest he farther should proceed,
Stop, restrain him, and defend,
Till the hour of darkness end.

Hide him from the thing design'd
~~Not according to thy mind~~
Save him from the purpos'd Ill
~~Not according to thy will~~.   After his own not thy will

We alas, can nothing do,
But present him to thy view
Weeping at thy feet complain
All the help of man is vain —

Gainst the truth he stops his ears,
Will not see his children's tears,
Shuts his eyes against the light:
Sure, that He alone is right.

13. An extract from the manuscript poem, now at the New Room, Bristol, written by Charles Wesley at the time of his disagreement with John about the ordination of priests for America. It is believed that it has never previously been published.

Saxon and his twenty or more varieties of metre, was among the pioneers, and John's remarks here on style find a natural place alongside Wordsworth's famous Preface to his *Lyrical Ballads* describing the true function of poetry.

John elsewhere characterized his brother's hymns as "some bad, some good, and some excellently good", but at his best, in vivacity, variety and lyrical power, Charles stands high in the Romantic tradition. And John's Preface, which has been described as one of the noblest pieces of English prose, deserves a place in prose anthologies. It ends: "When Poetry thus keeps its place, as the handmaid of Piety, it shall attain, not a poor perishable wreath, but a crown that fadeth not away."

Thus Charles was the poor man's poet, and, after the Bible, this collection of hymns served as the devotional classic of the Methodists. In Bernard Manning's words: "This little book— some 750 hymns (originally only 525)—ranks in Christian literature with the Psalms, the Book of Common Prayer, the Canon of the Mass. In its own way, it is perfect, unapproach- able, elemental in its perfection . . . a work of supreme devo- tional art by a religious genius."

And now, what of the hymns themselves? They express primarily the mood of the Revival. Hymn singing had hardly begun in the English Church. After the bleak paraphrases of Tate and Brady and Sternhold and Hopkins, Wesley's hymns, set to ringing tunes, met a popular need and revolutionized congregational worship. In this, Anglicans and Dissenters alike followed the Methodists; the cold formality of the worship of both needed and gained the stimulus of the Revival. And Charles met every occasion. Often the hymns were inspired by a local scene or situation. A story is told of him once hearing in a seaport drunken sailors singing a bawdy song, "Nancy Dawson", and within an hour or so producing for them his own words set to the same tune. The glow of furnaces at night in the Midlands inspired "See how great a flame aspires", which was eagerly taken up by the colliers of Newcastle-on- Tyne. In Portland he made a hymn for the quarrymen:

> Strike with the hammer of Thy word,
> And break these hearts of stone.

When in Georgia, standing on a narrow promontory, he wrote, echoing Addison and Prior,

> Lo! on a narrow neck of land,
> 'Twixt two unbounded seas, I stand.[1]

Lighter verse includes his "Man of Fashion":

> A busy man, without employment,
> A happy man, without enjoyment . . .
> In sleep and dress and sport and play,
> He throws his worthless life away . . .
> Custom pursues, his only Rule
> And lives an Ape, and dies a Fool!

And lines to his son Charles beginning:

> "Take time by the forelock," is old Charles's word,
> "Time enough," quoth his son, with the air of a lord.

Among his elegies is a fine one on Dr. Boyce with a picturesque reference to Handel greeting him in heaven, and equally good is one on Whitefield, who

> Nor ever more would for opinions fight
> With men whose life, like his, was in the right.

The hymns are loaded with Scripture, skilfully adapted and interwoven, and many carry classical and other allusions. From Ignatius he drew the refrain "My Lord, my Love is crucified", and from Augustine such themes as "I cannot see Thy face and live", and

> The ruins of my soul prepare,
> And make my heart a house of prayer.

Another reference is to the sword of Damocles:

> Show me the naked sword
> Impending o'er my head.

And there are echoes of Milton, from *Samson Agonistes*: "O dark, dark, dark, I still must say", and "A poor blind child I wander here".

From Milton also are: "With glorious clouds encompassed

[1] These lines are often mistakenly associated with Land's End.

round", "Loose all your bars of massy light", and Eve's words from *Paradise Lost*: "With Thee conversing I forget". From Dryden we have "Veiled in flesh the Godhead see"; and "Love Divine, all loves excelling" is a brilliant parody of his "Song of Venus"—"Fairest isle, all isles excelling". From Pope comes "Thine eye diffused a quickening ray", and there are many similar instances.

"If I had a thousand tongues," said Peter Böhler, "I'd praise Christ with them all", and Charles took this as the theme of a hymn on the anniversary of his conversion, "O for a thousand tongues to sing", which since has been the opening hymn in every Wesleyan Methodist hymnal.

His hymns on death are of victory: "Rejoice for a brother deceased", "Come, let us join our friends above", "What are these arrayed in white?", and "Happy the souls to Jesus joined". Even his morbid "Ah, lovely appearance of death" is in harmony with the sentiment of St. Francis: "And thou most kind and gentle death".

There is a charming baptismal hymn, now unfortunately out of use:

> Jesus, in earth and heaven the same,
>   Accept a parent's vow,
> To Thee, baptized into Thy name,
>   I bring my children now.

Some of the hymns are remarkably practical, often with a social content: "A charge to keep I have", and before going to work: "Forth in Thy name, O Lord, I go". There is his great morning hymn: "Christ, whose glory fills the skies", and some are full of healthy psychology:

> Arise, my soul, arise,
> Shake off thy guilty fears.

Others are mystical: "Open, Lord, my inward ear", "Come, Divine Interpreter", "Thou hidden source of calm repose", and "Thou great mysterious God unknown". Nor can we omit "O Jesus, full of truth and grace":

> Thou know'st the way to bring me back,
> My fallen spirit to restore,

and "Wherewith, O God, shall I draw near", full of mounting metaphor and antithesis: "Guilty I stand before Thy face", but

> See where before the throne He stands,
> And pours the all-pervading prayer.

This was a favourite device, of contraposition, of which "Jesus, Lover of my Soul" is a clear example:

> False and full of Sin I am
> Thou art full of Truth and Grace.

For sheer force of imaginative power in depicting the drama of the Passion we must turn to "And can it be that I should gain?", where every line is charged with dramatic vigour. Typical also of his hymns on the Passion are:

> Never love nor sorrow was
> Like that my Saviour showed . . .

> Depth of mercy! can there be,
> Mercy still reserved for me?

> O Love Divine! what hast Thou done?

and reminiscent of Crashaw and Quarles:

> Thy love is all my plea,
> Thy passion speaks for me,
> By Thy pangs and bloody sweat,
> By Thy depth of grief unknown . . .

A similar paraphrasing of the Litany occurs in

> Lamb of God, whose dying love
> We now recall to mind.

Such hymns are miracles of compression, incomparable in depth and clarity. He had a fine sense of rhythm and could take the loftiest themes and express, illumine and interpret them with the utmost felicity.

He wrote also some of the greatest festival hymns of Christendom: "Hark the herald angels sing!" (but more vigorously in the original, "Hark, how all the welkin rings!"), "Christ the Lord is risen today", "God is gone up on high" and "Hail the day that sees Him rise", with its Miltonic ring:

> There the pompous triumph waits,
> Lift your heads, eternal gates;
> Wide unfold the radiant scene,
> Take the King of Glory in.

We can almost hear the sound of trumpets and the roll of drums. Also "Jesus, the Conqueror reigns" and "Lo, He comes with clouds descending". What sweep and vigour we find here!

The early Methodists, as we have seen, attached great importance to the observance of Holy Communion, and the Wesleys published in 1745 *Hymns on the Lord's Supper*, which contained no less than 166 items. No hymns more clearly reflect the depth and mystery of the Eucharist or more faithfully apply its meaning.

> From house to house they broke the bread,
>   Impregnated with life divine,
> And drank the Spirit of their head,
>   Transmitted in the sacred wine.

> With Jesu's constant presence bless'd . . .
> They kept the eucharistic feast . . .

> Throughout their spotless lives was seen
> The virtue of this heavenly food.

With such strong devotional themes Charles nourished the piety and enriched the quality of Methodism, and his Communion hymns reveal, without ambiguity, his comprehension of catholic and apostolic truth.

> This eucharistic feast,
>   Our every want supplies;
> And still we by His death are bless'd,
>   And share His sacrifice.

Here is high doctrine, rooted in Scripture.

> Obedient to Thy gracious Word,
> We break the hallowed bread,

and

> Thy life infuse into the bread,
> Thy power into the wine.

The hymnals of Christendom can be searched in vain for Eucharistic hymns of such quality, whether of language or of doctrine, and in which the deepest mysticism is linked to evangelical appeal.

> Our hearts we open wide,
> To make the Saviour room;
> And lo! the Lamb, the Crucified,
> The sinner's Friend is come.

And in "Victim divine, Thy grace we claim":

> Thou standest in the Holiest Place,
> As now for guilty Sinners slain . . .

> To every faithful Soul appear,
> And show thy Real Presence here.

His hymns are remarkable for their natural flow and many are exuberant, such as: "Happy the man who finds the grace" and his lively anapaestics:

> Away with our fears,
> The glad morning appears.

Hymns on the Church are equally exhilarating, notably: "Christ, from whom all blessings flow" and "Head of Thy Church triumphant". So are his militant hymns and full of stirring metaphor, in which Christ is the Captain and Charles His standard-bearer. "Soldiers of Christ, arise," with its ringing challenge, is a magnificent paraphrase of Ephesians VI. We have seen Charles reluctant and depressed, but here he is the Happy Warrior.

In contrast is his mood of contemplation in a hymn which as much as any reflects his aim and character. It is based on Deuteronomy VI, showing again his unfailing use of Scripture.

When quiet in my house I sit,
   Thy book be my companion still,
My joy thy sayings to repeat,
   Talk o'er the records of thy will,
And search the oracles divine,
   Till every heart-felt word is mine.

"And when thou risest up" (Deuteronomy VI, 7):

Rising to sing my Saviour's praise
   Thee may I publish all day long,
And let Thy precious word of grace
   Rise from my heart and fill my tongue,
Fill all my life with purest love,
   And join me to Thy Church above.

It was his constant prayer and his whole life was spent in its fulfilment.

Chapter Fourteen

LAST PHASE 1786–1788

CHAPTER FOURTEEN

CHARLES FACED his decline with equanimity. Until his eightieth year he was still riding, versifying, visiting Newgate, and he preached until within a few months of his death. His little mare was grey with age and he himself was enfeebled. His habits had become peculiar through advancing weakness. In the pulpit his thoughts flowed less freely, his speech was slow, there were long pauses. He would preach with eyes closed, with fumbling hands, leaning heavily on the pulpit cushion; but at times his fluency returned, there was an outburst of his former power, and his sermon came again from an overflowing heart.

For some years difficulties had arisen over Charles' monopoly of the City Road pulpit, where he preached morning and afternoon every Sunday. In consequence the lay preachers were seldom heard there. Four preachers were attached to the London circuit, but with Charles and his team of curates, their services at City Road were unnecessary (and here was an anomaly, for one of them was Superintendent of the Circuit!). This naturally provoked friction, and all the more because the best of the preachers were no longer illiterate or unacceptable, but in some cases able and distinguished, who had matured appreciably in character and ability under the Wesleys' discipline. One of them, Pawson, expressed his feelings strongly, saying that it was well known that Mr. Charles Wesley was throughout his life prejudiced in favour of the clergy, that only hard necessity had obliged him to continue the lay preachers, that he would have disowned them if he could have found a sufficient number of clergy to carry on the work.

He recalled a Conference debate on the propriety of Methodist preaching in any parish which had an evangelical vicar. Charles with characteristic bluntness had said: "If I was stationed in a particular parish, you should not preach there." At which a preacher, Hampson, retorted rudely: "I would preach there, and never ask your leave, and I should think that I had as good a right for doing so as you had." This had roused Charles' anger, who replied sharply: "You are a grievous wolf; you will tear the flock when my brother and myself are dead, unless God give you repentance." The incident had evidently rankled, but it was this lack of tact and considerateness on the part of some of the preachers who, apart from notable exceptions, were mostly of limited backgrounds, which nettled Charles. Hampson, by the way, not only repented, but was glad enough in the end to be ordained and accept a Church living.

To return to Pawson's letter, he complained that Charles made a convenience of the preachers, glad enough of their help when he did not choose to preach himself or was otherwise engaged. He would always have one of them appointed as well as himself, lest a shower of rain or an agreeable visit should prevent his appearance. On the other hand Pawson cannot praise John Wesley too highly and in exaggerated terms that never from creation was any single person so highly regarded by any body of men, not even St. Paul himself. Pawson acknowledged, however, that the Methodists were too poor to supply a sufficient number of acceptable ministers to meet the needs of their congregations. "Common prudence, therefore, prevented them from wishing for that which they knew could not be accomplished."

Following these complaints Charles wrote to his brother (in 1779): "My reasons for preaching at the new chapel (City Road) twice every Sunday are 1. Because, after you, I have the best right. 2. Because I have so short a time to preach anywhere. 3. Because I am fully persuaded I can do more good there than in any other place. They, I know, are of a different judgment, and make no secret of it, declaring everywhere, that the work is stopping, the society scattering; and the congregation at the new chapel dwindled away and quite dead. I thank God the chapel is well filled. Last Sunday I preached twice, never with greater power, and seldom with equal effect. . . . You will inquire when here (only not of the preachers), and judge for yourself whether my persevering ministry at the chapel has done good or hurt. I think the preachers wrong, and in the greatest danger through pride; but I have, and will have, no quarrel with them. . . . The lay preachers affect to believe that I act as a clergyman in opposition to them." But, he continues: "if there was no man above them, what would become of them?" And he begs his brother to convince them of this and that he cannot long stand in their way, serving the chapel Sundays and holy days in all weathers. "If God continues my strength, I shall take the best care of the chapel I can till you return. Then I shall deliver up my charge to you and you alone."

It is the old story of declining energy and of the thrust and pressure of a new generation. Pawson himself was no brilliant preacher and he and his friends, for all their useful qualities, were in no way comparable, in personality or genius, to the poet preacher, despite the latter's failing powers. "Dry and lifeless", was Pawson's sneer at Charles. Disgruntled because Charles opposed the wish of the preachers to dispense the sacrament and casting a jaundiced eye on his social activities, he exclaimed: "How doth the fire of hell burn in that poor man's breast!" But Pawson was grave and unctuous, a narrow-minded ex-builder from Yorkshire, whose mischievous act in deliberately burning John Wesley's annotated copy of Shakespeare after John's death shows only too clearly his limited outlook.

Similar signs of the growing unrest of the preachers were seen later that year in Bath, where John had invited a clergyman to preach every Sunday evening in the Methodist chapel, to which a violent objection was made by the preacher there, McNab, who refused to accept the arrangement. John, incensed by his attitude, sent for Charles and rode with him immediately to Bath where he delivered a stinging rebuke to the Society and expelled McNab on the spot. He would brook no interference with his arrangements. Charles was delighted at his firmness, but disgusted when a year later he relented and reinstated the offending preacher. But Charles had done with controversy.

> Why should I longer now contend,
> My last important moments spend,
> In buffeting the air?

His last visit to Bristol was in 1787, five months before he died. He was joined there by his brother who had travelled up from Penzance, on his return from Guernsey. The brothers, now both old men, preached and shared their final joint activity. In the city which they had served so long they ministered for the last time together. Nearly half a century had passed since they had first come at the call of Whitefield to preach among the cockpits of Kingswood, and nearly forty years since Charles had brought his bride to the house in Stokes Croft. And in St. James's churchyard three of his children lay buried. Charles loved Bristol and always remembered it with affection.

The visit was in September and on his return, with the coming of winter, his strength declined. He still occasionally went out, but his condition gave growing concern. John wrote to him in February: "Dear Brother,—You must go out every day, or die. Do not die to save charges. You certainly need not want for anything as long as I live." Ten days later, in his eighty-sixth year and mobile as ever, he left for Bristol and the north. He was never to see his brother alive again. In his anxiety he wrote frequently and in the same strain, urging him to keep on his feet, to go out for an hour each day, and not to spare expense, and he conveyed to him the remembrance of old friends. "Never mind expense, I can make that up." And three days later: "I hope you keep to your rule, of going out every day, although it may sometimes be a cross. Keep to this but one month, and I am persuaded you will be as well as you was this time twelve-month." And he adds advice about Charles' sons, who are evidently still giving anxiety. "*Be master* in your own house. If you fly, they pursue. But stand firm, and you will carry your point."

But Charles was past standing firm. And his verse reflects his mood:

> When young, and full of sanguine hope,
>   And warm in my first love,
> My spirit's loins I girded up,
>   And sought the things above . . .
>
> And put forth every day and hour
>   My utmost strength for God . . .
>
> But now, enervated by age,
>   I find my fierceness gone.

In the Methodist Archives we find a note he wrote in reply to the demand of a music-seller for the balance of an unpaid account which he thought had been settled: "If there is the least doubt, Mr. Wesley always takes the safest, that is, his neighbour's side; choosing to pay a bill twice or twenty times, rather than not at all. He will be obliged to Mr. Wright for a line of acknowledgment, that he is now out of his debt."

Bracing injunctions still came from John; hardly a post without a line of comfort. Tough as ever, he pressed his spartan remedies: riding, vitriol, and beef and onion poultices. To his niece he wrote: "When my appetite was entirely gone, so that all I could take at dinner was a roasted turnip, it was restored in a few days by riding out daily, after taking ten drops of elixir of vitriol in a glass of water. It is highly probable this would have the same effect in my brother's case." And he begs her to call in Dr. Whitehead, the best physician, in his opinion, in all England, even though he did not know how to cure his own wife. But whatever happens Charles must be kept on his feet, lying in bed as little as possible in the daytime, otherwise he will not sleep at night. And Sally must tell her brothers that the best help they can give him is to ask his pardon and thereby may save his life. In a brief note to his nephew Charles he wrote: "Whenever it pleases God to call your father, Sammy and you while I live will find a father and friend in your affectionate Uncle."

But not all his well-meant remedies could save his brother whose life was drawing peacefully to its close. His physician, Dr. Whitehead, says that his body was reduced to extreme weakness and that to the end he showed the same unaffected humility and holy resignation which had characterized his life. There were no transports of joy, but solid hope and unshaken confidence in Christ, which kept his mind in perfect peace. As he had lived and as he had preached, so he died, with the sun shining in his heart, in sure and certain hope of the Resurrection.

Samuel Bradburn, one of the London preachers, who attended him frequently and sat with him through the night towards the end, records that he had no disorder but old age, and very little pain. "His mind was as calm as a summer evening. He frequently said, 'I am a mere sinner, saved by the grace of God'" and on that theme, even in weakness, he composed his final hymn.

For some months, according to his daughter, he had seemed detached from earth, speaking very little, nor wishing to hear anything read but the Scriptures. All his prayer was: "Patience and an easy death." When asked if he wanted anything, he answered: "Nothing but Christ." And when one of his visitors remarked that the valley of the shadow of death was hard to be passed through, he replied: "Not with Christ." It was with difficulty he seemed to speak. He prayed with tears for his enemies. He took a solemn leave of his friends and he spoke tenderly of his children. He called his son Samuel to his bedside—whose conversion to Rome had almost broken his heart—and taking him by the hand said: "I shall bless God to all eternity that ever you was born; I am persuaded that I shall." And when his daughter read out to him the letter her other brother had received from Uncle John saying that he would be a father to them, Charles answered: "He will be kind to you, when I am gone. I am certain your uncle will be kind to all of you."

A few days before the end he dictated to his wife the last lines he composed:

> In age and feebleness extream,
>   Who shall a sinful worm Redeem?
> Jesus, my only Hope thou art,
>   Strength of my failing flesh and Heart.
> O could I catch a smile from thee
>   And drop into Eternity!

He was then so weak he could scarcely articulate. His wife records (in her own hymn-book, preserved in the Archives— see Plate 14): "My good Partner desired me to transcribe them when he came in faint and drooping from taking an airing in a Coach, a few days before his End."

Towards the close he was hardly conscious. When asked if he had anything to say, he raised his eyes and replied: "Only thanks, love, blessing." On his last morning (March 29) his beloved Sally entreated him to press her hand if he knew her, which feebly he did and whispered: "Lord—my heart—my God". "He then drew his breath short, and the last so gently that we knew not exactly the moment when his happy spirit fled." He was in his eighty-first year.

All this his daughter wrote afterwards in a full account to her uncle, and Bradburn wrote at once to inform him of his brother's death. But owing to a misdirection the news did not

The following lines I wrote from
Revd Mr Charles Wesley's repeating, a
few days before he departed y.s Life

In age & feebleness extream,
Who shall a helpless worm redeem,
Jesus, my only Hope Thou art,
Strength of my failing flesh & heart
O! could I catch a Smile from Thee
And drop into Eternity!

14. Lines written by Sarah Wesley on the endpaper of her hymn book at the time of her husband's death.

15. The fine life-size bronze statue of Charles that stands in the courtyard of the New Room, Bristol, shows him in a characteristic attitude, with right hand outstretched in appeal.

reach him until a week later at Macclesfield and he was unable to attend the funeral. He wrote immediately to Charles' widow: "Dear Sister,—Half an hour ago, I received a letter from Mr. Bradburn, informing me of my brother's death. For eleven or twelve days before, I had not one line concerning him. The last I had was from Charles, which I delayed to answer, expecting every day to receive some further information. We have only now to learn that great loss, 'The Lord gave, and the Lord hath taken away; blessed be the name of the Lord'. If it had been necessary, in order to serve either him or you, I should not have thought much of coming to London. Indeed, to serve you, or your dear family, in anything that is in my power, will always be a pleasure to, dear sister, your affectionate friend and brother, John Wesley.'" Eight days later he wrote to her again, advising her to limit her acquaintance and "to keep little company".

He was not one to show his deepest feelings, but when preaching at the time in Bolton and announcing his brother's great hymn, "Come, O Thou Traveller unknown," on reaching the lines:

> My company before is gone,
> And I am left alone with Thee,

the aged apostle, unable to control his emotion, burst into tears, sat down and buried his face in his hands. The singing ceased, the congregation silently sharing his grief. When he had recovered, the service continued and was never forgotten by all who were present.

Unlike his brother, Charles chose to be buried in consecrated ground. As, in the education of his sons, he had ignored his brother's school at Kingswood, so now by his own wish he declined the grave provided by him at City Road. John expressed his displeasure to Peard Dickinson: " 'Tis pity but the remains of my brother had been deposited with me. Certainly that *ground* is *holy* as any in England, and it contains a larger quantity of 'bonny dust'." John was afterwards buried there like a prince among his preachers. But Charles before he died had sent for the parson of his parish and said, "Sir, whatever the world may have thought of me, I have lived, and I die, in the communion of the Church of England, and I will be buried in the yard of my parish church."

His funeral lacked the excitement of that of his brother. There was no burial at dawn to reduce the crowd, no souvenir biscuits engraved with his likeness in full canonicals crowned with a halo. Eight clergymen bore his pall, and his wife and children followed him to his quiet grave in the churchyard of Old Marylebone, which is marked today by an obelisk which has replaced the original headstone. His wife and two sons were later buried in the same grave. The obelisk bears the following lines which Charles himself had composed on the death of his Moravian friend, Mr. Latrobe:

With poverty of spirit bless'd,
   Rest, happy Saint, in Jesus rest;
A Sinner sav'd, through grace forgiv'n,
   Redeem'd from earth to reign in heav'n!
Thy labours of unwearied love,
   By thee forgot, are crown'd above;
Crown'd, through the mercy of thy Lord,
   With a free, full, immense reward!

The faithful (and eloquent) Bradburn preached his funeral sermon both at West Street and City Road on the Sunday following the burial to "an inconceivable concourse of people of every description". His text was: "A prince and a great man is fallen this day in Israel." The chapels were draped in black and the congregations were in mourning.

It is strange there is no record of any memorial tribute from his brother, apart from the cool obituary in the Minutes of the following Conference, which read: "Mr. Charles Wesley, who after spending fourscore years with great sorrow and pain, quietly retired into Abraham's bosom. He had no disease, but after a gradual decay of some months, 'the weary wheels of life at last stood still.' His least praise was his talent for poetry, although Dr. Watts did not scruple to say that the single poem, 'Wrestling Jacob', was worth all the verses he himself had written."

For Methodism's real appreciation of his worth we must turn to his memorial in Wesley's Chapel with its generous eulogy:

"God buries his workmen, but carries on His work."
Sacred to the Memory
of
THE REV. CHARLES WESLEY, M.A.

Educated at Westminster School
And sometime Student at Christ-Church, Oxford.

As a preacher
He was eminent for ability, zeal, and usefulness,
Being learned without pride,
And pious without ostentation;
To the sincere, diffident Christian,
A Son of Consolation;
But to the vain boaster, the hypocrite, and the profane,
A Son of Thunder.

He was the first who received the Name of Methodist;
And, uniting with his Brother, the Rev. John Wesley,
In the plan of Itinerant Preaching,
Endured hardship, persecution, and disgrace
As a good Soldier of Jesus Christ;
Contributing largely, by the usefulness of his labours,
To the first formation of the Methodist Societies,
In these Kingdoms

As a Christian Poet he stood unrivalled;
And his hymns will convey instruction and consolation,
To the faithful in Christ Jesus,
As long as the English language shall be understood.
He was born the XVIII of December, MDCCVIII,
And died the XXIX of March, MDCCLXXXVIII,
A firm and pious believer in the doctrines of the Gospel,
And a sincere friend to the Church of England.

John continued his kindness to his brother's family, writing affectionate letters to his sister-in-law, but concerned at the upkeep of her large house, and advising her to live within her means. "I have sometimes thought you are a little like me. . . . I know you are of a generous spirit. You have an open heart and an open hand. But may it not sometimes be too open, more so than your circumstances allow?" He is concerned also over his niece's health and thinks Harrogate might benefit her and will gladly give her ten or twenty pounds towards her going there. "In everything that is in my power you may depend upon the willing assistance of, dear Sally, Your affectionate friend and brother."

He was particularly fond of his niece, whom he took with him to Holland in his eightieth year, and his letters to her throw light on their easy relationship. When she visited Ramsgate, he looked forward to joining her, and advised her to bathe every day, but not to drink sea-water, adding in his dry way: "I am persuaded it was never designed to enter any human being for any purpose but to drown it." And when she is suffering from a skin ailment he recommends more of his odd remedies, and, of all things, a poultice of coal. "Pound common coal at fire, sift it through a sieve, mix this powder with warm water, put this poultice half an inch thick on the sore, changing it every four and twenty hours. But you will have need of patience. In a few days it will cure any sore in a human body. I scarce ever knew it to fail." He is pleased that she still finds her way to the services at City Road and she must regard his house there as her second home. Had she been his own daughter, he could not have been kinder.

He had intended to write his brother's life and asked her to help him. "Now, in this you may assist me much. You know as much of him as most people, and you have the pen of a ready writer. Set down everything you can recollect concerning this. I think that between us we shall be able to make something out." His plan, however, fell through. But when Dr. Adam Clarke was writing his biography of John Wesley she sent him interesting details in a letter which is preserved at Headingley College. She says she was accustomed to spend a few weeks every year with her uncle at the Foundery and at his City Road house. "His distinguished kindness to me from the earliest years I can remember made an indelible impression. I can retrace no word but of Tenderness, no action but of Condescension and Generosity. . . . No human being was more alive to all the tender Charities of domestic life than John Wesley."

Charles, unlike his brother, published few prose works and the only printed collection of his sermons is a modest volume produced by his widow, to which she prefixed a brief but generous and discerning tribute.[1] "It appears," she says, "that Charles was the first on whom the title of Methodist was

---

[1] One of his sermons (Awake, thou that sleepest!) is included in John Wesley's *Fifty-three Sermons* (since reduced to forty-four). In marked contrast to those of his brother, in its absence of argument, use of Scripture, and powerful appeal, it is perhaps the liveliest and most eloquent.

conferred. When in Oxford the Vice Chancellor issued his protest against those corrupting the students, the Methodists boldly raised the standard against infidelity and vice, were indefatigable in acts of charity, exercises of devotion, and habits of self-denial. . . . Accounts of their ascetic singularities spreading far and wide, their father took a journey to Oxford to examine himself whether they might not carry matters too far and injure their health and their cause by unnecessary rigour. . . . In a letter to Mrs. Wesley, he writes, 'I am well repaid for my expense and labour, by the shining piety of our two sons'."

Sally comments sensibly on their irregularities: "If the strict observance of the rule impedes the end, the end must be attained, though the prudential means, which are in some circumstances obstructive, be neglected. Deviations in non-essentials, if the end be promoted thereby, cannot promote a schism in any church. . . . The refusal of the clergy to admit them to their pulpits was the foundation of itinerant preaching. . . . They were neither to be intimidated by danger, affected or deterred by disgrace. And surely it required no common degree of resolution to expose themselves to the rude ignorance of the lowest of the people, the contempt of men of respectability and influence, and the censure of particular friends. It is not possible to imagine that, in their situation in life, men of learning and abilities, distinguished by academic honours, could have been activated by any motive but the purest benevolence."

She confesses that it was exceedingly irregular, but "let it be remembered that at that period there were no Sunday Schools, no Tract Societies, no propagation of Bibles. . . . The bigotry and opposition they met with at the beginning was unjustifiable by all the rules of charity. In 1738 the education of the labouring poor was totally neglected. It was a matter of national importance that so large a part of the community should be instructed in the principles of religion and the social duties of life." But happily they outlived enmity and prejudice and in the end received every mark of respect from all denominations.

She then draws an interesting comparison between the two brothers. In character they were entirely different. John had a disposition that scarcely any injury could provoke, ingratitude ruffle or contradiction weary. Though born to govern, he did so without arrogance, and showed remarkable gentleness and forbearance. He was amiable in his domestic circle and extremely generous to his relatives in need.

Charles, on the other hand, was full of sensibility and fire. "Tender, indulgent, kind, as a brother, a husband, a father, and master, warmly and unbelievably devoted to his friends, discerning in the character of men, incapable of disguise. . . . His most striking excellence was humility. . . . He not only acknowledged and pointed out, but *delighted* in the superiority of another, and if there ever was a human being who disliked power, avoided pre-eminence and shrank from praise, it was Charles Wesley. . . . As a preacher he was impassioned and energetic and expressed the most important truths with simplicity, brevity and force."

Samuel Bradburn described him in similar terms; candid without cowardly weakness, firm without headstrong obstinacy, free from both lifeless formality and wild enthusiasm. "He was never known to say anything in commendation of himself, and was never at a loss for something good to say of his divine Master." He was courteous, without dissimulation; honest, without vulgar roughness; a scholar, without pedantic ostentation. "He was a great Christian, without any pompous singularity; and a great Divine, without the least contempt for the meanest of his brethren."

All who knew him pay similar tribute. In preaching he had greater warmth and feeling than his brother, which the latter recognized. "You are made, as it were, for this very thing. Just here you are in your element. In connection I beat you; but in strong, short, pointed sentences, you beat me." His preaching was all light and fire. Reluctant though he was to face crowds, he had a remarkable gift of appeal, and few could withstand his compelling sincerity and persuasiveness. He never drove men to God, but drew them by warmth and affection. He was never remote from his hearers, but one with them in their need; like them, a sinner seeking mercy. He used no tricks of oratory, no ornaments of eloquence, but kept close to Scripture, applying Biblical texts with relevant and challenging directness. His sermons followed no ordered sequence, but were the overflow of a richly stored mind and of a full heart. Often he opened the Bible at random and preached from the first appropriate text that caught his eye, and so close was his knowledge of Scripture that he had no difficulty in its immediate application. Far from being at a loss or allowing himself to ramble, he showed, in the result, remarkable freshness and vitality, and through this spontaneity, his sermons were alive. It was this immediacy and directness, joined to natural warmth and fervour, that gained for him invariably a breathless hearing. His congregations literally hung on his words, spellbound, not by oratory, but by the grace of the preacher and the force of his appeal.

Nothing could be further from the truth than that Charles was a pale shadow of his brother or that he stands in the background of his brother's work. Though less dynamic, his genius in other directions was marked. And if he never occupied, like John, the centre of the stage, it was because he deliberately chose not to. He never liked the limelight. He would have preferred a country living (he refused more than one) or a settled academic life, but when God called, he never failed, no matter how reluctant, to respond. With the result that he, no less than John, established Methodism. Their work was indivisible. John organized; Charles provided the impulse. John was the head, Charles was the heart. The latter's contribution was immeasurable: in warmth, fervour and affection. And supremely there are his hymns, without which it is doubtful whether Methodism could have survived, at any rate in its present form. Charles set their converts singing and they sang throughout the century. In crowded chapels theology was expressed in exhilarating song. John, though no mean hymn-writer himself, had no such power. Charles gave wings to his brother's work, spreading it with a rapidity and gaining for it a popularity it could never otherwise have known. In Dr. F. L. Wiseman's words: "Methodism without Charles Wesley is just as unthinkable as Methodism without John Wesley," and he adds with truth that Charles has found but few to preserve his memory.

It would be foolish to suggest that Charles made the greater contribution, but we cannot escape the fact that his hymns preserve the spirit of Methodism. They carry it down the centuries, and though John Wesley did a great work, his brother's hymns remain as an imperishable legacy and as Methodism's greatest contribution to the treasures of Christendom.

The character of Charles presents an interesting enigma. What are we to make of his paradoxical nature—patient yet impulsive; retiring, yet resolute; frail, yet a fighter; controversial and hot-tempered, yet gentle and forbearing; otherworldly, yet intensely human; introspective, yet exhilarating; a rigid conformist, yet a bold pioneer; a strict Churchman, yet an ardent Methodist? In this mixed pattern we find his many-sided nature. He carried within himself the tensions and contradictions common to most of us. He knew both the heights and the depths, the glory of the morning and the dark night of the soul. John, for all his sociability, was remote, an austere and lonely leader, bearing problems he could not solve and responsibilities he could not share and consumed by a single and devouring purpose. But Charles was the pastor who shepherded the flock, closer to the penitent, more sensitive to the sufferer. John was respected, feared, venerated, but Charles was loved.

Again Charles usefully consolidated his brother's work. With unwearying devotion he helped to knit together the scattered Societies, especially in the earlier years when they were loosely associated, by sifting the faithless, recovering the lapsed, and confirming the faithful. And by his constant reiteration of Church principles he gave a balance and stability to the Movement which it might otherwise have lacked.

In appearance Charles was plumper than his brother, though, like him, well under middle height. He was short-sighted and his manner was abrupt. He had the same keen glance and aquiline nose. Contemporary portraits of him are few. John sat often for his likeness, which was widely reproduced, often in busts and medallions. This did not happen with Charles. Of his three main portraits by contemporary artists, that by John Russell, R.A. is probably the most life-like, at the age of sixty-four. In this he resembles his grandfather Annesley. Russell was a personal friend and a regular worshipper at City Road. This portrait hangs in the headquarters of the Methodist Missionary Society (see Plate 10).

The engraving by Jonathan Spilsbury, R.A., was exhibited at the Royal Academy. It has been described as the finest of Charles' portraits and was the only one published in his lifetime. The work most frequently produced is that by William Gush, dating from the early nineteenth century, showing Charles preaching, and is now in the possession of Kingswood School. Thomas Hudson's attractive portrait, at the Epworth Press (see frontispiece) shows the preacher full-faced, in his younger period, probably round the time of his marriage. A full-length picture of him in old age by an unknown artist depicts him in heavy cloak and buckled shoes, hat in hand and leaning on his stick.

In the north courtyard of the New Room in Bristol is his life-size statue in bronze (see Plate 15); and in the south aisle of Westminster Abbey is the well-known Adams-Acton memorial showing the two brothers in profile (see Plate 2b) and bearing a saying of Charles: "God buries his workmen, but carries on his work". Recently an excellent bust of him has been executed by Miss Erica Lee, commissioned by the World Methodist Council, and is now in America. So far as is known, there is no other bust or statue of him in existence.

An early anecdote about Charles is worth recording. The scene is the Hotwells, Bristol, the year 1748. Charles was taking a cure and encountered an Oxford acquaintance, Dr. Robinson, who afterwards became Primate of Ireland. They were glad to meet and talked freely. Dr. Robinson remarked that he had not believed many things he had heard about the Methodists and expressed surprise that they actually employed laymen. "It is your fault," replied Charles. "My fault, Mr. Wesley?" "Yes, yours and your brethren's." Dr. Robinson was taken aback. "How so, sir?" To which Charles answered: "Why, you hold your peace, and so the stones cry out." "But I hear they are unlearned men." To which Charles retorted: "Very true: in general, they are so; so the dumb ass rebukes the prophet."

It was characteristic of Charles, both of his ready wit and of his Methodist principles. His biographer is wrong who states that Charles stayed at home and nursed his theory, while John went throughout the country and saw what it was necessary to do. No judgment of Charles could be more mistaken. As we have seen, he travelled in his day arduously like his brother, shared the burden of persecution and disgrace, and at a time when Methodism needed him most bore his full share of labour. Methodism has never given him the place he merits. At the same time, it has never ceased to sing his hymns, nor indeed, has the Christian Church throughout the English-speaking world, and wherever Christians meet to worship, his memory is preserved.

But why, apart from his hymns, has he been neglected? It is only partly explained by his self-effacement and his brother's overshadowing influence. His zealous adherence to Church principles may be another reason. Consistency is rarely a popular virtue and in his case led to an inevitable clash with the more headstrong and radical of the preachers, who were only too eager to gain control, and whose views, after the death of the Wesleys, prevailed. Methodism then diverged increasingly from the mother Church; Charles' attempts to preserve its original aim had failed. As a result, his memory has suffered; with some there has remained a lingering coolness, while to others his logical emphasis has been unwelcome, and in general no popular or clearcut image has survived.

His virtues and achievement, however, deserve far higher recognition. He was a Methodist in the truest sense, not only the first Methodist, but the complete Methodist, whose character and career crystallize perhaps more than any other the authentic spirit of the Revival. Rooted in catholic principle, fervent in evangelical appeal, second only to Whitefield as an evangelist, his recurring theme was "O let me commend my Saviour to you!" No man preached more passionately the saving love of Christ. And though his memory has declined, his voice still speaks and with compelling relevance to our contemporary need:

> Why is the faithful seed decreased?
>   The life of God extinct and dead?
> The daily sacrifice is ceased,
>   And Charity to heaven is fled . . .
> But canst thou not thy work revive,
>   Once more in our degenerate years?

The work of the brothers was complementary, unique in the annals of the Church. Each supplied what the other lacked. And the synthesis at which they aimed, of high churchman and liberal evangelical, of flexibility within a framework of Church order and tradition, despite later deviations, remains a marked and agreeable feature of the Methodist Church and one towards which current ecumenical trends appear to be moving. The brothers hammered in vain at the doors of the Establishment, but they renewed the life of the Church. And, in spite of differences they kept together to the end in unbroken unity. In Sally's words, quoted from Scripture, "In their lives they were lovely, and in death they were not divided."

Index